The Machine Stops: the Mayan Long Count Through a Western Lens

History, 2012, and the End of (Some) Things

Tim Lyons

Copyright 2011 by Tim Lyons

No part of this book may be reproduced or transcribed in any form or by any means, electronic or mechanical, including photocopying or recording or by any information storage and retrieval system without written permission from the author and publisher, except in the case of brief quotations embodied in critical reviews and articles. Requests and inquiries may be mailed to: American Federation of Astrologers, Inc., 6535 S. Rural Road, Tempe, AZ 85283.

ISBN-10: 0-86690-628-2
ISBN-13: 978-0-86690-628-9

Cover Design: Jack Cipolla
Back Cover Photo: Bill Karelis

Published by:
American Federation of Astrologers, Inc.
6535 S. Rural Road
Tempe, AZ 85283

www.astrologers.com

Printed in the United States of America

To Lewis Mumford,
without whose scholarship and vision
I could not have written this book.

and to

E. M. Forster, from whom I have borrowed the title.

Introduction: Burdens

I. Bigness and the Garden

I went out the other day to water my garden as the mid-afternoon light slanted in from the southwest. The angle of the early-December sun, combined with the lushness of the northern Colorado garden, and even with the simple fact that I had not yet shut down the water to the outside spigots, gave me pause. Kale, spinach, turnips, carrots, beets, and chard all continued to thrive; only the zucchinis had given way to the cold, for we'd had only a few frosts, and only a few days when the night-time temperature dipped below twenty degrees. When I came inside, the television news told me that many so-called experts saw General Motors as "too big to fail," putting it into the same category, it seems, as the various banks and investment firms (two categories with plenty of overlap these days) that the government had already attempted to save.

We'll get back in a minute to the connection between my garden and General Motors. First, though, we should acknowledge that in many ways the so-called experts have a point: General Motors' tentacles extend into thousands of car dealerships, millions of car-warranties, and more sub-contracted suppliers than we care to count; this behemoth of a company employs many thousands of workers directly and many thousands more indirectly. The bank-mortgage fellow-behemoths also have a pervasive effect on countless areas of American life, not only through home-mortgages, but through their connection to the credit system that underlies so much of the United States' economy.

We can draw many conclusions from this, but an inescapable one involves bigness. Bigness characterizes so many of our institutions that we more or less take it for granted, forgetting that throughout most of human social development, people did just fine with smaller groups and different emphases—and that the switch from the simple life of the Neolithic village to the first large-scale structures and institutions took place comparatively rapidly. During one extensive period of human pre-history, people all over the world lived not in large cities but in small villages, their lives marked by patterns that still survive.

The durability of this culture might well, as Lewis Mumford suggests in *Technics and Human Development*, bear witness "to its having done justice to natural conditions and human capacities better than more dynamic but less balanced cultures."[1] In those ancient societies, Mumford tells us, "every member of the community had access to the entire cultural heritage, and could ordinarily master every part of it." Further, we find there an "easy interchange of skills and occupations, with a minimum amount of specialization," and "no hierarchy of precedence, except the natural one of age, since in such a community, he who lived the longest knew the most."[2] Yet within this balance we find, it seems, the seeds of change, for its conservatism ensured that change would surely come. When it did, it came accompanied by myriad changes not limited to the development of writing and metallurgy.

But that we see *some* kind of change as inevitable does not mean we should see the *type* of change that occurred as inevitable. Though we will look more carefully in the next chapter at the particular changes that took place in the 4th millennium BC, we can summarize them briefly here as a quasi-cataclysmic series of developments with repercussions in all areas of human life, repercussions still felt today even in events as apparently trivial as my garden-watering in late November or as apparently nontrivial as the proliferation of mega-companies allegedly "too big to fail" in the forefront of the current crisis, a crisis generally referred to as "economic" but that seems to extend to practically all areas of life.

As to the gardening, I should note that I have grown vegetables for nearly twenty years here in Colorado and that when I started, my gardening season generally came to an end in September, or perhaps October. Now, each year the growing season seems to get a bit longer, and though I might interpret this as resulting from a short-term fluctuation in weather conditions instead of from major and pervasive climatic changes, an overwhelming amount of evidence suggests the latter interpretation even as it suggests a connection between companies "too big to fail" that don't flourish, and vegetables, in December at 40N01 latitude at over 5000 feet of altitude, that do.

Though the pervasive influence of General Motors and mortgage-investment-banking conglomerates goes back only a hundred years or so, the trend they represent stretches back to the beginning of the Mayan Long Count over 5000 years ago, a period when the Neolithic village social structure metamorphosed into—or, some will say, was replaced by—what we now call "civilization." In this new mode of social structuring, the dispersed villages of the Neolithic period, based in democratic principles not yet enunciated, depending on "neighborly intimacy,

---

[1] Lewis Mumford, *The Myth of the Machine, Volume I: Technics and Human Development* (New York: Harvest/HBJ, 1967), 159.
[2] Ibid.

customary usage, and consent"[1] gave way to a structure based in authoritarian control, centralized bureaucracy, and a need to conquer other groups in order to insure the supply of those raw materials that ensured its dominance. Lewis Mumford writes:

> By perfecting new instruments of coercion, the rulers of this society had, by the Third Millennium BC, organized industrial and military power on a scale that was never to be surpassed until our own time.[2]

This shift was characterized by changes in both pattern and scale. We see the former in the increased emphasis on "mechanical order, mathematical exactitude, specialized skill and knowledge, and, above all, centralized intelligence" deriving from "the systematic observation of the heavens." We see the latter in the "quantification and magnification" that "are the marks of the new technology":

> Instead of the little Neolithic shrine, there stands a towering temple, the 'Mountain House,' and nearby a huge granary; instead of the cluster of frail, mud-walled village houses, for a score of families, a wall-engirdled city, with a thousand or more families, no longer merely a human home, but the home of a god; indeed a replica of Heaven.[3]

This change in scale resulted, primarily, from changes in social organization, not primarily from changes in tool-making. Though we see a quantum leap forward in size, from hut to ziggurat or pyramid, people constructed these larger structures with fairly primitive tools (e.g. wooden sledges to carry the pyramid stones). The significant changes had to do not with mechanical technology but with new ways of organizing human beings into quasi-mechanized units of production, for it took regimented work-gangs to move those stones. This change in social organization lies beneath the bigness that we see in current organizations deemed "too big to fail," and it appears in a hidden way in the health of my garden in early December, for from bigness came more bigness, until huge and highly organized conglomerates created a technology with enough power, and producing enough waste, to alter even the climate itself.

I don't know how much of this would have surprised the Maya astronomer-priests in their deliberations about their Long Count. Few of the Mayan records have come down to us, thanks in large part to the depredations of the Spanish Conquistadors and the ministrations of the priests who accompanied them in their conquest of Mesoamerica centuries ago.[4] However, I think that

---

[1] Mumford, 164.
[2] Mumford, 164.
[3] Mumford, 167-8.
[4] In one of the strange ironies of history, one of these priests, Father Diego de Landa, not only oversaw the destruction but also saved what of that record we still have today.

the Long Count itself has to do precisely with this change in pattern and in scale. The Long Count natal chart aptly symbolizes what came into existence over five millennia ago, and the transits and progressions to that horoscope show its development over the centuries.

II. Time and Burdens

In this book, we will use the tools of our own astrological tradition to examine the scope and significance of the ancient Mayan time-measurement known as the *Long Count*. In other words, we will use the tools of one very ancient system of time-analysis to examine another. Because both methods suggest that we can derive meaning from time-measurement, it seems appropriate to use one to look at the other—particularly considering the fact that although we know much of the Mayan measurements themselves, we do not have many direct statements about the meanings the Maya attached to those measurements, at least beyond the very general—such as, for example, that the Long Count's conclusion would supposedly bring something catastrophic. Much of what we know, we have derived from inference. (None of which means, of course, that we should deride the inference makers, a group including such figures as J. Eric Thompson, Frank Waters, and John Major Jenkins. To say that a writer makes inferences does not mean he doesn't offer something of value. I mean, here, only to distinguish between *reports* from Mayan texts and *inferences* from available materials.)

In applying the methods of our own astrological system to the Mayan time-measurements, I make no assumption that the Maya would have accepted any of my interpretations. Nevertheless, I apparently share some assumptions with the Maya who took it upon themselves to chart the heavens and measure time.[1] Both the Mayan method and the one I use deal with the curious, cryptic, and demonstrable relationship between time-cycles and events, and because as we approach the end of the Long Count we *do* see developments that could presage some catastrophe, we might derive great benefit from an attempt to interpret Mayan time-measurements by using our own astrological methodology. That the current period seems so fraught with dangers and difficulties that resist easy solutions should remind us that we can benefit from perspective wherever we can find it.

The Maya depicted the various units of time as burdens carried by the gods. This depiction suggests, among other things, that each moment of time has "weight," a quality or significance that we can perhaps unlock if we understand the symbols (gods, planetary or otherwise) that portray that quality or significance. We might note, here, a difference between this and our more common view that we can't derive meaning from time itself, but only from our ob-

---

[1] According to Leon de Portilla, the Maya word for time, *kinh*, has *sun* as its primary meaning. This might at first seem to differ from our word *time*, which seems to refer to something more abstract than *sun*. However, apparently *time* comes from the same roots as *tide* (Shipley's *Book of Word Origins*, page 357), and thus, like the Mayan term, refers to an observable, rhythmic movement in the environment.

servation of the events that happen *in* time irrespective of the symbols that we use to measure "time itself,"[1] the symbols having use only as measuring devices, not as carriers or symbols of significance. In what we might call the commonly accepted "scientific" view, the symbolism that we use to measure time does merely that: it measures; it does not, by itself, yield meaning or significance.

Astrologers, on the other hand, those outré cousins of astronomers, generally posit that time *does* have meaning, or, at least, that we can derive meaning by referring to the symbolism that humans (astrologers in particular) use to measure it. An astrologer would say that one can say much about the meaning or significance of an event merely by knowing its time and applying the appropriate symbolic vocabulary, though the astrologer would want to amplify, we might even say *ground*, that meaning by looking at the events themselves. Though we do not *need* astrology in order to find meaning (as millions of people seem to find sufficient meaning without any reference to astrological symbols), it seems that humans *do* need symbols of some sort, as what we call *meaning* doesn't seem to exist outside of the symbols we use to talk about it. Further, though advocates of the so-called "western scientific view" would say, "Use *our* set of symbols, not the one astrologers use," we would probably do better to use both.

In deriving meaning from the symbols used to measure time, astrologers will refer to at least two types of cycles: those derived from the observable movements of the heavenly bodies, and those derived by numerical measures or divisions without reference to celestial movements. We find the former not only in our day-night pattern, but also in our lunar "month," our solar year, and in other planetary and inter-planetary cycles, though lay-people generally leave this last group to the astrologers. We find the latter in our centuries and millennia. We also find it in some Mayan cycles, for in their measurements the Maya used not only planetary cycles, but also cycles apparently without precise astronomical referents. Astrologers in the western tradition take a similar approach, though the particulars differ a good deal, as we will see.

Like the Maya astronomer-priests, contemporary astrologers accept the notion that time has to do with the gods, or at least with a set of symbols named *after* gods. We might say, for example, that Saturn, which through its movement offers a definite measure of time, also carries forth a meaning, and that we cannot separate the meaning from the time-measurement, for meaning works itself out through time and crystallizes in characteristic ways at particular points in Saturn's cycle. We might also say that Saturn "bears" the burden of his own symbolism, so that as we look at Saturn's various cycles (e.g. his movement through the zodiac, his cyclic relationships with other planets, his movements through the houses of a natal horoscope, as well as the cycles formed by various directions and progressions), we see that burden—that weight of

---

[1] It seems that this term lacks a definite referent; hence the quotation marks.

meaning—moving forward, expressing itself in the world. And we also see that at the end of each cycle, something gets released or unburdened.[1]

Having "weight," time's moments have "moment," or significance, have enough weight to bring forth, symbolically speaking, the course of events. If we look into both past and present cycles of the planets, we see the past carried forward, so that the burden of the past appears in the present: karma ripens; people go through experiences to which they attach significance. In general, we carry forward the human and non-human inheritance of the past, its own kind of burden. As each cycle comes to a conclusion, we should, like the Mayan gods, let go of our burden as preparation for the new cycle.

We can see the same process at work in longer cycles such as that symbolized by the Long Count. A process or series of processes begins, develops, comes to fruition, and dissipates. Because the Long Count has to do with processes integral to what we call "civilization," we can expect much breakdown as we approach the end of the cycle, as if the gods, weary of their burdens, begin to set them down. In some cases, Maya astronomer-priests posited a resting period between one cycle and another. This suggests that we can observe in collective matters what we so often experience in personal ones: as one cycle of activity draws to a close, we let go of old attachments, opening up space for new activity or new creative possibility; and if we look carefully, we will see falling into the ground seeds that will develop during the next cycle.

III. Destruction, Transformation, and the Long Count

The Long Count began back in 3114 BC and comes to an end in 2012 AD. Its midpoint around 500 BC coincides with what many consider the highest point in human cultural development and/or greatest period of spiritual awakening in recorded history; its end seems destined to coincide with collective changes of an unprecedented nature, among which may number the pervasive climatic changes looming as a result of global warming, the altering of the human genome, possibly massive starvation, and other developments that we can see as the natural, karmic results of processes begun at the end of the 4th millennium BC. That the end of the Long Count closely coincides with the end of our own Age of Pisces should alert us to the importance of the contemporary period.

According to Robert Sieck Flandes' interpretation of the Sun Stone, or "Aztec calendar," we should translate Nahui-Olin, the name for the fifth and final period of the present cycle, as "Earthquake Sun"; he sees this as referring to "the next and last destruction of human life in the

---

[1] During the last phase of any cycle, we can observe people letting go of various attachments, apparently because their experience pressures them to do so. Because we find ourselves at the end of the Mayan Long Count (and at the end of the Age of Pisces), we see around us much letting go of burdens and reaping of karma (i.e. experiencing the results of causes). It accounts for much of the chaos we see in the world.

world," a cataclysmic destruction of earthquakes.[1] Though we might wish to take such a prediction symbolically rather than literally, expecting "earth shaking developments" rather than actual earthquakes, we still should pay it some heed. Certainly as we approach the end of the Long Count, we see major changes in the earth itself. We might, on the one hand, expect the end of what we call "civilization," or we might expect a major shift in the values, priorities, and assumptions that underpin that civilization. The symbolism strongly suggests major and pervasive changes in social structure, some so far-reaching and of such depth that "changes in social structure" might amount to "the end of civilization as we know it" simply because so many of the structures of that "civilization as we know it" will change. We might expect the destruction of all that gives a sense of security and identity. Though until quite recently many might have taken millennial thinking as primarily delusional, brought about by fear and having its locus inside the minds of people instead of in the evidence from the world, recent developments (e.g. climate change) seem to suggest that we can see the signs of "millennial change" by simply looking around us.[2]

Nevertheless, we may wish to start by taking the images of destruction as metaphors for the collective demand for transformation. Certainly back when western archaeologists first published their understanding of the Long Count, this symbolic-explanation seemed the most plausible interpretation, and it may yet prove more accurate than a literal interpretation. However, with the accelerated (and perhaps irreversible) melting of the polar ice caps, increasing climatic instability, the political and scientific implications of current genetic research, and what appears as an ever-increasing possibility, even likelihood, of some sort of global epidemic, we might lean more and more toward the literal interpretation: that we will witness the destruction not only of many forms of social organization, but also of homo sapiens altogether. Some interpretations of global climate changes suggest this latter interpretation. I don't have the qualifications to speak with authority on such scientific matters, but I do think that the symbolism, drawn from our own astrology as well as Mayan calendrics, strongly suggests that our social structures will change radically, for we have come about as far as can go in a certain direction.

Civilized living promises a kind of security. We see this promise in the very first civilization—or, what we might call the very first living situation commonly accepted as a civilization: the Sumerian. Arnold Toynbee, in arguing that we should see the Sumerian civilization in this light, points to one of its defining characteristics:

---

[1] Robert Sieck Flandes: "The Sun Stone or Aztec Calendar: Literature and Drawing Reconstruction of the Original" (Mexico: Lito Selder, 1936).

[2] We can see external signs when Ages change. Around the time of Jesus, whose name means *fish* and whose birth coincided with the beginning of the Age of Pisces, fish symbolism pervaded the eastern Mediterranean area. Now, we see in our environment power lines whose supports closely resemble the glyph for Uranus, co-ruler of Aquarius, sign of the impending Age. Further, Mary, allegedly a virgin, reminds us of Virgo, Pisces' polar opposite, while the heat from the Sun, ruler of Leo, Aquarius' polar opposite, serves as the source of present climate change. See chapter one.

> In bringing the alluvium under cultivation, the Sumerians were the first society in the Old-World Oikoumene to produce a surplus, over and above the annual requirements for bare subsistence....[1]

Surplus, of course, brings the promise of security; it provides a buffer against uncertainty. In Sumeria, as in ancient Egypt and subsequent societies, it also gave birth to hierarchy, to a managerial class, for if you have a surplus, you must presumably find someone to manage it. We see, here, the relationship between "civilization," hierarchy, and security. As we will also see, this "civilization," this particular approach to social structuring, has from the beginning carried the problematic seeds that we now see coming to flower.

If we look at civilization as an ongoing attempt to provide security, we may interpret the end of that civilization as the death of that promise. An earthquake certainly brings radical insecurity, as we tend to depend on the ground beneath our feet remaining firm and reliable. Similarly, we expect the oceans to stay in their places and the continents not to drift about noticeably. We also expect the social forms around us to continue pretty much unchanged and for biological patterns to go on as they have. Finally, we expect to find congenial the same states of mind, what we might call the same *habitual patterns* of mind, for when these change, we don't feel secure no matter what external situation we encounter, as any person in psychological crisis will attest.

Of course, we might take all of this metaphorically. We might say that the end of the Long Count (or the closely coinciding end of the Age of Pisces) will bring radical psychological insecurity; if we view things that way, we would take the threat of earthquakes, floods, or other physical cataclysms as metaphors for this process. As we will see, this facile distinction between inner attitudes and outer events doesn't really stand up very well to examination—an idea that I take as central to our discussion—but we will begin by discussing them separately. We may wish to psychologize everything, to see the external only as a metaphor for the internal. Certainly "the end of civilization" would require everyone to let go of psychological attachment, but quite likely it would also result in millions of deaths, a consequence we should certainly not take as mere symbol for some inner development. Still, we may find it useful to say that the external destruction will result from mankind's collective refusal to let go of attachment, for the forms to which we remain attached will have much to do with the destruction that we face.[2]

---

[1] Arnold Toynbee, *Mankind and Mother Earth* (New York: Oxford University Press, 1976), 53. (On page 27 of the text, Toynbee says the following of the word *Oikoumene*: "[It] is a Greek term which became current in the Hellenic Age of Greek history.... Its literal meaning is 'the Inhabited (Part of the World)'....")

[2] For example, current social, economic, and political structures resist the changes necessary to slow or halt global warming, so it seems all but inevitable that the process will continue. As of this writing in 2009, the north polar ice cap has been reduced by an area greater than that of Texas, and many scientists suggest that the process may well accelerate, largely because the resultant open seawater absorbs so much more sunlight than does the polar ice. Yet current policies seem woefully inadequate to address this

I don't wish to deny the power of collective projection, by which the similar projections of millions appear in the world as events. In fact, in previous publications,[1] I have emphasized that power. Just as an individual's experience reflects, in myriad and important ways, that person's unconscious mind, so the collective experience reflects the unconscious of the collective (not synonymous with Jung's "collective unconscious"[2]): that which millions of people reject from consciousness.[3] Humanity has collectively rejected the energies symbolized by the outer planets, particularly Saturn, Chiron, Uranus, Neptune, and Pluto. As people reject these energies from their inner world, which they do because these planetary energies threaten ego and its security, they appear, in their rejected form, in the collective situation. In that situation, we see that Saturn (fear) has co-opted the energies of Uranus (insight), Neptune (spiritual yearning and imagination) and Pluto (power). We therefore confront a situation in which those with authoritative positions in the prevailing hierarchies (Saturn) control and make their own use of human inventiveness (Uranus) and, through an ongoing process of deception (Neptune), disempower the people while empowering plutocratic agencies of all sorts (Pluto).

We could see this as the basic Jungian idea of projection taken to a collective level and leavened with astrological symbolism. We have, as a result, a symbolic picture of the demands confronting humanity as a whole; further, we have information relevant to the decisions necessary to prevent catastrophe. The planetary symbolism gives us guidelines for a collective approach, but one that remains centered in and relevant to each individual, whether he has a position of power or not. Simply put: each individual must work to recall these projected planetary energies, valuing these energies as inner potentials so that they don't appear in the world as outer threats. Otherwise, we just perpetuate chaos, no matter how sophisticated our historical, occult, or astrological knowledge.

IV. Millennial Thinking

As I write this, we approach the end of two aeons, the Age of Pisces and the Mayan Long Count's Age of Ollin ("Movement"). To some, this assertion will only restate the obvious and they will find meaning in it; to others (e.g. those who "do not believe" in astrology), it will seem to contain all sorts of unexamined assumptions, particularly the assumption that investigation of these aeons brings us any useful information whatsoever. Some in this latter group will see astrologers' claims about aeons as indicating nothing more than human credulity, a hangover

---

potentially catastrophic problem. The problem lies not only, or primarily, in any purported lack of technical expertise on these matters, but in failures due to social organization.

[1] *Astrology Beyond Ego* (Quest Books, 1985; reissued by The American Federation of Astrologers in 2010), *Your Hidden Face: Projection in the Horoscope* (unpublished manuscript), and numerous articles.
[2] According to Jung, the collective unconscious does not consist of repressed contents.
[3] Astrologers often, and with good reason, discuss the unconscious by discussing the energies of the outer planets and Saturn, sometimes Mars and Chiron, as well as other forces during specific periods. More on this as we proceed.

from superstitions that scientific knowledge has replaced but for some reason not uprooted completely from credulous minds.

Even those who find much significance in the Long Count should acknowledge the errors arising from past millennial thinking. Perpetrators of the French Revolution saw it as the beginning of a new and more enlightened era. Similarly with the American Revolution, as Thomas Paine announced by saying, "We have it in our power to begin the world over again."[1] In retrospect, we can see not only that the world did not "begin . . . over again," but also that those two developments perhaps don't deserve the name "revolution" at all. The French reverted to an authoritarian state under Napoleon, and the Americans adopted a constitution without the word "rights" in it, passed a law against sedition, and failed to recognize the rights of non-white non-property owners and non-males whether they owned property or not. Some historians have argued that after their respective counter-revolutions, both countries perpetuated the kind of oppressions that the "revolutions" had purportedly uprooted. Small wonder, then, that people look with skepticism upon all discussions about new ages, new worlds, or idealized ways of structuring society.

I don't intend, at this point, to offer any theoretical defense of "millennial thinking." We should examine the evidence before we decide. However, as it seems wise to offer a thesis early in an essay rather than later, I will say that the evidence suggests at least two conclusions: first, that humankind has come about as far as it can in a certain direction—the direction taken, largely, by what we can loosely refer to as *the mechanized and industrialized societies*, representatives of what Lewis Mumford calls the *power system*—without courting its own destruction; second, that we can describe this development not only accurately, but in a way suggesting praxis, by referring to our own astrological symbols as we analyze the Mayan Long Count. However, if we say that we have come to the end of civilization, or of "civilization as we know it," we should recognize that such statements suggest a kind of dualistic mind-set that does not help us to think clearly about the relevant material.

If we ask whether we will have civilization after 2012 or not, we suggest two alternatives, both of them based on the term *civilization*, an abstraction of a rather high order. If we ask questions of that type ("Will we have civilization, or will we not have civilization?"), we may blind ourselves to alternatives not based on that dualism, fail to acknowledge the complexity of the situation we face, and conclude that the world must fit into the categories that our language says it must have. In the symbolism of the Long Count, we find that the Mayans referred to the current 5125-year period as the *Sun of Ollin*, which Frank Waters described decades ago (in *Mexico Mystique*) as a symbol for interlocked and inter-weaving polarities.[2] The symbol suggests that we must step beyond dualistic thinking.

---

[1] Qtd. in Michael Grosso's *The Millennium Myth* (Wheaton: Quest Books, 1995), 106.
[2] Frank Waters, *Mexico Mystique: The Coming Sixth World of Consciousness* (Chicago: Swallow Press, 1975), 119.

Our own system of Ages seems to measure the evolutionary development of humankind altogether, at least since the previous Ice Age, a subject to which I will return in chapter one; the Mayan Long Count seems to measure the development of systems of power that, though they begin with the individual, express themselves in modes of social organization.[1] Though historians say that "civilization" began back in the 4th millennium B.C., we should perhaps more accurately say that the mode of social organization that we call "civilization" crystallized around then. That this occurred doesn't mean that what happened before then, or what will happen after December 21, 2012, couldn't also qualify as "civilized."[2] One could make a pretty good case that Neolithic village culture seems much more civilized than our modern version, as the former lacked the latter's emphasis on organized barbarity and wanton destruction.

If we step away from the high level abstractions and look to operations—if we look, that is, at what people *did*, not at what category we use to analyze that activity—we find ourselves looking again at bigness, for in the 4th millennium BC, people began making big things of all sorts. Not only did they start making structures like the ziggurats and pyramids, they also organized society on a much vaster scale than any had done before. Not only did they build bigger buildings, they farmed bigger fields, made bigger walls, and fenced off bigger territories. In other words, we see during that period a rapid increase in the size of dominant social institutions and of the physical things constructed *through* those social institutions. Though we can see a gradual increase in size and complexity in the millennia leading up to that period, we see a quantum leap forward around the Long Count's start-date, a leap that looks like the crossing of a threshold point. Just as water cooling to 32 degrees Fahrenheit undergoes a change in form in the midst of an ongoing process, so around 3114 BC we see a change in the form of social organization from Neolithic village culture, in which smallness and intimacy pervaded everything, to the Sumerian and Egyptian mode of social-organization, in which bigness predominated.

With the change of size came a change of function. The functional change had to do with hierarchy and central power, matters to which we will return; as a result of these functional changes, people could build such things as pyramids. People also began to organize themselves into hierarchical, pyramidal structures emphasizing dominance-submissive modalities not only in the relationship between ruler and subject, but also in the relationship between the society as a whole and nearby social groupings not yet subsumed into the larger organization.

The end of the Long Count doesn't necessarily presage the end of civilized living or the end of culture—though, as we will see, it presents some daunting challenges related to the environ-

---

[1] This sentence reflects the Mayan emphasis on the numbers 5 and 7, a matter to which we will return in chapter two.
[2] Nor does it necessarily mean that we couldn't find other "civilizations" in existence long before 3114 BC, perhaps long before the previous Ice Age. I make no comment on any claims made about whether or not such "civilizations" existed. See below.

ment upon which civilized living and culture seems to depend. It suggests, rather, the end of what we might call an era of bigness in which we see dominance-submissive modalities and hierarchical structures integral to a larger power-system.[1] Large institutions will no longer promote healthy development, will no longer effectively facilitate problem solving, and will no longer alleviate our adjustment to our environment. Some will say, "But have large institutions *ever* done so? Couldn't we say that the Neolithic village social structure served—and still serves—human needs better than does the power-system that in large part replaced it?" These questions have value, but again they steer us toward a dualistic thinking that we should stay clear of. We can all bring to mind situations in which large institutions seemed to produce benefit. Even back in Sumer, the larger social ordering helped insure people against want, for the social structure grew from and then ensured an ongoing agricultural surplus, and it promoted kinds of cultural and intellectual developments, whether in expression, thinking, or feeling, that the earlier mode had not. We can acknowledge these benefits even as we say that the era of bigness has run its course and must give way.

The problem presents itself not only through the plethora of institutions deemed "too big to fail," but in the simple fact that the problems besetting us show the Hydra-like tendency of these institutions: because all the problems seem interconnected, if you fix one, two more spring up. As the members of the Club of Rome wrote back in 1972 of the five major trends of global concern—"accelerating industrialization, rapid population growth, widespread malnutrition, depletion of nonrenewable resources, and a deteriorating environment"—all are "interconnected in many ways."[2] We see in this description that each of the five "trends" has to do, though in different ways, with the *size* of human institutions. Many of the problems cited resist solutions not so much for technical reasons as for what we might call institutional ones: the large institutions that could in theory solve the problems always resist doing so because of something in the internal logic of the institutions themselves.

The predictions of the Club of Rome, made decades ago, now seem prescient—and perhaps even understated even though many at the time found them radical and far-fetched. We see a depleting ozone, melting polar ice-caps, retreating glaciers, rising temperatures, depleted soil, the destruction of the rainforests, water shortages, storms of increasing severity, almost continual and widespread famine, and governments that seem powerless to do much about any of this. Certainly some leaders have made some efforts at weapons control, and many have signed on to the Kyoto Accords and similar agreements, but these efforts seem a classic case of "too little, too late." The process seems to have its own momentum, as members of the Club of Rome predicted, and would seem daunting even if nation states demonstrated the will to sacrifice national

---

[1] I have borrowed this term from Lewis Mumford. As will become evident, I have borrowed much material from Mr. Mumford's various writings, writings without which I could not have written this book.
[2] Donella H. Meadows, Dennis L. Meadows, Jorgen Randers, William W. Behrens III, *The Limits to Growth* (New York: Signet, 1974), 27.

interest in order to slow the process. We hardly need the rhetoric of occultists, astrologers, or examiners of things-Mayan to tell us that we have come to a fork in the road—or, perhaps, the end of the road altogether. That so much resistance comes from nation-states directs us back to the Long Count, for the Long Count's beginning brought on the mother of all such states.

When we speak of the rhetoric of occultists, though, we might wish to put to the side some notions for which we have little empirical basis, as for example the claims about the "occult" connection of present times to goings-on in ancient civilizations, either recognized like Egypt or disputed like Atlantis. We have heard that the latter destroyed itself because of overweening pride, and we may see a connection to the contemporary crisis; we have also heard that people now alive have reincarnated from either Egypt or Atlantis. I have no position on these matters, partly because of the aforementioned empirical problems, and partly because I don't see how it matters whether people in our society have reincarnated from Atlantis, Egypt, or any other ancient society.

I do, however, take a position on some of the ideas often brought forth regarding the Age of Aquarius, for I think we have good reason to suspect that this "New Age" will not necessarily bring a period only of enlightened brotherhood, beneficial technical progress, and amity as some have suggested. Though it may bring some of that, it will probably bring a good deal else besides, and we will probably not characterize this "good deal else" as altogether "enlightened" or as connected seamlessly with brotherhood. I discuss these matters more fully in chapter one.

Using Mayan terminology, we can say that any aeon carries the burden of its own symbolism. We can see this symbolism as multi-leveled, and by itself it contains no value-judgments: we would not say that Aquarius "is better" than Pisces, for with each symbol arise elements that we will categorize as "positive" and elements that we will categorize as "negative," and sometimes these two mix together, apparently inextricably. We might say that we shouldn't throw out the beneficial babies with the problematic bathwater, but when dealing with collective trends, we find it more difficult to separate the relevant elements as easily as we do in our private bathtubs.

We can see this difficulty in the symbolism from our own tradition. People speak of Aquarius' connection with friendship, brotherhood, networking, new technology, and group-relationships. We may see all of these as positive. However, none of this speaks of fertility or organic growth, and if we look into the world, we see that people's use of new technology has often led to decidedly negative effects on the ecosystem and that one person's sense of brotherhood looks to another like rabid aggression. In addition, though Aquarius' penchant for forming groups based on shared ideas may seem beneficial, if we gravitate toward such groups, we may gravitate away from either the family (a group based on affinities other than those generated by ideas) or the home ground; and when we think of "new ideas," we may equate them with "progress" and hold to them even though their consequences seem in many ways quite problematic. The "best and the brightest" have not always led wisely.

Though Aquarius has much to do with the new and the groundbreaking, as a barren sign it carries within its symbolism the suggestion of a barren earth, one perhaps crisscrossed by wires carrying information, but one also characterized increasingly by deserts beneath the wires. And though we may see much group-affinity, we may also see one group opposed to another, particularly during periods of acute shortage. As for Leo, Aquarius' polar opposite and another barren sign, it brings in the idea of autocracy, suggesting the danger of increasingly autocratic forms of government as a response to environmental crisis.[1] Neither Leo nor Aquarius has a reputation for empathy or a connection to organic growth; farmers do well, when the Moon passes through these signs, to destroy pests or pull weeds, not plant seeds. These observations should give us pause as we enter the new age.

I remember an older historian, admittedly of the armchair variety, saying to me, years back, that humanity was "headed for the technological millennium," which he apparently saw as a good thing. However, neither *technology* nor *millennia* seem valuable in themselves. Each technology has its own bias,[2] and some have a bias that we may find problematic. And as we approach the end of an era, particularly one of our astrological ages (not really *millennia* in the strict sense, of course), we don't necessarily approach a period we will enjoy living in. The shift in Ages tells us only that we will enter a period in which the symbolic dominants will change dramatically. The lives of individuals will take on different emphases; the collective life will move in a different direction. Perhaps more importantly, we will find that the old ways of solving problems will no longer serve; they may well exacerbate rather than ameliorate.

IV. The "Why?" of It All

I once met a Lakota Indian who, noticing that the cows had long coats and that sunflowers covered the fields in unusual profusion, correctly predicted a particularly hard winter characterized by lower-than-usual temperatures and heavy snowfall. Not all of us read the signs so well as that Lakota man, either as regards the weather or as regards the future generally: we may not observe carefully enough, or we may not have any reliable way of analyzing the given facts, whether those facts have to do with meteorology, eschatology, or a nation's future. To analyze accurately, we first need to know which facts to take as significant, and then what significance to attach to them. Further, because the matters that concern us develop in periods "measured in decades or centuries, rather than months or years,"[3] we can't always get the facts just by looking around us; we need to look at the historical record.

---

[1] As we will see in chapter three, Leo plays a prominent role in the horoscope for the Long Count.
[2] If you doubt this, try hitting a baseball with your kitchen knife. Interested readers might wish to read Neal Postman's *Amusing Ourselves to Death* (Penguin Books, 1985 and 2006), to which I owe a debt.
[3] *The Limits to Growth*, 27.

Astrological analysis of the Long Count can help us in all this, for a horoscope, when analyzed using techniques with a proven track record, will help us to find these general patterns "measured in decades or centuries" and to know which ones to take as important and which ones to ignore. Because we have cast the horoscope for an aeon instead of for an individual, the astrological factors will point to general patterns that we can discern in the historical record. Because astrological analysis can inform us not only about behavior (what has happened in the past), but also about how to work with present problems, our analysis of the Long Count may point to creative possibilities not yet discerned.

Presumably, individuals come for astrology readings when they feel that they can benefit from the objectivity that astrology provides, for what Jung called the "effective determinants" of one's fate beyond the reach of one's conscious intention.[1] If the objectivity gained from such a discussion seems beneficial, then the reading will generally prove helpful. It seems that the "client" for the present reading—what we might call *the dominant human social formation*, as well as the group of human beings either directing it or influencing it—stands in dire need of some of that objectivity. As I write this, the counsel of such people as Al Gore has had insufficient effect. The megamachine—a term I borrow from Lewis Mumford and to which we will return—goes on as it always has, preventing the effective taking of alternative measures. But if enough people offer cogent analyses of our current situation, perhaps we will see some change; and if an argument based in astrological symbols can explain things more effectively in some ways than do other arguments, then why not offer it?

So we can ask, "Beyond the conscious intention of governments and leaders, what seem the *effective forces and determinants* of the collective fate?" Hopefully the following astrological analysis of history will offer us an objective description of our situation, a description we can see as a *diagnostic* one. A different description of a problem, one given using a different set of symbols arising from a different tradition, often suggests a unique set of possible solutions. For example, a practitioner of Chinese medicine will describe breast cancer quite differently than will a Western allopathic practitioner. From a Chinese medical point of view, breast cancer arises as the result of a long train of causes that the person and/or the Chinese medical practitioner can interrupt at various points (though better sooner than later), whereas most Western doctors talk only about what the practitioner of Chinese Medicine would see as the *result* (the formation of a tumor). The description offered by a practitioner of traditional Chinese medicine will suggest different ways to treat the condition.[2]

---

[1] C.G. Jung, *Modern Man in Search of a Soul* (New York: Harcourt Brace Jovanovich, 1933), 208.
[2] See, for example, Honora Lee Wolfe's *The Breast Connection: A Laywoman's Guide to the Treatment of Breast Disease by Chinese Medicine* (Blue Poppy Press, Boulder, Colorado, 1989), and other publications either by the same author or by her husband, Robert Flaws.

Here, we can hope that if we describe the problem in astrological terms, we may see different solutions than those we will see if we describe the problem only in, say, political terms, or only in terms of economic factors. Not that the astrological symbolism ignores these factors. On the contrary, it should include and integrate them. But it links these factors to inner, psychological referents. Also, because it speaks in terms of patterns, the astrological analysis will direct us to causes far in the past, particularly when we connect this analysis with the analyses of some historians (e.g. Toynbee and Mumford) who have offered concise summaries and interpretations of what occurred over the past several thousand years. From diagnosis can arise recommendations for treatment. Both diagnosis and treatment result from a coordinated explanation of relevant astrological factors.

Of course, we will find that our analysis involves various factors that we will evaluate in different ways. Certainly it will extend beyond the "sun sign astrology" available in many newspapers. Furthermore, it will involve the integration of a wide variety of astrological factors, not just one or two (as in Sun-sign astrology). We won't say, for example, "It all has to do with Leo and Leo only" (though, as we will see, Leo plays an important role). Just as a historian will look at economic factors, political factors, environmental factors (etc.) and from the *combination* of factors form conclusions, so here we will look at various interrelated astrological factors. However, astrological symbols have a particular facility for showing the connection between psychological elements and behavioral ones, between personal issues and collective developments, between what we might call neurosis or psychosis and what we might call intelligence or wisdom. Further, astrological techniques enable us to tell *when* specific developments will come to fruition or demand attention. It seems that only such an integrated approach will serve us at all well at this time.

VI. Procedures

We will begin our investigation by looking at Western astrology's notions about Great Ages, tracing those aeons (e.g. The Age of Pisces, The Age of Aries, The Age of Taurus, etc.) through thirteen thousand years of history, attempting to set the Mayan Long Count, with its birth date in 3114 BC, into the context of that historical pattern. In the second chapter, we will look at the similarities and differences between our astrology and Mayan calendrics, trying to see where the Maya focused their gaze and if it differs from where we generally focus ours; we will use principles of our system to draw inferences about Mayan concerns. Having done that, we will, in the third chapter, take a long look at the natal horoscope for the Long Count. In chapter four, we will do a time analysis of that horoscope, using standard astrological techniques to focus on several key periods and examine developments related to what we can loosely call "civilization." Finally, we will look to the future symbolized in the horoscope for the next Long Count. From these analyses will come both prognosis and praxis. Though not all scholars of things-Mayan will agree that the Maya predicted a Long Count following the present one, every ending brings (as far as we know) a beginning, and the precise end point of one cycle seems to qualify as the precise beginning point of the next one.[1] We can therefore interpret the planetary positions at the end of the present Long Count not only as indicators about developments in that Long Count, but also as indicators for the future.

---

[1] The Maya astronomer priests might not agree with this assertion, as we find in some Mayan cycles a "resting period" between one cycle and the next. In this book, though, we apply *our* practices to *their* measurements.

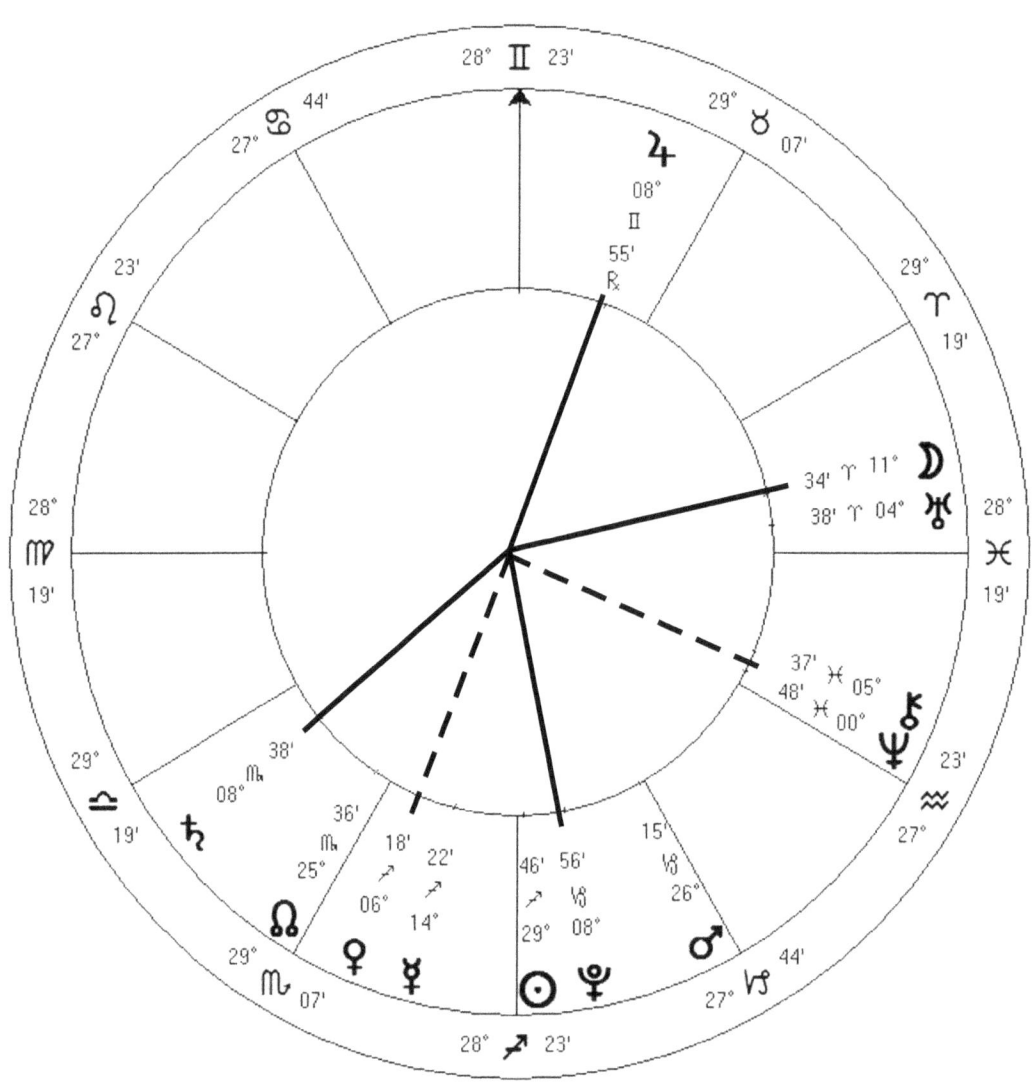

Long Count Next. December 21, 2012, 12:00 am, Palenque, Mexico

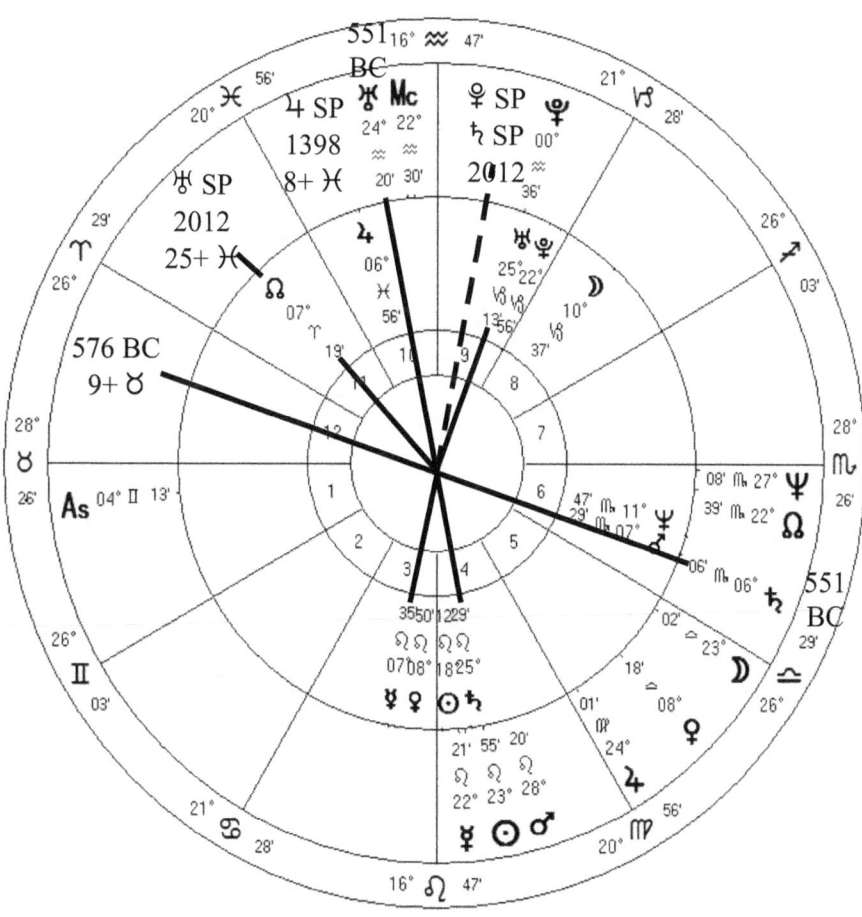

Inner Wheel: Long Count Gregorian Mayan, August 11, 3114 BC NS, 12:00 am, Palenque Mexico

Outer Wheel: Long Count Gregorian Mayan Progressed, January 1 551 BC

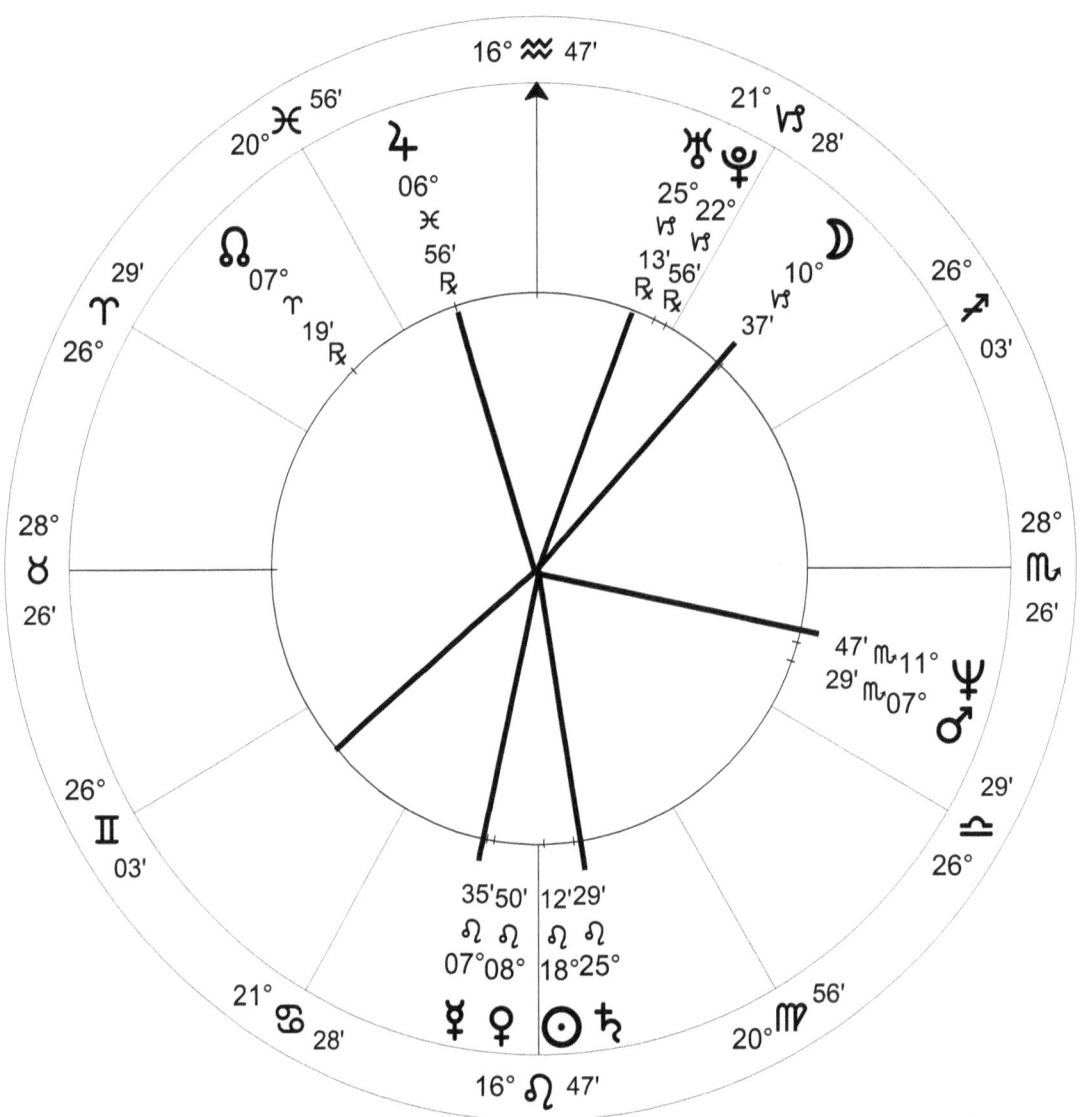

Long Count Gregorian Mayan
August 11, 3114 BC NS, 12:00 am, Palenque, Mexico

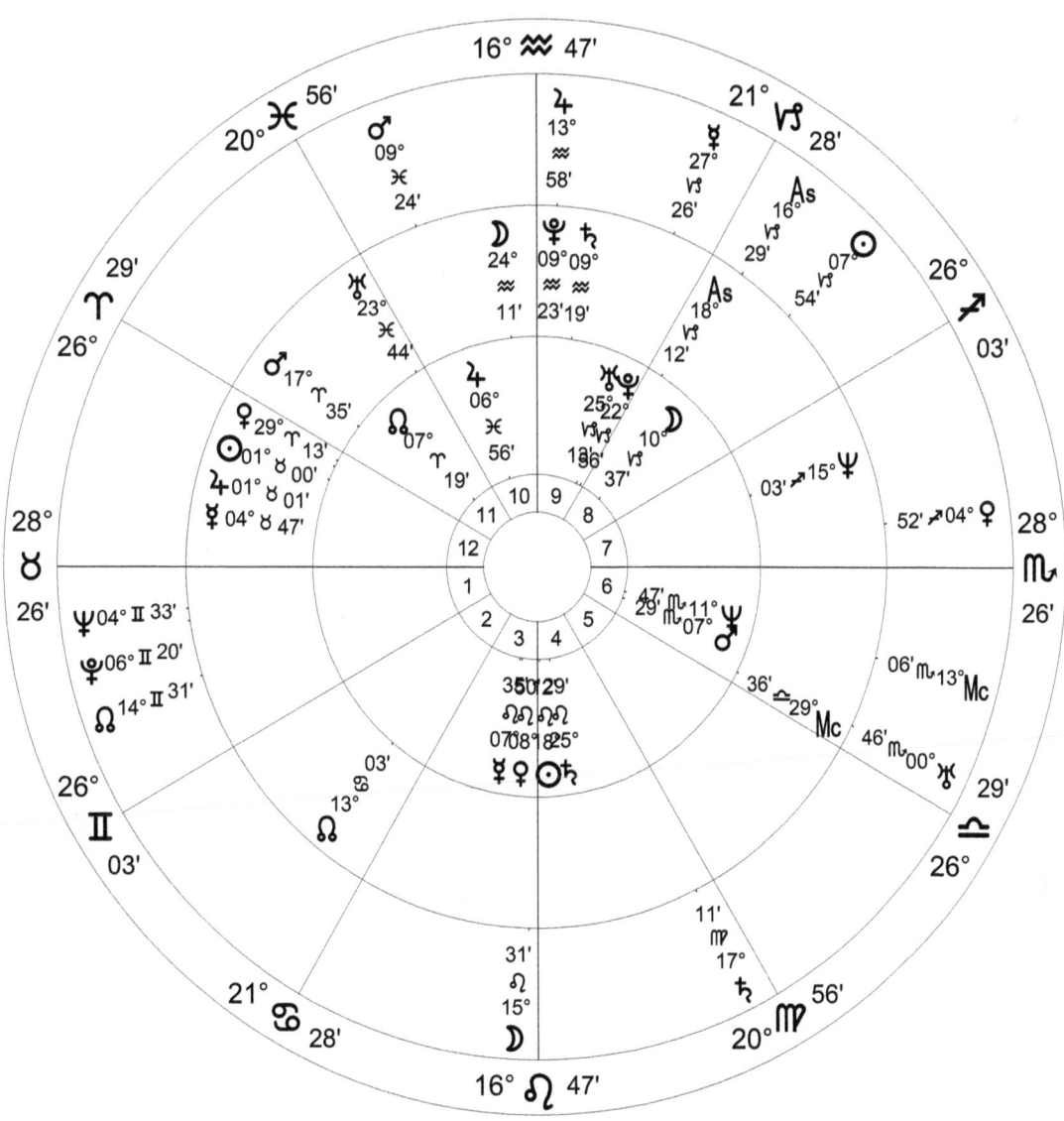

Inner Wheel: Long Count Gregorian Mayan
Middle Wheel: Progressed to December 29, 1890
Outer Wheel: Wounded Knee, December 29, 1890, 8:00 am, Wounded Knee, South Dakota

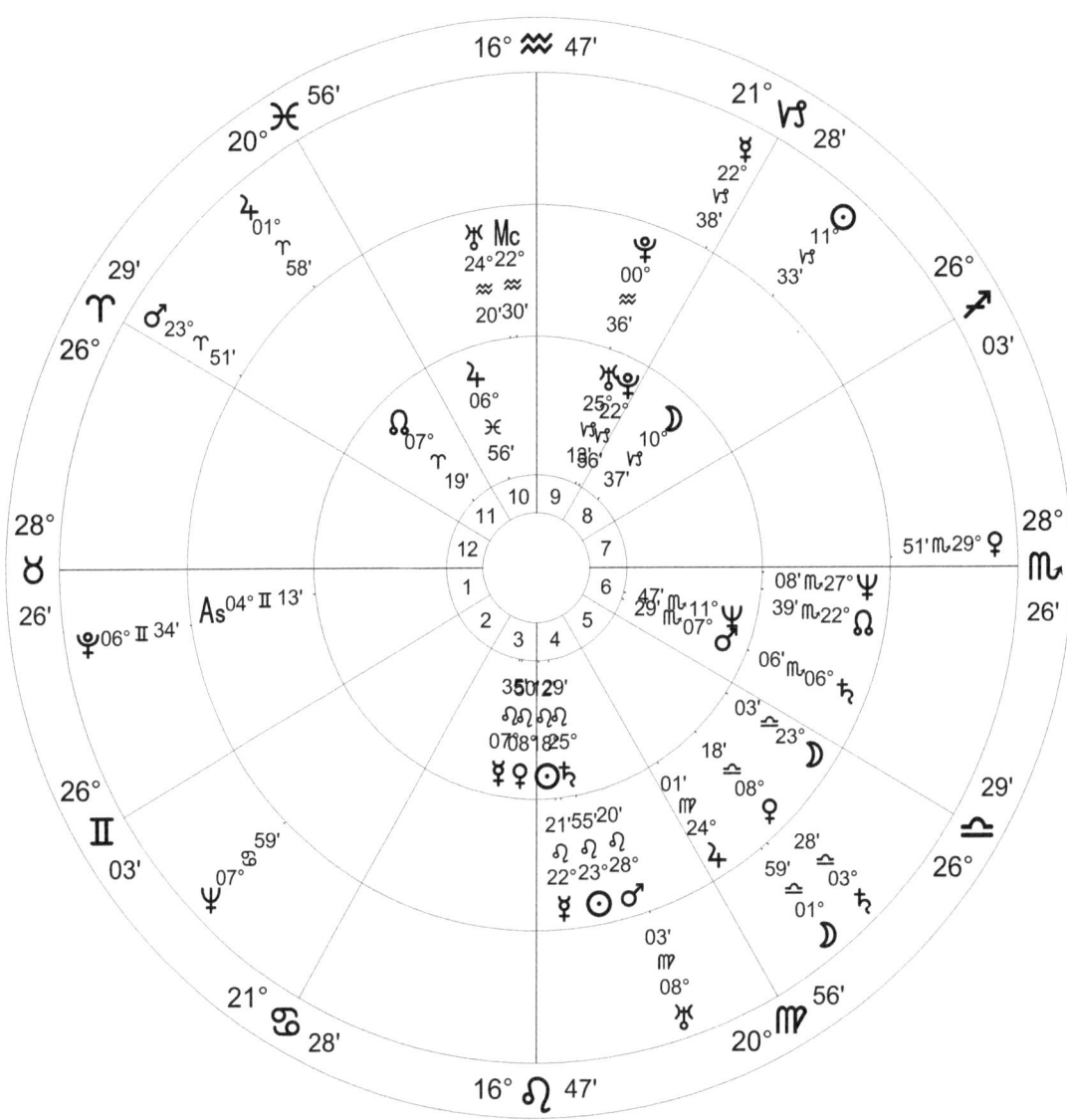

Inner Wheel: Long Count Gregorian Mayan
Middle Wheel: Progressed to January 1, 551 BC
Outer Wheel: Long Count Midpoint 551 BC Transits, Palenque, Mexico

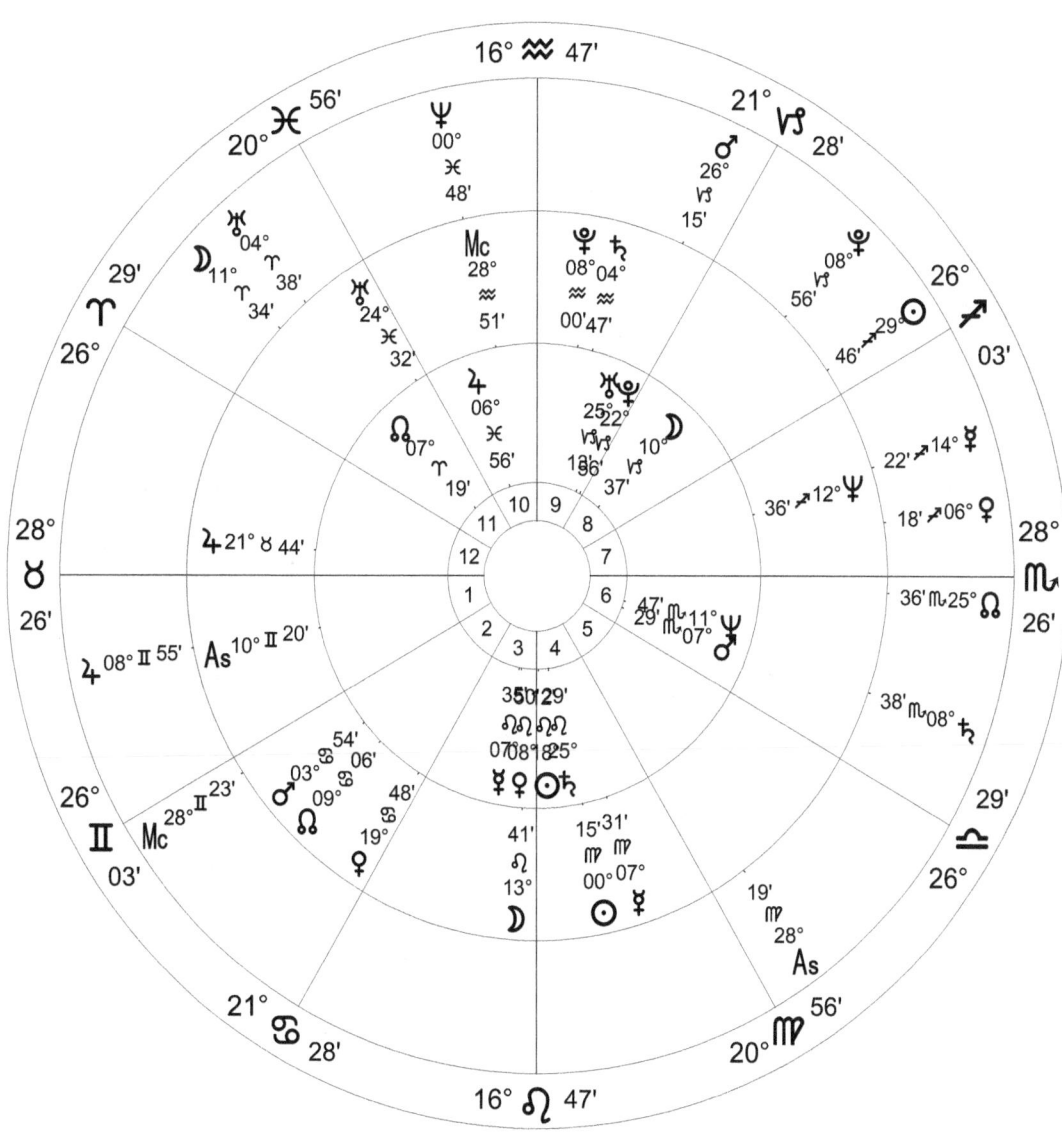

Inner Wheel: Long Count Gregorian Mayan
Middle Wheel: Progressed to December 21, 2012
Outer Wheel: Long Count Next, December 21, 2012, 12:00 am, Palenque, Mexico

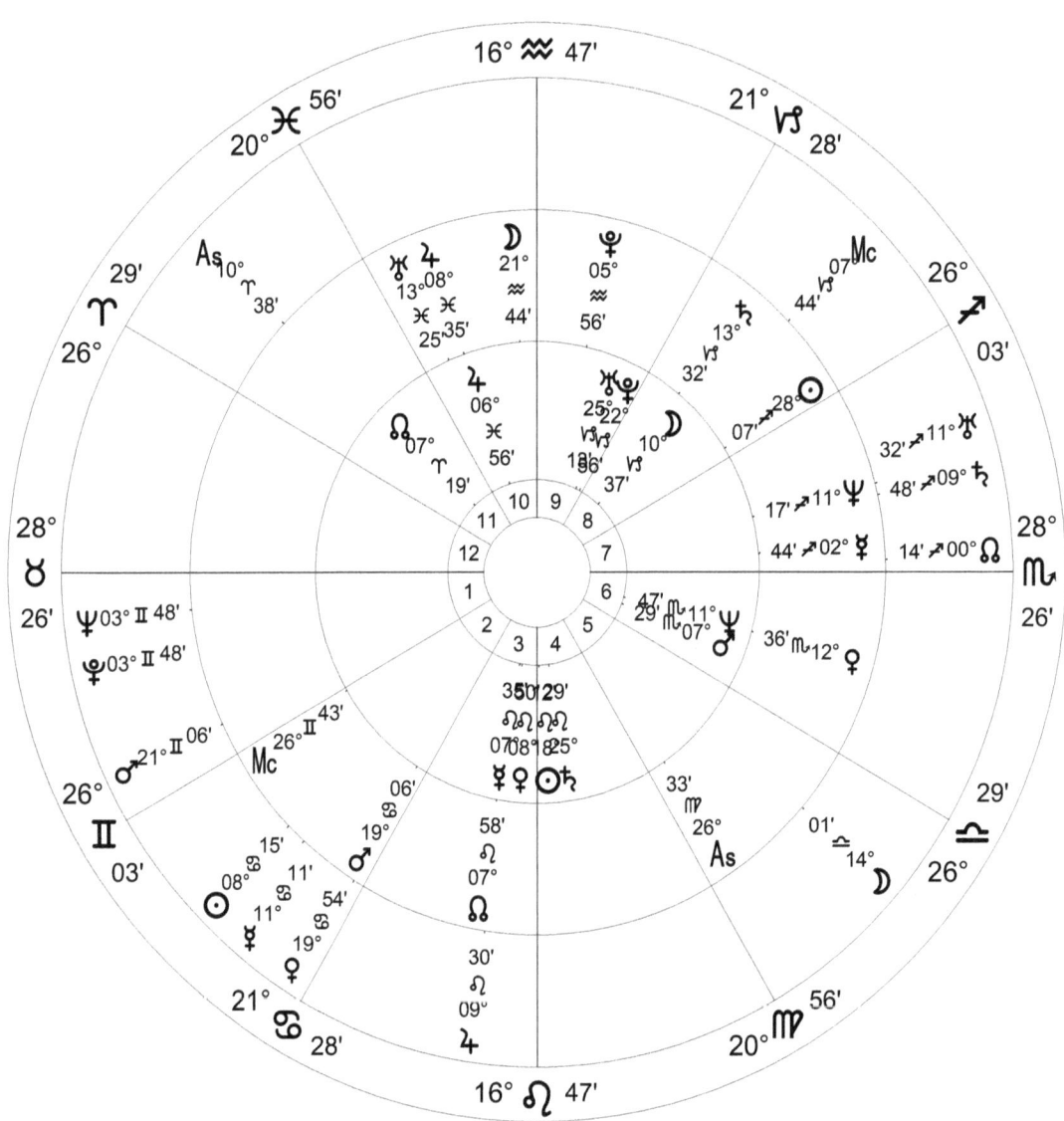

Inner Wheel: Long Count Gregorian Mayan
Middle Wheel: Progressed to June 22, 1398
Outer Wheel: Renaissance, Long Count 1398, June 22, 1398, 12:00 am, Palenque, Mexico

Chapter One

Astrology's Evolutionary Timepiece

IF WE WISH TO VIEW the Mayan Long Count through the lens of our own astrology, we should begin by seeking some points of connection. We find an important one in the concept of Great Ages and another in the observation that Western Astrology and Mayan Calendrics both apparently measure the same Great Year of over 25,000 years. Whereas we arrive at our figure of 25,920 years by dividing the Great Year into twelve Ages, the Maya apparently arrived at their figure by dividing the Great Year into five ages, or Suns. We will discuss the meaning of these different divisions in chapter two, noting here only that astrologers in both systems concerned themselves, at least in part, with long-term trends.

Astrologers measure the astrological ages by the movement of the equinoctial point backwards, via precession, from one astrological sign to the previous one: from Taurus to Aries to Pisces to Aquarius to Capricorn and so forth. In speaking of these Ages of 2160 years, we should see the figure as approximate: the constellations do not have fixed boundaries and so have different extensions in the sky. The figure 2160 comes from dividing the Great Year by twelve, not from any precise idea of when the equinoctial point "leaves" one constellation and "enters" another. For this reason, we hear much discussion in astrology circles about just when our present Age of Pisces ends and the Age of Aquarius begins.[1] In speaking of the ages, we should therefore rec-

---

[1] We can contrast this with the precision of the Mayan Long Count, a period for which the Mayans gave a precise beginning. Yet whereas our measurements have a loose connection to the constellations, theirs may have none at all. (Note the "may" in the previous sentence. John Major Jenkins has argued for a connection between the Long Count and the dark rift in the center of the Milky Way as seen from earth, though we may wish to distinguish between this rift and the constellations proper.)

ognize a transition period between one aeon and another, a period that some have called the "cusp" period.[1]

This imprecision—this recognition of transition-periods—reflects the nature of historical development: major shifts take place gradually, often over many centuries, not on precise dates. While historians may delineate threshold points in such processes, we should not expect sudden changes. We shouldn't reject the imprecision in the astrological system in a misguided search for some precise proof not reflected in the available evidence.

Keep these points in mind in looking at the following chart, considering the dates as rough guidelines only. I have arbitrarily chosen 0 AD as the beginning of the Piscean era, and have added or subtracted 2160 years for each succeeding or preceding age. A shift of a few hundred years one way or the other makes little difference to the material that follows.

Age of Virgo	12,960 BC-10,800 BC
Age of Leo	10,800 BC-8,640 BC
Age of Cancer	8,640 BC-6,480 BC
Age of Gemini	6,480 BC-4,320 BC
Age of Taurus	4,320 BC-2,160 BC
Age of Aries	2,160 BC-0 AD
Age of Pisces	0 AD-2,160 AD
Age of Aquarius	2,160 AD-4,320 AD

The Long Count—the "Sun of Ollin"—began about the middle of the Age of Taurus. An overview of the astrological aeons will help us to place this date into context.

The Pattern of History

To begin, a few technical and historical notes:

Technical notes: As the following evidence suggests, we see in each astrological age the symbolism not only of the dominant sign, but also of its polar opposite. So in the Age of Virgo, we find symbolism related to both Pisces and to Virgo; in the Age of Leo, we see symbolism related

---

[1] Astrologers use "cusp" in many ways, most obviously in their discussion of the houses of a horoscope. If a planet falls within 5 degrees of the house-boundary, most astrologers will interpret that planet as "on the cusp" and therefore as influencing the succeeding house as much as the house in which the planet actually lies. More generally, the term refers to a transition area or transition period between one period or cycle and the next.

to both Leo and Aquarius; and so forth. Second, the terms "trine" and "sextile," referring to aspect measures of 120 and 60 degrees respectively, generally refer to a harmonious relationship characterized by helpful developments *within* a given form, whereas the terms "square" and "opposition," referring to aspect measures of 90 and 180 degrees respectively, generally refer to challenging relationships or changes *of* form (because current forms cannot accommodate the changes taking place). Squares often point to specific structural developments (e.g. new social structures developing); oppositions often bring culminations or evident splits.

Historical notes: Archaeologists and historians don't entirely agree on all of the matters discussed here, so some will dispute some of my conclusions. However, I've drawn from scholars whose work has gained respect even when disputes remain. Some astrologers may feel troubled that I omit from this discussion many occult theories, particularly those dealing with ancient civilizations (Atlantis, Lemuria) that purportedly existed in ancient times. I neither accept nor dispute ideas related to these ancient civilizations. I have focused on what we might call the "generally accepted theories" of non-occultists—of scholars who swim in what we might call the mainstream of academic opinion. As I will show, this mainstream point of view accords well in many ways with the pattern suggested by the astrological ages.

The most recent ice age gave way to warmer temperatures back during what we now refer to as the Age of Virgo, about twelve to fourteen thousand years ago. The receding icecaps uncovered new (virgin) earth in northern latitudes. At the same time, due to the melting ice, the oceans rose—suggesting watery Pisces, Virgo's polar opposite—flooding many coastal areas. That we see rising oceans again here at the end of the Age of Pisces, half a precessional year later, should give us pause even if we see different causal factors at work.

As the ice melted, our ancestors developed hunting tools to survive in a period of scarce game, a development that seems to reflect Virgo's well known penchant for precision and practical efficiency. At the same time, the rebirth of vegetation in temperate zones as the glaciers retreated seems to reflect Virgo's connection to the Great Mother, symbol of vegetation and the natural world, and to the harvest. As we come to the end of the Age of Pisces, half a Great Year later, we see quite clearly not only the result of the skillful tool-making, but also the widespread destruction of vegetation.

We see in Virgo what we will see in Taurus, the next earth sign: development in practical, "earthy" affairs related to survival, feeding, and stabilizing, though we see more of the stabilizing in the fixed earth sign (Taurus) than we do in the mutable one (Virgo). During the Age of Virgo, self-discovery (Leo) had to play a subservient role to the rituals, disciplines, adjustments, and technical developments necessary to ensure physical survival. However, as the Age of Virgo moved into the Age of Leo, questions of identity surely rose increasingly to the forefront. With basic survival more certain (relatively speaking) due to comparative mastery over the immediate environment, people quite likely began to reflect, to see themselves as individuals, as separate and isolated.

In his controversial *The Origin of Consciousness in the Development of the BiCameral Mind*, Julian Jaynes speculates that names were invented between 10,000 and 8,000 BC, dates approximating those of the Age of Leo.[1] Names suggest an emphasis on personal identity, and with that identity comes personal pride along with the barrenness of the resulting isolation. Leo is generally known as the most barren sign of the zodiac, connected with the sun, heat, evaporation, and desiccation. During the Age of Leo, the earth continued to warm, suggesting the influence of the Sun, traditional ruler of Leo. Some occultists and astrologers have interpreted Leo's barren pride as indicating that during the Age of Leo, Atlantis fell due to the overweening pride of its leaders, a pride that set one person against another. Man's growing technical capacities (Aquarius, Leo's polar opposite), these occultists say, combined with human arrogance (Leo) and led to ecological destruction. Technology plus arrogance, in this equation, equals barrenness and a fall from grace. The theory goes further, in some cases, postulating that the people presently in power have reincarnated from Atlantis and now play similar roles in our society. In one version, these reincarnated Atlantians, having learned their lesson, will make a wiser use of power than they did back in the Age of Leo.

Whether or not Atlantis actually existed, and whether or not it fell back into the ocean, and whether or not this resulted from humans using their inventions unwisely, and whatever we say about Jaynes' ideas regarding names and their function, we can reasonably conclude that once humans gained some degree of mastery over the external environment during the Age of Virgo, they had time to make additional discoveries about themselves. And so we see Leo following Virgo: the development of individualized self-identity follows from some degree of practical acuity.

Whether we discard or accept the "occult" interpretation sketched above, we can accept the ideas as metaphorically true: we stand in a rather interesting relationship to the people who lived at the cusp of the Virgo-Leo ages. Like them, we confront problems related to human pride, technical mastery, and the natural hierarchies of the world; like them, we live on a warming planet. During the earlier period, humans experienced for the first time the results of limited technical mastery; the hunt no longer required full-time participation of the entire clan, and so humans' excess consciousness, not needed for simple survival orientation, began (so to speak) to survey its personal realm, and, in experiencing the isolation of personal identity, to seek shared goals or ways to participate more consciously in group (Aquarius) activities, particularly through hunting, an activity associated in myriad ways with Leo, a matter to which we will return, and to Aquarius, for people often hunted in groups.

---

[1] Julian Jaynes, *The Origin of Consciousness in the Breakdown of the Bicameral Mind* (Boston: Houghton Mifflin Company, 1976), 135.

With these shared goals, people began to form the Neolithic villages associated, appropriately enough, with the Age of Cancer. The birth of the town or village seems to have occurred by 7000 BC, the period that some have termed the "Neolithic Revolution":

> Around 8000 B.C., the initial steps were taken, in a few localities in the Near East, toward the greatest revolution humanity had yet experienced; the development of agriculture. Very likely the revolution resulted from the ingenuity of women, gathering wild grain while the men were off hunting, and discovering the uses of seed.[1]

Domestication and the emphasis on women surely reflect Cancer, primary sign of the mother, the most fertile sign in the zodiac, the sign of nurturing as well as of the home, the clan, and the family groups that form the basis for communal living. We can find corroborative evidence for this in Jaynes' work, for he writes of Natufian culture ("the best defined and most fully studied Mesolithic culture"):

> In 10,000 B.C., like their Paleolithic predecessors, the Natufians were hunters…often living in the mouths of caves…By 9000 B.C., they are burying their dead in ceremonial graves and adopting a more settled life.[2]

Jaynes goes on to speculate that without names (Age of Leo), leaders could not have controlled entire towns (Cancer) because the people needed a way to keep the ruler or king in mind when he was not physically present:

> Of course it is not impossible that one chief could dominate a few hundred people. But it would be a consuming task if such domination had to be through face-to-face encounters repeated every so often with each individual, as occurs in those primate groups that maintain strict hierarchies.[3]

Though not all historians will accept this explanation, and though it seems that the major authoritarian impulse became clearly visible during the Age of Taurus, most will agree that the period-in-question saw a shift from a predominately hunting economy to one more dependent on settled agriculture practiced on a small scale. They see this period as characterized more by egalitarianism than by the drive for authority and control. Nevertheless, Lewis Mumford acknowledges that as the centuries passed, the non-warlike farmers of the Neolithic villages probably found themselves threatened by the more aggressive hunters, and that the two split apart. This split seemed to develop flagrantly during the Age of Gemini, a sign associated with splits

---

[1] C. Warren Hollister, *Roots of the Western Tradition: A Short History of the Ancient World* (New York: John Wiley & Sons, 1982), 7-8.
[2] Jaynes 138-9.
[3] Jaynes, 140.

of various kinds, though it probably had its roots earlier. In any case, the Age of Leo, particularly in its later stages, brought a transition from food-collecting economies, largely hunting-based and thus related to Leo, to food-producing ones, largely farming-based and thus associated with Cancer, generally considered the most fertile sign in the zodiac for planting food-crops.

We see creativity (often associated with Leo[1]) in activities indicating that *homo-sapiens* had achieved some degree of mastery of the environment. Lewis Mumford writes of the period associated with the Magdalenian cave paintings, which many archaeologists place from 17,000 to 11,000 years ago—that is, from 15,000 BC to 9,000 BC, the later date placing it at the end of the Age of Leo:

> Along with [the] symbolic concentration on sex,[2] the first evidences of hearth and home as central to a settled life appear: a mutant in hunting culture that became a dominant in the succeeding phases of Neolithic culture, and has remained persistent since. And not without further technical significance is the fact that the first use of clay, apart from the hearth itself, is its employment as a material for art, as in the bisons of Tue d'Audoubert cave, thousands of years before there is evidence of pottery. The suggestion here is plain: Paleolithic man began to domesticate himself before he domesticated either plants or animals. This was the first step, beyond ritual, language, and cosmetics, in transforming the human personality.[3]

The connection to Leo seems clear here: an emphasis on creativity instead of domesticity, on the personality instead of the home itself. Mumford goes on:

> And here, precisely at the point where the symbolic arts join together and supplement each other, Homo Sapiens—Man the Knower and Interpreter—appears in the character that marks all his later history: not just doggedly scratching for a living, grubbing and picking, tool-making and hunting, but partly detached from those animal necessities, dancing, singing, playing, painting, modeling, gesturing, mimicking, dramatizing, conversing—certainly conversing!—and perhaps for the first time laughing. That laughter would identify him and certify his mastery better than tools.[4]

---

[1] We should distinguish, here, between creativity in the sense of "creating one's life, moment to moment," and creativity as it relates to "creative artists." Leo has a close connection to the former.
[2] Lewis Mumford, *The Myth of the Machine, Volume One: Technics and Human Development* (New York: Harcourt, Brace, Jovanovich, 1967), 123.
[3] Mumford here refers to the "imaginative transformation of art and sex that accompanied the improvement of weapons and collective hunting techniques." He sees this transformation in the "distribution of the female figurines" found in the period. See *Technics and Human Development*, c. page 122.
[4] Ibid.

By 7000 BC, settled villages had definitely established themselves, suggesting the symbolism of Cancer. The Age of Cancer brought the development of pottery, the remains of which archaeologists use as a major means of dating the distant past. The pottery both symbolizes and points to the containment of the community and its relationship to Mother Earth, both obviously related to Cancer.

This period apparently brought humanization of the environment. Mumford describes the changes that occurred as the Paleolithic shifted into the Neolithic:

> Partly because living conditions were so formidable during the Ice Age, Paleolithic man, apart from playing with fire, largely took his habitat as given, and bowed to its demands, even becoming a specialist in one particular mode of adaptation—hunting. Such shaping as was open to him . . . had mainly to do with his own body and mind. But the Neolithic cultivator made numerous constructive changes in his environment, aided by the warming of the climate and—after the great melting and flooding that followed—by the drying up of the swamps. With the aid of the axe he opened up the heavy forest, built dams and reservoirs and irrigation ditches, erected stockades, terraced hills, staked out permanent fields, drove piles, built clay or wooden dwellings. What neither the miner nor the hunter had been able to accomplish, the woodman and the farmer, able to support larger numbers in a small area, actually achieved: an increasingly humanized environment.[1]

So we see, as we might expect, that the Age ruled by a cardinal sign brings important new beginnings. Because we have to do with Cancer, these beginnings had to do with the development of settled communities. With that settled community came, not the excitement of dramatism (as in the Age of Leo), but predictability, particularly the kind that comes from the application of a person to a specific task. And whereas in the Paleolithic we see an emphasis on what we might call "male prerogatives," in the Neolithic we see women taking on a more important role, hardly surprising when we consider Cancer's connection to the feminine. We can see this in connection with activities in which people worked not to gain immediate satisfaction but to achieve more long-term goals, behavior patterns generally associated with Capricorn, Cancer's polar-opposite:

> . . . a new trait appears in Neolithic culture: 'industriousness,' the capacity for assiduous application to a single task, sometimes carried over years and generations. The intermittent technical activities of paleolithic man no longer sufficed: it was by prolonged, dogged, unremitting effort that all the typical Neolithic achievements, from breeding to building, were accomplished. Paleolithic males, if we may judge by most surviving hunting peoples, had an aristocratic contempt for

---
[1]Mumford, 127.

work in any form: they left such drudgery to their womenfolk. So when Neolithic peoples turned to work, one need hardly wonder that woman, with her patient, inexorable ways, took command.[1]

We also see during this period an increased emphasis on patterns of behavior associated with Capricorn, Cancer's polar-opposite, a sign associated with the willingness to work carefully and with discipline towards long-term goals. Mumford tells us that during this period we see for the first time what we might call "daily work"—along with a loss of dramatic display and excitement, not surprising for a shift from Leo, sign of the hunt, to Cancer, the dimmest constellation in the zodiac:

> In this transformation, from a predominately hunting economy to an agricultural one, much was gained; but also something was lost. And the contrast between the two cultures underlies a large part of human history; it can still be seen in more primitive communities even today. A modern observer in Africa, innocent of any of my present preoccupations, noticed a difference between the Batwa hunters, "gay with an uncomplicated cheerfulness" and the "rather sullen demeanor of the average Bantu" in his employ. And he asks himself, "Is it possible that the hard but unfettered life of the hunter brings a freedom of the spirit that the sedentary agriculturalists have lost?"[2]

The Age of Cancer brought rapid increases in the domestication of both animals and plants, and to effect these changes, Neolithic people had to have a settled life in which to apply steady attention toward tasks that would bring about desired ends:

> For the first time, under Neolithic cultivation and building, man began deliberately to change the face of the earth. In the open landscape, the signs of man's year-round occupation began to multiply: little hamlets and villages made their appearance in every part of the world.[3]

This is not to say that the entire process took place during the Age of Cancer; rather, the Age of Cancer brought the visible consequences of a process with its roots in the past. As Mumford points out, though there is "still a tendency to date the great agricultural advance from 9000 to 7000 BC," dates that place it within the Age of Cancer, "we now have reason to see that it was a much more gradual process. . . ." He divides this "gradual process" into several phases, the first of which involved increased familiarity with the material people would eventually domesticate: both foraged plants and wild animals. Then came the actual domestication of both animals (e.g.

---

[1] Mumford, 128.
[2] Mumford, 128
[3] Mumford, 129.

first the dog, later such animals as the pig and duck) and plants (perhaps first such starchy roots as yam and taro). Periods after this saw the development of mixed farming and more types of nutritive plants. Finally, "on the eve of civilization" (the Age of Taurus; see below) came the "last stage in this complex, long-pursued process": the domestication of cereals "and the beginning of large-scale open-field, clean-drop agriculture" that brought about an immense increase of food in the rich lands of Mesopotamia and Egypt, for the very dryness of the cereal seeds makes these grains storable at ordinary temperatures for a longer period than most other foods except nuts; and the richness in proteins and minerals gives them exceptional food value.[1]

It may seem but a short step from the development of settled communities (Age of Cancer) and non-vagrant agriculture—both of which suggest land and home that one could pass on to one's descendants—to the stage of civilization that we find in Sumer (Age of Taurus) just before 3000 BC. Yet this step took over 3000 years and

> . . . must have been planned by leaders who had the imagination, foresight, and self-control to work for returns that would be lucrative ultimately but not immediately. The leaders' plans would have been no more than unfulfilled dreams if they had not been able to induce large numbers of their fellow men to pursue objectives which were probably incomprehensible to them. The masses must have had blind faith in their leaders, and gods whose potency and wisdom were realities for both the human leaders and their followers. The one indispensable new tool was a script. The leaders needed this instrument for organizing people and water and soil in quantities and magnitudes that were too vast to be handled efficiently by the unrecorded memorizing of oral arrangements and instructions.[2]

Though the script had its practical effect and formalization during the Age of Taurus, the period during which the Sumerian and Egyptian civilizations took shape, it quite probably had its inception during the Age of Gemini; the generally accepted date for the first formal writing seems to fall between 3500 and 3000 BC. Toynbee notes that unlike the Egyptian script, which he describes as "devised suddenly," the Sumerian script went through "a gradual evolution...out of antecedent pictographs."[3] Astrologers will see this pattern as appropriate to Taurus and Gemini, for they consider Gemini as a mutable sign, having to do with movement from one state or stage of action or awareness to another, and Taurus as a fixed sign, having to do with the development of stable forms. So we see the development of writing during the Age of Gemini, a sign generally associated with written and other forms of communication, and the formalization, through practical activities, during the Age of Taurus, a sign associated with grounding and resource-management. The Gemini-Taurus connection seems more compelling when we consider that

---

[1] Mumford, 130.
[2] Arnold Toynbee, *Mankind and Mother Earth* (New York: Oxford University Press, 1976), 51.
[3] Toynbee, 56-7.

"the earliest uses of writing were not to convey ideas, religious or otherwise, but to keep temple records of grain, cattle, pottery, fabricated goods, stored and disbursed,"[1] Taurean matters all. And, it seems, to record the taking of prisoners, a matter to which we will return in our discussion of Scorpio, Taurus' polar opposite, a sign traditionally ruled by Mars, the planet associated with militarism.[2]

The Age of Gemini saw not only the development of writing, but also of a marked bifurcation of society, with the farmers on the one hand and the hunters on the other: the twins appearing in the developing dualism. Though hunters and farmers can obviously develop a symbiotic relationship—the farmer benefits when the hunter kills animals that would otherwise threaten crops or livestock; the hunter benefits from the regular food supply supplied by the farmer—the split eventually became an egregious one, finally leading to major alterations in social structure. On the one hand, the hunter "fared best when he entered into symbiotic relations with the new peasants and builders, and helped to create a new economy and a new technics." On the other hand, because that technics involved weaponry, the hunter with his "imagination and…audacity," eventually emerged as "an aristocratic minority" who gained "control over a large population."[3]

We can add three points. First, the act of writing seems to require a separation of the writer from his experience, an inner division for which Gemini stands as an apt symbol: the writer must stop and recollect past experience; the writing and the events written about take place separately. As we will see, this kind of objectivity also seems necessary to the development of metallurgy, a process that spanned the same two ages.

Second, though many new species of plant came under cultivation during what Mumford calls the "agricultural transformation," that process "soon reached a climax" after which the "original impulse toward domestication was exhausted."[4] After that, we see, instead, "both in nature and on the farm . . . an increasing proliferation of new varieties of existing species." This variety seems to reflect Gemini, as does the process, for it involved observation and clear communication. Mumford's description shows us, though unwittingly, the symbolism of Gemini, for we see in the process the result of "causal insight and relevant correlations, passed on by speech," resulting in "large accretions of positive knowledge" arising from "pre-scientific lore."[5] So, not surprisingly, we see the major initiatives taking place during the Age ruled by a cardinal sign (Cancer: initial domestication), and further developments, adjustments, and variation taking place during the age ruled by a mutable sign (Gemini: proliferation). We see this latter kind of

---

[1]Mumford, 192. The following argument owes much to Lewis Mumford's account in *Technics and Human Development*.
[2]As we will see, too, Scorpio has a prominent position in the Long Count horoscope, with Mars and Neptune conjoining there, indicating obsessive aggression based on idealism and delusion.
[3]Mumford, 132.
[4]Mumford, 130.
[5]Mumford, 134-5.

development not only in the various kinds of, say, squash or dogs, but also in the development of numerous folk remedies and tonics.

Third, the domesticity indicated by Cancer suggests that people, no longer nomadic, applied themselves to specific tasks, among them the kind of "grinding, boring, and polishing" that characterized Neolithic tool making:

> Only groups that were prepared to remain long in the same spot, to apply themselves to the same task, to repeat the same motions day after day, were capable of gaining the rewards of Neolithic culture. The restless ones, the impatient and adventurous ones, must have found the daily routine of the Neolithic hamlet intolerable, as compared with the excitement of the chase, or of fishing with net and line. Such people reverted to the hunt or became nomadic herdsmen.[1]

The task-orientation suggests Capricorn, Cancer's polar opposite and therefore implicated in the Age of Cancer. Capricorn, ruled by Saturn, has to do with tasks undertaken not for excitement but for practical reasons or purposes, activities not necessarily experienced as rewarding in themselves, but undertaken for a long-term goal. We also see once again the contrast between the exciting dynamism of the fire-ruled Age of Leo and the more domestic Age of Cancer, between a period apparently dominated by men and a period apparently dominated by women, for as Mumford tells us, as "homemaker, house-keeper, fire-tender, pot-molder, garden-cultivator, woman was responsible for the large collection of utensils and utilities that mark neolithic technics."[2] This pattern remained in effect until the end of the period. From this dynamic dualism arose the increasingly flagrant split between farmer and hunter.

This last point shows, though indirectly, the influence of both Gemini and Sagittarius, for Sagittarius wants expansion and space to roam, whereas Gemini wants space for intellectual curiosity. We will see these influences if we follow Mumford's argument.[3] In the "last stage of domestication" with its "patriarchal pastoral specialization"—for as the garden gave way to or found itself in cooperation with the larger grain field, men again found themselves as the sowers of seed, just as they found themselves working with the animals—men regained dominant, or at least equally prominent, positions in the Neolithic domestic economy. In short, ". . . the repressed male element recovered lost ground in every part of the economy." As a result, "woman, freed from her masculine obligations to work and govern, no longer crippled physically by excessive muscular effort, became more enchanting not just for her sexuality but for her beauty."[4]

---

[1] Mumford, 137.
[2] Mumford, 141.
[3] The following, and the entire chapter, owes much to Mumford's argument, even in sections in which I do not cite him directly.
[4] Mumford, 155.

We see here described a more clear differentiation in gender-roles, with the men having more to do with the bringing in of food and women relegated, perhaps for the first time, to the status of something separate and distinct. Again, we see the mark of Gemini's dualism.

Further, during this period, as the villages became more secure from want and invasion, and with the increased emphasis on sexual attraction, we would find more children. And with more children in a family or community, those children learned more quickly:

> [T]here would be a larger number of siblings in the same nest and this would accelerate the pace of learning almost as much as grandparental care and example—for more of the old, too, would be likely to survive. Though the first dolls were probably Paleolithic, the appearance of children's toys indicates not merely a greater margin for playful activity but a growing interest in children's needs—and, it seems, connected with some clear sexual differentiation, with the males functioning as hunters and the women as watchers of the garden.[1]

Much of this bears the mark of Gemini, for Gemini, partly through its connection to the third house, has to do with siblings and the immediate community, and with the mind in its immediate application to experience, gathering information and learning through play—all suggesting Gemini's love of curiosity, of immediate communication, and of learning through community connections. Whereas children would handicap a hunter, they proved valuable at home, not only for the enjoyment they brought, but also for help in domestic tasks such as husking vegetables (Gemini rules the hands and fingers). So again and again, we see, in the period after the Age of Cancer, the marks of Gemini: of duality; of language and learning; of curiosity; of community and communication; of play within the daily round with neighbors and siblings.

Astrologers call Gemini a sign of "mutable air," which we might translate (admittedly, a bit over-simplistically) as "restless mind" or "restless curiosity." Fittingly, then, as the Age of Gemini drew towards its conclusion and the Geminian gods wearied of their burden, we see a curious lack of dynamism. It seems that the Gemini drive had exhausted itself:

> Once formed, the Neolithic culture lacked the very qualities that had made it so attractive in the beginning—its exploratory curiosity and its adventurous experiments. In many parts of the world, an elaboration of neolithic technics took place; but further human development, though it always fell back on the neolithic stabilities when threatened with extinction, took a different route, exploiting not sex but power: the route of civilization.[2]

---

[1] Mumford, 157.
[2] Mumford, 162.

This brings us to the Age of Taurus, and, about halfway through it, to the Long Count, for during the Third Millennium BC, a profound change took place in human culture.[1]

The Age of Taurus brought a new kind of social organization, one based not in "neighborly intimacy, customary usage, and consent," but on "collective power," power as a fundamental value. In this we see Scorpio, polar opposite to Taurus, as well as Taurus itself, for power-seekers couldn't have accumulated power unless the social group had available an agricultural surplus. This surplus came about because of the large-scale, field–agriculture that came to replace the gardens of the Neolithic village. The developing power-complex also had metallurgy as a basic component, and language as a necessary glue. Certainly we can see the Age of Taurus as a period that brought the formalization (fixed earth sign) of earlier mental developments (mutable air sign).

Scholars seem to agree that metallurgy first appeared about 6000 years ago, which would place it right around the time when the Age of Gemini gave way to the Age of Taurus. We can see metallurgy as a preeminently intellectual (Gemini) process, one requiring an objectivity and curiosity (Gemini) regarding the items of experience. Earth itself appeared as something separate, something one might work. Here, as in the series of Neptune-Pluto conjunctions in Gemini that we will discuss later, Gemini arises as a split in which humans took a more objective view of the world in which they lived: seeing the world as "other," they saw it as something one might work at with one's hands, through one's curiosity, and with one's knowledge. Humans would never have learned to work metals unless they used all these capacities:

> Metallurgy is the end-product of a chain of successive discoveries, and the concatenation was not self-evident. Each link was added by a stroke of intellectual genius. Neolithic man first noticed lumps of more or less pure metal exposed to view on the . . . land-surface. He first treated these lumps of metal as stones and discovered that, unlike ordinary stones, they were malleable. He then discovered that, if heated, they became temporarily pliable and that they liquefied if the temperature were raised to a high degree. Thus, in metal, Man had hit upon a raw material which, like clay, was much more amenable than stone to being shaped.[2]

If, as Toynbee suggests, the development took place gradually, it seems reasonable to place most of it back in the Age of Gemini, with its emphasis on division, objectivity, curiosity, and intellect. This could not have occurred without the settled communities that arose during the Age of Cancer, for without a settled community working in pottery, you have no kiln; with no kiln, you can't heat the potentially malleable metals. So Cancer led to Gemini, but with metallurgy as with writing, the formalization took place during the Age of Taurus. In *The Astrology of*

---
[1] Mumford, 163.
[2] Toynbee, 42.

Fate, Liz Greene connects Taurus to Hephaestos, the "divine smith" and husband to Aphrodite, the "cow-eyed one,"[1] emphasizing the connection between Venus-ruled (and therefore Aphrodite-ruled) Taurus and *making* through the shaping of metals.

Metallurgy and the surplus forced upon people some basic dilemmas regarding the distribution of wealth. Astrologically, we again see in this the movement from Gemini to Taurus, from idea and intelligence to the need for management based on acceptable values—management, we might say, of value, of a kind of wealth that in theory belonged to everyone equally but which eventually came to serve a power-system (Scorpio) that seemed to promote inequality. Toynbee writes:

> The division of labor was the technological consequence [of metallurgy]. The social corollary of this was the exchange of the products of diverse kinds of work; and this in turn created a still unsolved, and perhaps insoluble, ethical problem. On what principle is the total product of society to be distributed among the various classes of producers?[2]

We see in Toynbee's description various Taurean elements in combination: the need for management; questions of value; the importance of resources. Toynbee also notes that metallurgy brought the demand for a "non-replaceable and scarce raw material." As we have moved through the Age of Pisces (one-quarter of a Great Year later: Gemini squares Pisces[3]), we have experienced a plethora of difficulties related to this problem: the demand for limited resources has brought about international conflicts (suggesting Sagittarius, Gemini's polar opposite) that have obstructed humans' efforts to deal with the ecological crisis brought about by the use of those limited resources; we see similar conflicts in the 4th millennium BC, for when the metallurgy-producing people ran out of the necessary raw materials, they often moved into other areas.

During the Age of Pisces, humans have experienced difficulties (square) related to the dualism inherent in Gemini: the division of person from person, of person from environment, of nation from nation, this last reflecting Gemini's polar opposite Sagittarius, a sign associated with matters-foreign (and, like Pisces, ruled by Jupiter, a planet associated with expansion). At the end of the Age of Pisces, we have experienced these as a crisis related to the earth itself; and this, too, we find reflected in the astrological symbolism, for in Alice Bailey's occult system of rulerships, the Earth rules Gemini, and astrologers have always referred to Taurus as a *earth*-sign. As

---

[1] Liz Greene, *The Astrology of Fate* (York Beach, Maine: Samuel Weiser, Inc., 1984), 188-9.
[2] Toynbee, 42-3.
[3] Hard aspects bring challenges. The square indicates a need for new venues. Note in this discussion of Ages how what we might call the major karmic consequences of something developed in an earlier Age come due or appear clearly during an Age that either squares or opposes the earlier one.

we enter the Age of Aquarius, a quarter of the zodiac from Taurus, we experience problems related to the forms of social development connected to metallurgy and large-field agriculture: global warming, battles over resources, and soil-depletion.

The Age of Taurus brought what many historians often refer to as the "birth of civilization." Toynbee points to agricultural surplus and the development of a managerial class needed to manage the surplus as essential to this development, so again we see the marks of Taurus: agriculture, abundance, and decisions regarding the use of resources. And as we have seen, the managers required a script (Gemini) in order to manage these resources.

Scorpio, Taurus' polar opposite, appears partly in the cults of the dead that arose in Egypt.[1] We see in these cults the influence of both Taurus and Scorpio, for the deceased was provided with abundant material goods (Taurus) for his journey through the land of the dead (Scorpio). The trine from Taurus to Virgo emerges because the surplus created in Taurus released people even more from the demands of survival orientation, and the square from Leo emerges in the structures (society, cults of the dead, connection to kings) developing in the new social organizations as a result of self-identity (for the idea of a *soul* depends upon and develops from the idea of self-identity) and as a result of the dominance of the hunter class. The civilizations that developed during the Age of Taurus presented new structures (square) through which people in that class found an outlet for their abundant energy—for it seems that the hunters came to dominance during the Taurus aeon and have remained there ever since—though now, as we come to the Age of Aquarius, 180 degrees from Leo, we see the culmination, and perhaps the downfall of that class, a matter to which we will return.

The Ages of the Leo and Taurus, fixed signs, brought different stages of release from the bondage of necessity. Now, as we move into the Age of Aquarius, scientists have developed genetically-engineered seed-strains, but this probably will not lead to the abundance evident during the Age of Taurus, for whereas astrologers have traditionally seen Taurus and Scorpio as fruitful signs and thus friendly to organic growth, they have seen Aquarius and Leo as "barren" signs. These notions suggest that contemporary technical developments will increase barrenness instead of providing abundance. We can also say that civilization (Age of Taurus), with its subordination of the individual to collective concerns, challenges individual identity (Leo)—and that the dominance of group concerns (Aquarius) can bring dire consequences when combined with unbridled egoism or self-concern (Leo).[2]

We can also see the surplus as a harmonious and beneficial result arising from settled living.

---

[1] Alan Oken, *Complete Astrology* (New York: Bantam, 1988), 519-20.
[2] Of course, people with Leo strong in their horoscopes will not necessarily display more self-concern or egoism than others (though I know of no reliable way of measuring these matters). Signs and planets in the horoscope of a collectivity generally manifest in the most problematic ways. The reader should bear this in mind in all of the discussions that follow.

Though we might object to many of the ways in which the dominant class made use of this surplus, the surplus itself seems a clear benefit resulting from human ingenuity. This reflects the harmonious sextile (ingenuity) between Cancer and Taurus,[1] the latter sign suggesting the practical result of that ingenuity: what began in the cardinal sign (Cancer), and what developed through the mutable one (Gemini: a sign associated with ingenuity), takes on a more stable form in the fixed sign (Taurus). We see further benefits from surplus in the tremendous material and cultural advances of the Age of Pisces (trine Cancer; sextile Taurus). Still, the results of individualism and regality within civilization (Leo square Taurus) will demand attention during the coming Age of Aquarius, a period that will bring the structural results, tangible and evident in the world around us, of ego ego-driven materialism (Leo plus Taurus). Two barren signs, Leo and Aquarius, square Taurus: we can expect dire consequences to the earth and our living environment, for an Age ruled by a barren sign could surely bring ecological barrenness.

Toynbee sees war and class-differentiation as the two "congenital evils" of civilization. Neither could have arisen without the mentioned surplus, for "[i]n a community in which the working time of every able-bodied participant is fully occupied by the task of producing food, there is no spare time for the maintenance of even part-time administrators, priests, artisans or soldiers."[2]

With the arising of warfare we see a change in the nature of the gods from representatives of natural forces to representatives of the "collective human power of some particular Sumerian city-state."[3] These gods served as focal points for both the individual and the state as the former began to identify with the latter. We see, here, the shift from the Age of Taurus into the Age of Aries: once civilization develops, one sees class-differentiation; and once class-differentiation arises, ruling and warrior classes develop; and once these develop, wars and battles seem inevitable. But before we move on to the Age of Aries, let's take a final look at the Age of Taurus, particularly at the peculiar kind of social development that Lewis Mumford refers to as the *megamachine*.

Underneath all the developments that we call "the rise of civilization," we find an emphasis on order:[4] ordered fields, an ordered hierarchy, the keeping of orderly records (with the script, developed during the Age of Gemini), apparently the standardization of wheel-sizes, and, perhaps supporting them all, an orderly view of the cosmos, this last suggested by the rise of the sun-god, embodied in the human king. This last kind of order came from observation of the heavens, where people saw the orderly movement of planets and stars. Not everyone had suffi-

---

[1] It also suggests Gemini, the sign between Cancer and Taurus, a sign generally associated with ingenuity and with a symbolic connection to the sextile (because Gemini begins 60 degrees from the beginning of the zodiac at 1 Aries).
[2] Toynbee, 54.
[3] Toynbee, 54.
[4] I have borrowed much of the following historical material from Lewis Mumford.

cient knowledge of these matters to make predictions, but a small group did, and this gave that group a good deal of practical and persuasive power.

We see here the development of a priesthood, a group with "an exceptional power of astronomical and then meteorological prediction" that "was a source of their supernatural authority."[1] During this period, in both the heavens and on earth, people saw and sought order. Those who perceived that order apparently put it to ego-driven ends so that the understanding of the cosmic order metamorphosed, through ego-driven alchemy, into social control. No wonder, then, that we see arising here the new institution of kingship as a central organizing principle for the megamachine. Viewed from an astrological perspective, this shift represents the square (new structures) from Leo (hunting bands) to Taurus ("civilization"): the hunters found a new structure through which to exert their dominance, the desire for such dominance having arisen during the increasingly flagrant hunter-farmer split of the Age of Gemini. (As we will see in chapter three, Leo plays an important role in our discussion not only because of what occurred during the Age of Leo, but also because the Long Count horoscope has four planets in Leo—the Sun, Saturn, Mercury, and Venus—each of which plays a prominent role in the interpretation.)

This machine did not have metal or inorganic parts. Those lay far in the future. It had human parts, and it built the pyramids, the great temples, and the great walled cities that represented a quantum increase in size from the Neolithic villages. The shift from village to city, from a kind of participatory democracy to the hierarchy controlled by the king, took place when the hunting chief took "to his own person all the powers and prerogatives of the community," for as Mumford tells us:

> [as] to the origin of the king's unconditional supremacy and his special technical facilities . . . , there is no room for doubt: [I]t was hunting that cultivated the initiative, the self-confidence, the ruthlessness that kings must exercise to achieve and retain command; and it was the hunter's weapons that backed up his commands, whether rational or irrational, with the ultimate authority of armed force: above all, the readiness to kill.[2]

We see here the uneasy, stressful relationship between Leo and Taurus, signs in a square (stress, challenge) relationship and thus resulting in structural change: in the Age of Leo, the hunter dominated; in the Age of Taurus, with its new agricultural abundance, the hunter returned to dominance through a change in social structure even though the abundance had come about largely through the work of others. Thus the hunter emerged as the king, a connection that has come down to us through the centuries, evident during some periods in such notions as "the king's forest" or "the king's beasts," and today in the ruler or king's ability to set armies marching.

---

[1] Mumford, 167.
[2] Mumford, 169.

Five thousand years ago, as in the myth of King Minos and the Bull, the king took as his own what belonged rightfully to the people. Taurus, here, suggests the management of resources; Scorpio suggests the rising of power, particularly the power to kill, but including the power that transformed the social conditions in which people lived. Notable here, is the relationship between Scorpio and Aries, the two signs traditionally ruled by Mars, a planet serving as the shadow-ruler of the Age of Taurus and as the acknowledged ruler of the succeeding Age of Aries, two periods characterized by a practice heretofore unknown among humans: organized and large-scale warfare. Though archaeologists have found no trace of weapons in the Neolithic village, Mumford tells us that Egyptian kings boasted of their prowess as lion hunters.

In the Age of Taurus, the kings resolved, after a manner, the split associated with the Gemini period: from the hunters came courage, weapons, and the habit of violence and killing; from the villagers came "the punctual, prudent, methodical life of the agricultural community" with its habits of persistence and discipline. From the combination appeared the military class. Those in power effected the change, augmenting their power by demanding the cooperation and "awed submission and passive consent" of the entire community. The hunting chief metamorphosed into the high priest; he lived in the walled temple, from where he controlled the grain and allocated it according to plans of his own or his subordinates' devising. So it seems that the king maintained power partly by the knowledge of the heavens that enabled him to make predictions, and partly by his control of the food supply. In this we see the mark of both Scorpio and Taurus, power and plenty:

> This fusion of sacred and temporal power released an immense explosion of latent energy, as in a nuclear reaction. At the same time, it created a new institutional form, for which there is no evidence in the simple Neolithic village or Paleolithic cave: an enclave of power, dominated by an elite who were supported in grandiose style by tribute and taxes forcibly drawn from the whole community.[1]

We see, in this description, the two rulers of Scorpio, Taurus' polar-opposite. In the traditional system, Mars, associated with warfare and hunting, rules Scorpio. In the contemporary system, Pluto also rules Scorpio. Pluto's symbolic connections include the night sky, from whose movements the priests drew some of their power, the unconscious, the source of the primitive power-drives that arose at that time, and the sense of secrecy that surely characterized the actions of those who retreated into their priestly enclaves. Finally, as ruler of plutonium, Pluto has a close connection to all "nuclear" reactions, even the symbolic type of which Mumford speaks.

The sun-god (Leo)[2] appears in the emphasis, even insistence, on order, for the priests could make predictions related to the cosmic order: they could predict the movement of the Sun, in re-

---

[1] Mumford, 170.
[2] See chapter three for further discussion of Leo's importance to the period in question.

lation to other bodies in the heavens, and from that movement they could predict some yearly patterns of weather, on which the crops depended, and perhaps other things as well. However, we see a new power emerging from the knowledge of the night sky (Pluto, and thus Scorpio). Eventually, the power of physical coercion and the power of prediction fused in the sun-god-king. And so we see the temple of Atum-Re, the sun-god in Egypt:

> Out of [a] multiheaded family of gods, with its swarm of distant relatives in every little village, the Sun God had in Egypt become pre-eminent; and the new authority of kingship was sustained, not by brute force alone, but by its representation of the eternal power and order of the cosmos.[1]

And from this cosmic order derived other kinds or methods of order: counting, measuring, exact notation—"attributes without whose early development no such consummate monuments as the pyramids could have been built."[2] We see here once again the formalization in the Age of Taurus of processes that dominated the Age of Gemini: writing found its use in the very practical Taurean affairs of the new social order.[3] We also see the development (Gemini: a mutable sign) of the village (Cancer: the preceding cardinal sign) into the fixed, grounded form (Taurus: fixed earth sign) that seems not just a sequential development from the village, but an unprecedented kind of social order altogether.

Though all of this certainly suggests Taurus, with its emphasis on the management of earthly resources and its longing for higher truths, it suggests Scorpio as well, for "the gods are in fact the kings of the unconscious, enlarged, as the kings in turn became incarnate dream gods, exercising visible supremacy over waking life, transmitting their claims of inviolable sovereignty to the whole apparatus of the state."[4]

Settled civilization, based on surplus, seems to generate aggression. Epitomizing this shift we find the monotheism developed by the Israelites, Jahweh serving as the "focal point of identification" *par excellence*. Moses, traditionally considered an Aries, served as Jahweh's spokesperson and presided over the shift in identification (Aries) from the bull-god (Taurus) to the lamb-god (Aries), a process described in Genesis.

---

[1] Mumford, 172.
[2] Mumford, 173.
[3] Mumford notes, in a passage of interest to astrologers, that the Babylonians "introduced the same concept of predetermined order into the seemingly irregular events of daily life: they plotted the course and position of the planets and associated this with the hour of a person's birth in order to predict the entire course of his life. The biographic data needed for such plotting was based on systematic observation." And: "With this new office came a comparable enlargement of the sense of time. Egyptian, Mesopotamian, Hindu, and later Mayan religions all embrace cycles of thousands of years. . . ."
[4] Mumford, 177.

By all accounts, the Age of Aries had more than its share of war and aggression: the Hittites (c. 2000 BC), the Babylonians (c. 1200 BC), the Philistines, the Persians, the Hyksos in Egypt, the Greeks and the Trojans, and, perhaps cruelest of all, the Assyrians, whose reign peaked in the second half of the Age. What is new here is not aggression, for surely that had existed long before, but aggression organized and expressed on a vast scale: aggression based in law, hierarchy, and a drive for security (terms reflecting the three other cardinal signs: Libra, Capricorn, Cancer) driven by aggression (Aries).

At the same time, law codes, a balancing factor, arose in Babylon, among the Israelites, and elsewhere. This reflects Aries' polar-opposite, Libra, a sign concerned with fairness and with weighing (the scales) within so-called "civil society," for in all regulated social relations, people must refer to what Dane Rudhyar called a "socially accepted standard weight."[1] Thus the last half of the Age of Aries saw cruel wars balanced, after a manner, by the wisdom of Pericles, and the examination of law and civil systems that we find in Plato, Aristotle, and others. Even Alexander tried to balance conquest with learning and culture.

With Aries comes pioneering. You don't have physical pioneering unless you have a civilized area from which to pioneer, and you don't have intellectual pioneering unless you have some area referred to as "the known" and some other area referred to as "the unknown." The pioneer calls the known area "civilization"; he generally designates the rest as "un-civilized." People in the former generally see themselves as more advanced than people in the latter, and they maintain that point of view largely because military power (Aries) enables them to do so. That military power can arise only from a large and stable state (Taurus) that enables the creation of a military class (Aries), and it generally expresses itself against peoples considered barbarous by the purportedly civilized (Libra).

In any case, it seems that kingship continued to develop, now in association not only with the use of force or the notion that to identify (Aries) with the king or pharaoh meant to identify with the deity, but also that the king had to administer justice (Libra). Mumford writes of kingship:

> At the beginning, such power was associated with the idea of stewardship and responsibility to the gods. By 2000 BC, no Pharaoh could hope for immortality unless he had served the cause of righteousness and justice (Ma'at). In a text from the Middle Kingdom, Atum declares, "I made the great inundation that the poor man might have his rights therein like the great man. I made every man like his fellow." In this declaration one sees a recognition of a persistent pressure not only to legalize but to moralize power: to keep it within bounds and make it respect the human condition.[2]

---

[1] Dane Rudhyar, *Astrological Signs: The Pulse of Life* (Boulder: Shambhala, 1978), 85.
[2] Mumford, 182.

Yet, as Mumford notes in the next paragraph, we also see a consistent "ambivalence in this relationship" because "the kindliness of the ruler that is emphasized in the Egyptian texts goes along with his emphatic capacity to rouse terror and inflict death."[1] We can see, again, the union of Libra with Aries. So just as we see much to admire in the intellectual developments of the Aries-Libra age, we also see, as Mumford summarizes from Herodotus' history, "revolting descriptions of the rabid violence of kings."[2] And sometimes the legal and the terrifying went hand in hand, it seems, for "the number of crimes increased and the punishments became more terrifying" as disobedience to a superior's orders "was the worst of sins; and even 'answering back' was a serious offense." Further:

> Even under the relatively benign code of Hammurabi, the systematic infliction of punishment by torture and the permanent maiming of the body was sanctioned, though such practices were quite foreign to the archaic small community before the iron age.[3]

Despite the law codes, "every royal reign was a reign of terror." In theory, we might say, the rise of war and widespread, "civilized" aggression required or generated the message of compassion symbolized by Pisces, the sign ruling our current age. From one point of view, Jesus ushered this age in by supplementing the old law (Libra) of an eye-for-an-eye (balance: Libra; plus Arien aggression) with the law of universal love (Pisces) and service (Virgo). At the same time, though, the Age of Pisces brought not only widespread and unexamined delusion (Pisces), often in the name of one's chosen god, but also all sorts of problems related to purity (Virgo) or its lack, whether we consider that purity as related to moral virtue or to the ecosystem.

Many have noted that Jesus' name means "fish," appropriately enough for someone ushering in the Age of the Fishes. In *Aion*, Carl Jung noted, in addition, that fish symbolism pervaded the Middle East around the time of Jesus' birth. But we should note, in considering the boundary between Aries and Pisces, that we see not just a simple progression, but also a marked reaction to what has gone before.[4] Up to this point, we have seen a somewhat sequential and non-reactive development from survival to self-awareness to settled living to script-writing and invention to "civilization" to warfare. But with Pisces we enter a new cycle,[5] and as we do, we see a new "law" emerging as a reaction to the abuses of previous Ages.

---

[1] Mumford, 182.
[2] Mumford, 184.
[3] Mumford, 185.
[4] C.G. Jung, *Aion* (Princeton: Princeton University Press, 1959), chapters V-XI.
[5] In the "western" astrology system, the Age of Aries concludes a cycle of precession. After the Age of Aries, we pass from the first sign of the zodiac to the last, as the equinoctial point moves backwards through the zodiac.

The darker side of Pisces has emerged as mass-delusion and pollution. Pisces' rulers—Neptune (orthodox), Pluto (occult),[1] and Jupiter (traditional)[2]—aptly symbolize the unchecked expansion (Jupiter) of "civilization" based on or driven by underworld gods (Pluto) among which we can number oil (Neptune). Jupiter symbolizes expansion, confidence, and faith; Neptune rules not only oil (partly), but also any movements based on delusion; Pluto rules obsessions, the underworld, and power. Thus we see, during the Age of Pisces, the exponential expansion of the power-system, an expansion that has, by the end of the Age, well nigh taken over the entire planet and that has certainly affected the planetary ecosystem; the industrial age, powered by oil, has developed into the nuclear age, powered by plutonium. All of this has occurred during the Age of the Fishes, a period purportedly emphasizing love and compassion (Neptune), but one in which we see an evident split. Though we see evidence of the new "law of love" spoken of by Jesus, we also see the power of the status quo, the Saturnian imperative that underlies all the other manifestations of the Piscean era, a period ruled by Saturn's three sons: the aforementioned Jupiter, Neptune, and Pluto.

We also saw a split in Gemini, the previous mutable sign and the only other zodiac sign whose glyph consists of two distinct creatures. Under the sign of the twins, we saw human beings gain objectivity regarding their environment—and we saw a widening split between the hunters and the food-growers, a split that festered within the social forms that developed during the Age of Taurus. In the Age of Pisces, a mutable water sign symbolized by two fishes, people have found themselves immersed in a psychological dualism from which they have difficulty extricating themselves. Jung spoke quite extensively about the Piscean split, seeing it as inherent in the Christian myth and productive of a great deal of misery in the world. Of Jesus he said that . . .

---

[1] Many astrologers recognize at least four rulers for each sign: the traditional ruler, the contemporary ruler (which often coincides with the traditional one, though not for Scorpio, Aquarius, and Pisces), the occult ruler, and the exalted ruler. For Pisces, astrologers have assigned, in order, Jupiter, Neptune, Pluto, and Venus. I tend to see Pluto as having a particularly strong connection to Pisces, for oil, generally connected to Neptune, comes from the underworld, darkens the world, powers big business, and has, in our era, to do with power and brutality generally—Plutonian matters all. (Some astrologers recognize the various medieval rulers; some also recognize, following Alice Bailey, three occult rulers instead of only one. For information on medieval astrology, interested readers should consult the relevant writings and translations of Robert Hand.)

[2] In the traditional system, the Sun and Moon ruled one sign each (Leo and Cancer respectively), and the other planets ruled two signs each. Jupiter ruled Pisces and Sagittarius, a notion that, in itself, suggests dualism, for we may see these two signs as having to do with two approaches to what we might call "spirituality": the devotional approach and the rational approach. People generally connect Jupiter/Sagittarius with religion. After Neptune's discovery and subsequent assignment to Pisces, the dualism seemed complete. When Neptune was discovered, Darwin found himself working on the manuscript that he would eventually publish as *The Origin of Species*. (Stephen Jay Gould (*Ever Since Darwin*) reports that Darwin wrote preliminary sketches in 1842 and 1844 but waited twenty years to publish, his hesitation coming not from any lack of clarity or of material, but because of a variety of what we might call social factors.) The book highlighted for many the distinction between a spirituality based on devotion and yearnings (Neptune) and a spirituality based on learning, logic, and rational thinking (Jupiter).

> the dogmatic figure of Christ is so sublime and spotless that everything else turns dark beside it. It is, in fact, so one-sidedly perfect that it demands a psychic complement to restore the balance. This inevitable opposition led very early to the doctrine of the two sons of God, of whom the elder was called Satanael. The coming of the anti-Christ was not just a prophetic prediction—it is an exorable psychological law whose existence, though unknown to the author of the Johannine Epistles, brought him a sure knowledge of the impending enantiodromia.[1]

Jung goes on to link the coming of the Antichrist with the Protestant Reformation, which dawned as the equinoctial point entered the commissure that joins the two fishes in the constellation Pisces. Thus we see the inherent dualisms of the current Age: faith and reason; religion and science; good and evil; god and the devil; mind and phenomena. If faith ruled the period until the equinoctial point reached the commissure, reason challenged faith in the period afterward. Arnold Toynbee writes that between 1563 and 1763, Western civilization made

> . . . a greater mental and spiritual revolution than any that has ever been made by this society at any other previous date since it has arisen among the local debris of the Roman Empire. Western thinkers now refused to take their heritage from their predecessors on trust. They decided that henceforward they would test inherited doctrines by examining the phenomena independently, and that they would do their own thinking.[2]

The later discovery of Pisces' occult ruler, Pluto, coincided with the rise of quantum theory and Jung's analytical psychology, two major scientific developments, one having to do with mind and one having to do with phenomena, that call into question the facile separation between mind and world. We can add Edward Sapir and Alfred Korzybski to this list, for in the years to either side of the discovery of Pluto both men warned against the facile assumption that what we call "reality" arises as a thing in itself unconnected to the languages that, through their unique structures, enable us to form concepts about it. These schools of thought suggest that perhaps we don't see the world accurately at all, but that we see largely our projected version of things, a version that contains the dualisms just enumerated. The period around Pluto's discovery brought about a fusion (Pluto) of the prevailing dualisms of the Piscean era.

All of this has import for our discussion of the Long Count, for the Sun of Ollin, the final eon of the five that make up the great round of Mayan chronology, symbolizes movement arising from the union of opposites.[3] We see in our own culture, and in the Age of Pisces itself, ideas that seem very similar to the Mayan conception, for, as we approach the end of the Long

---
[1] Jung, 42-3.
[2] Toynbee, 536.
[3] Frank Waters, *Mexico Mystique* (Chicago: Swallow Press, 1975), 119-120.

Count and the Age of Pisces, we see accelerated movement driven by these unexamined dualisms. We also find in Pluto's symbolism the notion that such dualisms promote a kind of illusion and that if we insist on seeing the world in their terms, we don't see accurately and hinder progress.

The Age of Pisces has also brought motifs, issues, and problems related to Virgo, Pisces' polar opposite. Most obviously, we have at the beginning of the era the Virgin Mary, mother of Jesus. Much later, we find daunting problems related to purity and impurity, not only as points of emphasis in the dominant Christian religions—and, it seems, in the dominant Pisces Age theistic religions altogether—but also in the physical environment, with the world getting more and more impure as the years go on, with a host of attendant problems. We see impurity (pollution) related to an oil-based (Neptune/Pluto) economy in which plutocrats have power to exert hidden or not-so-hidden control over political processes that thrive on and promulgate inequality (Virgo). As noted earlier, all of the relevant gods (Jupiter, Neptune, and Pluto) are Saturn's children. Saturn has much to do with hierarchy. That we have to do with his children suggests that these planetary energies—the human energies that we connect with the planets—will often find themselves in a close relationship with prevailing hierarchies: working *within* hierarchies, controlled *by* them, and perhaps springing *from* them.

All of this seems foreboding enough in itself, but it takes an even more threatening form when we connect it to the coming Age of Aquarius. Though we hear a lot about the Aquarian Age of brotherhood and social improvement, of universal brotherhood and group unity based on technical advancement and more sophisticated communication systems, we should remember again that astrologers have always categorized Aquarius as a barren sign. Though this barren air sign may suggest fertile minds with a plethora of new ideas, it doesn't in any way suggest *organic* fertility. It suggests, rather, barrenness resulting from fixed ideas (Aquarius as the fixed air sign of the zodiac).

So though we will certainly see and have already seen improved communication, helpful technologies, and some sense of human brotherhood, Aquarian developments all, we also face environmental difficulties heretofore unprecedented and possibly catastrophic. We will and already do find ourselves on an increasingly barren earth, and, in a troublesome parallel to what occurred so long ago during the age of (polar opposite) Virgo, we see the waters rising as the polar ice-caps melt, the present situation bringing a culmination from the earlier one, when *homo sapiens* began to create the kind of world we see today. Pisces, after all, opposes Virgo: what begins in Virgo culminates in Pisces.

We should not feel surprised if, during the Age of Aquarius, many of our cities, descendants of the cities of Sumeria and Egypt, find themselves under Piscean waters. Nor should we feel surprised as one species after another goes extinct, as the planet gets hotter and hotter (suggesting sun-ruled Leo, Aquarius' polar opposite). The astrological situation suggests that things will get much worse as the Age of Aquarius proceeds. We might say that Aquarius suggests a much-needed brotherhood among humans; unfortunately, the current situation indicates that we will need all the brotherhood that we can muster. The primary symbols of an Age tell us what humans must and should cultivate, not what they will achieve. (Thus during the Age of Pisces/Virgo, humans strove for and spoke a lot about universal love and purity, but the evidence—e.g. from either the physical or moral climate—suggests that they did not achieve it.)

Because Leo suggests heat and Aquarius suggests technology, and because both suggest barrenness, we should expect a time of technical mastery but depleted fertility, and we should expect to see a connection between the heat and the technical mastery. Because human relationship has so much to do with the richness of earth (Venus, ruler of earthy Taurus, symbolizes love and bonding), we should also expect "relationship troubles" on a collective scale, as between nations or other collectivities. This, too, may connect to Leo and Aquarius: to Leo because it suggests overweening ego; to Aquarius because it emphasizes the one-to-many relationships (as distinguished from one-to-one partnerships or intimacies) that make up human society. On a collective level, this combination can indicate either the clarification of self-consciousness within group endeavors, or the ruling of autocrats over groups: the power of the group or the power of rulers *over* groups. On an environmental level, we find in the symbolism another pair of power-sources: power from the sun, suggesting Sun-ruled Leo, and the power of Uranium, suggesting Uranus-ruled Aquarius. Like Gemini and Pisces, Aquarius has a glyph with two parts. This suggests the dualisms that will surely pervade the coming era. However, whereas the glyphs of Gemini and Pisces consist of pairs of living beings, Aquarius' glyph consists of symbols representing non-living energies; this suggests not only Aquarius' emphasis on technology, but also Aquarius' barrenness.

Leo suggests kingship, and we carry with us the remnants of long-ago notions about the role of the king: about his closeness to the deity, about obedience to him and his commands, about loyalty to the realm he rules, about his close connection to the heavenly order. The king still has his allegiance to the hunters, and vice-versa: powerful rulers set armies in motion armed with weapons descended from those long-dead hunting bands. Aquarius-Leo suggests the relationship between the community and the power-system it adopts or gets co-opted by. On an individual level, this pairing can suggest ego and ego's world; on a collective level, it can suggest the ruler and the community. In times of difficulty, human beings have often turned to autocratic rulers.

The Long Count and the Age of Taurus

The spring equinoctial point precessed over 15 Taurus around[1] 3114 B.C., the beginning of the Sun of Ollin, the final eon in the Mayan cycle. Thus the Long Count began in an Age ruled by Taurus and Scorpio: Scorpio-Taurus; Taurus-Scorpio.

Scorpus: Scorpio-Taurus

Scorpio and Pluto have much to do with power, particularly hidden power; they also rule (along with Saturn), excrement, which according to many alchemical teachings has the same nature as the gold of enlightened consciousness. These teachings speak of the transmutation of the *nigredo* into the philosopher's stone, of darkness into light. This brings us back to the notion of power, and if we paid attention during our high school physics classes, we remember that physicists define *power* as the rate of doing work and *work* as a function of change. So the "transformation" that astrologers speak of in connection with Scorpio and Pluto has to do with the rate of change, not only in the external world, but also in the mind, for Pluto symbolizes fusion. Thus *transformation*—a change in form—involves a fusion, a recognition that external and internal arise together even if we give different labels to each realm: through its connection with fusion, Pluto reminds us of the inseparability of external and internal change.

As we will see, this reflects important factors in the Mayan time-measurements, particularly the Mayan emphasis on the numbers 52 and 72, numbers with symbolic connections to our septile and quintile aspects, and thus to matters related to collectivities (septile) and power (quintile). When we look at the horoscope for the Long Count, we will find important placements in Pluto-ruled Scorpio, and important transits involving polar-opposite Taurus.

At the same time, the emphasis on power and transformation, symbolized by Scorpio and its ruler (Pluto), reminds us of the powerful people and impetuses that have played such important roles in human cultural development, a development that seems to have come to either an impasse or a fork in the road during the current era, in the predicament that the Long Count seems so precisely to measure. Taurus, a sign associated with accumulation (as in the achieving of an agricultural surplus, mentioned above) appears in the grandiosity that characterizes contemporary civilization, a grandiosity that presents, we might say, such daunting obstacles in our efforts to solve many of the problems that beset us, particularly the Taurean problems related to money and natural richness.

---

[1] I say "around" because of a matter discussed above: that we don't know exactly when each constellation "really begins" or "really ends." We can say that in terms of precession, 3114 BC lies pretty close to the middle of Taurus, but we can't say exactly where the middle of Taurus lies. On the other hand, when we do time-analysis of the Long Count (in chapter four), we will have an exact mid-point for each period, for the Mayans gave us a precise birth-date for that era.

As I write this, hundreds of United States congress-members find themselves grappling with the financial problems of companies or banks deemed "too big to fail." Because these organizations command so much money and inter-link with so many other agencies, companies, workers, and markets, to let them go under would affect millions of people. And yet the organizations themselves seem completely dysfunctional in a world in which bigness so often proves problematic. Taurus and Scorpio, as any astrologer will tell you, have many connections to "big finance" and the banking system. Taurus has to do with the bigness and material value; Scorpio has to do with the interwoven and unseen connections in the underworld of financial conglomerates.

If we wish to look for the silver lining in the dark cloud, we will find it in Pluto's relationship to mind and its products. Pluto suggests, first of all, that we should not facilely distinguish between the phenomenal world and the mind; Pluto suggests, further, that you can't have one of these without the other, that they arise fused, and that if we look for a praxis, we would look first to the area in which we can bring about a change. Pluto suggests that widespread changes result from what might appear as very small causes. We can take the plutonium bomb as one example and an individual's change in awareness as another. All of this reminds us of the Mayan symbol *Ollin*, describing the modern era: the movement (power) that arises from the interweaving of opposites. That this movement may prove catastrophic should not blind us to the possibility that it could produce helpful, even necessary changes in approach.

The symbolism suggests that we will not deal effectively with the current crisis merely by making structural adjustments, whether through treaties or international agreements. We will not make the necessary external changes without the necessary inner changes—without, we might say, integrating the energy of Pluto. We know that the discovery of a new planet suggests that human beings must integrate that planetary energy into their personal growth; however, world history since 1930 strongly suggests that very few people have done this.

In other words, humanity has rejected Pluto; or, we might say, billions of individuals have done so. So the world seems ruled by a plutocracy in which we see signs of both Scorpio and Taurus: hidden power and abundance, or hidden power *in* abundance, or hidden power related to wealth, or any other combination of those terms you care to use. We may take this plutocracy as a collective projection arising from billions of minds. Humanity must withdraw this projection; or, individual people must do so, one by one. I suppose we might call this "power to and from the people," but it will look like powerlessness unless people do the necessary inner work and withdraw the projection, a process that must begin by revaluing within ourselves the Plutonian insistence on transformation, a process that fuses emotional and logical capacities and that effects a pervasive change in our ideas about the world and how it functions. Thus we "re-collect" (to borrow a term from Marie Louise von Franz[1]) Pluto from the world. The process again suggests

---

[1] Marie Louise von Franz, *Projection and Re-Collection in Jungian Psychology* (London: Open Court, 1985).

Ollin, for we generally take *mind* and *world* as opposites, though the closer we look, the more they seem to fuse.

Taurpeo: Taurus-Scorpio

Taurus tells us that the root of external power lies in the valuing of materialistic development and the management of material resources as ends instead of as means. Recall, here, what was said above about social and cultural developments of the Age of Taurus, when the power to manage resources taken from the earth (Taurus) gave political, military, and psychological power to the people doing the controlling. We might consider this as one of Taurus' messages: that we must address issues related to the management and distribution of resources, of the earth-based wealth that belongs to all humans. Though we must do so by taking Scorpio into consideration, recognizing the fusion mentioned in the previous paragraph, we needn't succumb to the dualistic thinking that tells us that we must work on either mind or on practical affairs, for the two arise together. To deal with wealth-distribution, a Taurean matter, we must deal with power and plutocrats, a Scorpionic one; and we must do so not merely by seeing them as projections of mind, but as people with projectiles whom we must deal with mindfully.

Another Taurean message: we must return to some sense of grounded value, ensuring that we don't let our values, statements, or policies get too abstract, too far away from what we might call "facts on the ground." Buddha—according to myth a Taurus with a Scorpio Moon: born on the full moon in May—living at the midpoint of the Long Count, pointed to the earth as "witness" to the truth of his teachings, teachings that enable people to work more effectively with mind. Certainly if the ground no longer yields plenty, we will have all sorts of perhaps insoluble difficulties; just as certainly, we will not solve our problems simply by managing external resources. The old dualisms, including the one dividing mind from world, must give way if we wish to deal with the problems confronting us.

During the Age of Taurus, human desire directed itself toward enduring materialistic concerns; desire took form in materialistic ways. We might say that the drive for security, not an evil in itself, got out of hand. During this period, humans demonstrated greater collective organization and management than they ever had before, and in doing so, they transformed their connection to the material world by liberating themselves from its more obvious demands. They achieved a surplus; they organized themselves to manage that surplus; and they (some of them, at any rate) found themselves with a newfound leisure. This in turn gave birth to new cultural potentials, many of them of great value.

This kind of cultural development couldn't have taken place if humans had not developed some security against the vicissitudes of nature. However, those who took control apparently began to see power as an end in itself, so they created a social situation through which they could maintain that power. We have discussed this above in connection with the class system, the return of the sun-god, the dominance of the warrior-class, and creation of grandeur that would awe those not part of the ruling class. We still have these problems today.

Though Taurus often manifests as a desire to accumulate material goods and satisfy physical desire on all levels, it can also manifest as the equanimity of the Buddha (traditionally considered a Taurus) who saw through the illusion of desire and who had what we might call a grounded wisdom, one that requires a firm connection to the earth. Apparently, too, if a civilization does not take this wisdom as its goal, it ends up as a rather unfortunate manifestation of the Taurean energy, for though Taurus emphasizes earth, it also symbolizes growth, organic or otherwise, that continually augments, whether in oak trees or in banking-institutions—or, we might say, whether in the organic world or in human institutions, and if we have too much institutional growth, we may have too little of the organic variety This seems to have occurred, and we can expect that developments begun in the Age of Taurus will reach crisis-proportions as we enter the Age of Aquarius, for we have a ninety-degree relationship, suggesting that to go forward requires major changes in social structuring.

"Civilization"

As I will explain more fully in chapter three, I take the Mayan Long Count as symbolizing the birth of those social forms that we now call "civilization." At the Long Count's beginning, the equinoctial point had moved to around the middle of Taurus. Though we can't pinpoint the date when this occurred, we might still note some prognostications from antiquity. In *Aion*,[1] Carl Jung cites a passage from the Talmud telling of time-measurements taken from "the Creation." The text reads that "only after seven thousand years will the Holy One, blessed be He, set up his world anew." Jung then tells us that "[I]f we take the 7,000 years mentioned in the prophecy as *anno mundi*, the year denoted would be AD 3239" and that by then "the spring point will have moved from its present position 18 degrees into Aquarius, the next aeon, that of the Water Carrier." And:

> As an astrologer of the second or third century would be acquainted with the precession, we may surmise that these dates were based on astrological considerations.[2]

From the point of view of our own astrology, the period around the middle of the Age of Aquarius would seem to have enormous significance, suggesting as it does structural challenges (square) to long-standing principles of social structure (fixed cross). The present period, as we move from the Age of Pisces into the Age of Aquarius, seems important for different reasons: we find ourselves at the simultaneous shifting point of two aeons, one measured by our own as-

---

[1] Jung, 80.
[2] Jung, 82.

trology and one measured by the Mayans; the coincidence of the two changes gives additional weight to both. Though the two traditions seem to measure different aspects of social development (see chapter two), they agree that major changes will take place during the current era. I suspect that even if the physical shell of present social formations continues in some manner until the precessed square (about a thousand years from now), the end of the Long Count will bring a cataclysmic shift in humans' view of the world in which they live—and, quite likely, of the world itself, insofar as we can separate those two. The end of the Long Count suggests a shift to a less dualistic view; nevertheless, we should expect that a shift in consciousness (so-called) will take place together with a change in form. This "form" will manifest in the physical environment, for humankind's tendency to continuously augment, whether in population or buildings, has had unfortunate, even disastrous consequences for the health of the planet. We will return to this discussion in chapter five.

As we have seen, the development of metallurgy during the Age of Gemini led to its more widespread application during the Age of Taurus. We have seen, too, that metallurgy required the transformation of a non-renewable resource. Metallurgy required continual prospecting for new sources of ore to replace existing but exhausted reserves.[1] Because of metallurgy's connection to military power, the exercise of that power at the end of the 4th millennium BC began to require that people take from the earth what they could not return, a process that has obviously continued to this day. The same period saw, not coincidentally, a shift in Sumerian civilization from female goddesses to dominant male gods.

The coincidence of widespread metallurgical practice with this mythological shift suggests that the ecological revolution coincided with a psychological one; disconnection from earth seems to have indicated a disconnection from those inner drives, instincts, and feelings that had kept each human being intimate with the earth and with himself. Metallurgy robs and depletes the Great Mother, a symbol for earth and of something deep in each person's unconscious. Domination by male gods seems to have meant attempted domination over natural processes—or, we should say, illusory domination.

During the Age of Taurus, beginning at about the time of the Long Count's start-date, humans passed a threshold point on the long road that has led us to our current state, one characterized by such daunting problems as the Greenhouse Effect, climate change, depleted ocean-life, and a host of related difficulties that defy easy or one-dimensional solutions. The same road, the one that began with metallurgy, has led to high-tech weaponry used to protect and promote the rich nations' more efficient continued robbing from the Great Mother's storehouse, a storehouse that does not seem infinite, despite its enormity. At the same time, the emphasis on individuated consciousness has set us down the road to the alienation that seems to prevail now, at the Long

---

[1] Toynbee, 43.

Count's end, an alienation from earth and from ourselves, leaving many people and their societies in a state of disassociation and dislocation.

In the present era, the plutocracy's information-bureaucracy has obviously aided and abetted this process, for as Edward Herman, Noam Chomsky and others have pointed out again and again, this bureaucracy works very hard to make the unthinkable seem ordinary. Division of labor proves essential in this process, as some people do the actual killing, others provide food and medical care to those who do the killing, and yet others manufacture the weapons and work to improve the technology. This seems quite in line with Mumford's remarks about the megamachine.

This dualism seems quite old, stemming back at least to the Age of Gemini, when people began to abstract themselves from the world. As we have seen, the Age of Taurus then cemented those developments into forms that we have come to call "civilization," which had as one of its characteristics the division of labor, stressed by Toynbee in his discussion of that period. Unfortunately, those forms have too often shown Taurus' "lower" side, its tendency to take the public good and hoard it as private gain, a process described in the mythic tale of King Minos of Crete. Poseidon gives the king a sacred white bull and subsequently asks Minos to offer the bull to him in sacrifice. Minos wishes to keep the bull for himself, so he substitutes another white bull from his herd. Poseidon quickly sees the subterfuge and curses Minos. The curse comes down through Minos' wife, Pasaphae, who develops an uncontrollable passion for the bull and asks Daedalus to figure out a way that she may have sexual relations with the creature. Daedalus fashions a great wooden cow, and inside it the queen receives the bull. From their union comes the Minotaur, to whom the king must feed the youth of the kingdom, and then the youth of other kingdoms.

The children fed to the minotaur—a creature born because of a curse, because of an imbalance—seem analogous in many ways to the children fed to the current industrial-economic system, an imperialistic system (as in the myth) that has resulted from dangerously narrow values in which the bounty belonging to everyone ends up in the hands of those with power. We might also see the devoured children as any kind of natural and new growth, living things constantly fed into the hungry maw of the monster called "production," a monster that has come into existence because the rulers and moneyed elites sought their own benefit instead of the common good, and that takes living "raw materials" and turns them into non-living commodities.

Though we surely could have witnessed barbarity and cruelty before the Sumerian civilization arose, the period around 3114 BC saw that barbarity metamorphose from a type confined to villages or towns into a kind of "civilized" barbarity with an exponential growth curve. Barbaric behavior had seemed inimical to the community, for obvious reasons, but during the Age of Taurus, it developed into state policy. If we wish to see how far we've come, we need only look at the United States' brutal foreign policies, at the treatment of Palestinians, at suicide bombers throughout the Middle East, at the massacres in East Timor and elsewhere, and at a multitude of other events that have dominated the final decades of the Sun of Ollin, events millions take as "normal."

So the heritage from the Ages of Gemini and Taurus still seem with us as we move from Pisces into Aquarius. The squares (from Gemini to Pisces, from Taurus to Aquarius) suggest that we face challenges directly related to social structuring (square) resulting from developments in the earlier ages. The squares also suggest that we need major changes in the venues through which we try to address these problems. Most likely this will mean changes in the form of government, changes in communication and in the management of resources, and changes in the relationship between invention and power, between individual and collective.

Some will say that the end of the Long Count will bring a return of the Great Mother, the natural, organic, life-affirming energies of the natural world and of the unconscious. Perhaps, but Aquarius doesn't have much affinity with that kind of energy. One of his rulers, Uranus, wanted to bury his children back into the earth, preferring to dwell in the realm of ideas instead of in the lived world of organic growth in which each living being works out his or her karma. Aquarius' other ruler, Saturn, wanted to devour his children, as if he had learned his lessons from his father. Both mythic figures seem to harbor a dislike for the Great Mother, aligning themselves more readily with the father, connected with the Leo and Capricorn complex of symbols that, as we will see, play such an important role in the Long Count horoscope and that will continue to play an important role in our lives as we enter the Age of Aquarius. Perhaps the Great Mother will return in a wrathful form.

Like Aquarius, Leo doesn't seem at home with the natural and organic energies of the world. As we have seen, Leo has a strong connection to hunting, the military, and kingship; long known as a barren sign, Leo seems the most barren of all. (As anyone who has gardened according to astrological principles will attest, if you plant food-crops while the Moon passes through tropical Leo, you will generally not get a very bountiful yield.) In his *Occidental Mythology*, Joseph Campbell speaks of a Sumerian terra cotta plaque, dating from around 2500 B.C, depicting the "lion headed solar eagle" devouring "through all time" the "ever-dying, ever-living lunar bull."[1] The bull "fecundates the earth," in sharp contrast to Leo's emphasis on desiccation. We may also wish to take the bull as a symbol of domestication and the lion as a symbol of energies not yet domesticated.

If we follow the line of thought suggested above, though, we will not so facilely separate the domesticated from the wild, the feminine from the masculine, the bull from the lion. Perhaps, in

---

[1] Joseph Campbell, *Occidental Mythology* (New York: Penguin Books, 1964), 54ff.

the end, the figure Campbell depicts represents one process involving all of the above elements. If the Lion must devour the bull, perhaps we should expect those human tendencies indicated by the lion to devour everything initiated during the era of the bull, the Age of Taurus—or, we might say, to complete the devouring-process already begun. This could mean that because of global warming (obviously related to the sun, ruler of Leo), human beings cannot maintain the kinds of social structures that first arose over 5000 years ago.

If we take the symbol of the Lion, and its ruling planet, the Sun, as representatives of potentially awakened self-consciousness, then we might suggest that the present forms of civilization must fall apart because humanity has grown beyond them. Even so, we should acknowledge that the devouring of the fecundating bull could presage a period of ecological barrenness: these days, the sun *does* seem prepared to devour earth's fertility. (Consider, for example, the depletion of the soils (Taurus) in so many parts of the world.) Even if we see the bull as "ever-dying" and "ever-living," we might conclude that we find ourselves in the death-phase, at least if we take the lunar bull as connected to the sub-lunar realm of organic growth.

Certainly the Great Mother symbol reminds us of the ever-returning, ever-fertile aspects of the human potential, not only through organic renewal and the birth-and-death process altogether, but also through the immensely fertile unconscious mind in each person. The fertility of that realm seems well guarded by demons that do not take well to humans robbing the bounty of the great storehouse, and it seems likely that before we can access those riches, we must loose the demons on the world. This seems another way of predicting a great destruction of some sort, probably one resulting at least partly, perhaps predominantly, from the various ecological factors already mentioned. Some scientists now speak of an ecological crisis from which the earth may not recover, suggesting that the Great Mother, heretofore seen as ever-returning, ever being reborn, will pass on, leaving only a barren planet.

We shouldn't assume that we can judge present developments by past ones or that we should see those past developments as precedents for our current situation. On the other hand, we would do well to acknowledge the powers of nature altogether. We may interpret the ecological crisis as the wrathful arising of the Great Mother energies. This might give us hope for renewal. On the other hand, the ecological crisis might suggest not a wrathful arising but a withdrawal, or even the death, of the Great Mother. It seems to me that the symbolism of the Mayan Long Count—or, the symbolism we get when we apply our methods to Mayan measurements—suggests that the Mayan aeon measures the effect of human creative power on the presenting situation. These two—human creative power and the presenting situation, the numbers five and seven respectively—lead us into the next chapter, a discussion of Mayan calendrics through the lens of our own astrology.

Chapter Two

Mayan and Western[1] Astrologies

DUE TO THE DECIDEDLY MIXED ministrations of Father Diego de Landa in 1552, we have the Mayan texts that we have and don't have the ones we don't have: much of what we have, he saved; much of what was destroyed was destroyed by his instruction. In the general decimation of Meso-American culture in the 16th century and thereafter, the invaders consigned to the flames texts considered sacred by the Maya and idolatrous by the invaders. In retrospect, we might say that the Mayan material smacked of a kind of idolatry different than the strain practiced and fancied by the Spaniards.

As a result of these events, when we speak of Mayan astrology or Mayan calendrics, we know much of the *what* but not as much as we would like of the *why*: we can read their measurements from inscriptions on innumerable stelae that show the meticulously carved glyphs for dates (the "what") extending far into the past or future, but to fully understand their intended meanings (the "why"), we would have to recover much Mayan material from ashes of invasion.

Still, though many specifics about Mayan culture remain unknown, we can sketch a general picture. Originally a group of scattered Yucatan tribes hunting with spears, arrows, and bark-less dogs, by around 200 AD the people we now know as the Maya had begun building cities, which

---

[1] This term may seem the wrong one to use, as many elements in our astrological system came from the Near East. By "Western" I mean the astrology practiced in what we generally refer to as "The Western World," even though the Maya lived thousands of miles west of the places where that astrology practice developed. Nevertheless, I haven't been able to come with a more apt term and so have stuck with "Western," despite these problems.

also served as ceremonial centers, on the Yucatan peninsula. They ate such staples as beans, corn, and squash and had developed at least rudimentary weaving. They organized their society according to kinship, and because the different sub-groups had a common language, they traded ideas as well as goods.

The different city-states seem to have had more of a cultural connection than a political one. Some scholars have surmised that they had no capital or centralized ruling situation, and while we know them largely for the magnificence of their cities and the precision of their astronomy, their neighbors apparently knew them as a sea-faring people who traveled far up and down the coast and throughout the Caribbean.

Around 1000 AD they abandoned their cities, some would say mysteriously or for reasons unknown, while others would say because they had exhausted the local ecological resources. The jungle re-enfolded the meticulously built cities and pyramids and the mystery went into a long sleep. Though scholars can offer only inferences about the cause for this decline, they agree that the Maya had built an extraordinarily sophisticated civilization, one in which scientist-priests could direct the construction of stone cities the equal of any in the old world, and perhaps surpassing them in their astronomically oriented architecture. The so-called Maya astronomer-priests could compute, apparently without the aid of sophisticated technology, the length of planetary cycles to within a small fraction of present measurements, and far exceeding the precision of any of their European contemporaries, or anyone in Western civilization until the past few decades. Yet despite all of this—or perhaps because of it—perhaps because of the prophecies connected with the time-measurements[1]—the people abandoned their cities, dissolving back into the jungle, as if to justify the name given to them so many centuries later by people with little understanding of their way of life. Maya. A mystery waiting investigation, it seemed.

In 1552, Bishop Diego de Landa publicly burned an undetermined number of Mayan writings along with a hefty number of statues and other works of art. Ironically, the same Bishop de Landa serves as our major remaining source for information on the Maya, for he recorded even as he destroyed, putting his observations down in his *Relacion de las Cosas de Yucatan*. J. Eric Thompson saw this work as the most important of our written sources of the Maya. He refers to it as

> . . . a mine of information on Maya customs, religious beliefs, and history, together with a quite detailed account of the Maya calendar, illustrated with drawings of the glyphs. This was the indispensable foundation on which to reconstruct Maya hieroglyphic writing, and is as close to a Maya Rosetta Stone as we are ever likely to get.[2]

---

[1] Some historians would offer more down-to-earth reasons.
[2] J. Eric Thompson, *The Rise and Fall of Maya Civilization* (Norman: University of Oklahoma Press, 1954), 35.

Arising from the earth and culture of the New World, Mayan astrology and calendrics seem at first to have little in common with our own, and it often seems that such parallels as we find arise not from cross-pollination, but because adepts in the different cultures uncovered parallel truths by living on the same planet. Many authors[1] have described the Mayan calendrical system quite extensively, and I will draw on their work in this chapter as we examine the not-entirely-obvious parallels between Mayan notions and time-measurements and our own.

The calendar system seems to have arisen between the 3rd and 1st centuries BC. In its most developed form, it consisted of both astronomical cycles (e.g. the synodical cycle of Venus, the solar year, the lunar cycle) and cycles not apparently based on astronomical measurements (e.g. the twenty day signs used in the *tzolkin*, or "Sacred Calendar"). As do contemporary astrologers, the Maya measured and analyzed time by weaving together astronomical and non-astronomical cycles. First, they used a 365-day solar calendar called the haab (which John Major Jenkins refers to as the "cycle of rains"[2]) that served as a basis for practical measurement. The Maya knew quite well that the 365-day cycle, like the 360-day *tun* that plays such an important role in the Long Count, served only as an approximation, for they had measured the year at 365.2430 days, remarkably close to the modern calculation of 365.2422 days. They kept close records of the accumulated discrepancy.[3] They also used the 260 day *tzolkin*, often referred to as the "Sacred Calendar," which they interlocked with the solar calendar and which may not measure any particular planetary cycle.[4] Its component parts do not seem to refer to planets at all, as the tzolkin consists of 13 numbers and 20 symbolic day-signs. When interlocked, these two cycles produce the 260 day calendar, which some have interpreted as a divinatory almanac. Apparently the Maya priest-astronomers consulted it and could interpret its meaning.[5]

By combining these two calendars, the Maya derived a vast array of more encompassing time-cycles. For example, if we begin both calendars today, they will not begin together again for 18,980 days: 52 calendar years; 73 *tzolkin* (52X365 = 73x260). This 52-year calendar round seems to have occupied a central role not only in the Mayan calendrics, but in Mayan and MesoAmerican life as a whole. Frank Waters writes of the Aztec customs related to it, apparently derived from older Mayan practices:

---

[1] For example: Frank Waters' pioneering *Mexico Mystique*; Jose Arguelles' controversial *The Mayan Factor*; John Major Jenkins' *Maya Cosmogenesis 2012*; Carl Johan Calleman's *The Mayan Calendar and the Transformation of Consciousness*; Bruce Scofield's *Day Signs*; Miguel Leon Portilla's *Time and Reality in the Thought of the Maya*.
[2] John Major Jenkins, *Maya Cosmogenesis 2012* (Rochester, Vermont: Bear and Company, 1998), 19.
[3] Frank Waters, *Mexico Mystique* (Chicago: Swallow Press, 1975), 226.
[4] However, John Major Jenkins notes that because "two tzolkin periods (520 days) equal three eclipse half-years (during which exactly three eclipses will occur), the tzolkin was used to predict eclipses." (See page 19 of *Maya Cosmogenesis 2012*). Several writers have noted that 260 days equals about nine months, the period of gestation for a human fetus.
[5] See Brian Scofeld's *Day Signs: Native American Astrology from Ancient Mexico* (Amherst: One Reed Publications, 1991).

As one ended, the people extinguished their fires, broke their cooking pots, lamented and fasted. When the calamity did not come on the last night, priests ascended to the temple on the mountain Huixachtecatl, Mountain of the Sun, sacrificed a human victim, and kindled a new fire on his breast. From this, fire-brands were carried to the great temple in Tenochatitlan and from there to other temples. From these, householders in turn carried torches to light new fires on their own hearths. The Calendar Round of fifty-two years the Aztecs called Xuihmolpilli, marking its beginning with the symbol of a fire-drill.[1]

The number 52 reminds us of the Long Count, a period consisting of 5200 tun—and 7200 tzolkin, matters to which we will return, for 52 and 72 (or 73) keep reappearing in Mayan time-measurements.

The 52-year ceremony may symbolize many different things, but it certainly suggests the sacrifice of the individual will to the collective demand, rhythm, or pattern, to a pattern with which the individual cannot negotiate. Collective destiny dwarfs that of the individual: social functionaries, purportedly acting on behalf of or as priests, purportedly with some connection to collective forces, sacrifice the individual heart to (again purportedly) attain the wider good. From that heart comes the ceremonial fire that unites the community. All of this took place on top of pyramids, suggesting hierarchy; and to build a pyramid one must have a strong, hierarchical setup akin to that which Lewis Mumford calls the megamachine, a matter to which we will return in chapter three in our discussion of the Long Count natal horoscope.

The longer time-cycles derive largely from a base-20 system:

1 kin = 1 day
20 kin = uninal
18 uninals = 1 tun = 360 days.

From the tun, the Maya went on to longer and longer spans:

20 tuns = 1 katun = 7200 days
20 katuns = 1 baktun = 144,000 days
20 baktuns = 1 pictun = 2,880,000 days (8000 tun; just over 7890 years)

And so forth. The multiples of 72 appear clearly. The multiples of 52 appear in the *tun* and year counts for the Long Count, for it consists of 5200 tun, or 5125 years,[2] which equals 7200 tzolkin

---

[1] Waters, 227.
[2] 5125 x 365.2430 = 1,871,870 days. 360 x 5200 = 1,872,000 days. And 260 (tzolkin) x 7200 = 1,872,000

(260 day periods). Thus: 5200x360 = 7200x260 = 1,872,000 kin (days) = 5125 years plus 132 days.

These measurements enable us to offer some connections to the aspect-measures of our own astrological system. Most contemporary astrologers use aspects derived from a division of the circle by whole numbers:

Aspect	Degrees	Division of 360 by
Conjunction	0/360	1
Opposition	180	2
Trine	120	3
Square	90	4
Quintile	72	5
Sextile	60	6
Septile	51.4285….	7
Semi-square	45	8
Novile	40	9
Semi-quintile	36	10[1]
Semi-sextile	30	12

Almost all astrologers use the conjunction, the opposition, the trine, the square, and the sextile; most also use the semi-square. If we ask, "Why these and not also the quintile and septile?" we can offer an at-least partial answer: not only do astrologers get demonstrably accurate results when they use the conjunction, opposition, trine, and so forth, but they also find these aspects easy to see on the horoscope wheel. Not nearly as many astrologers make extensive use of the quintile and septile, probably because they don't get the same demonstrably accurate results and because they don't find them as easy to discern on the horoscope wheel. Whereas the first group of aspects consists mostly of easy-to-see multiples of 10 degrees, the septile and quintile present apparent anomalies.

While acknowledging that astrologers find the first group of aspects easier to discern in a horoscope, we still might find it strange that the quintile and septile get used so much less often. Af-

---

days. We can account for the discrepancy of 130 when we realize that the Long Count began on August 11 3114 BC and ends on December 21, 2012. From August 11 to December 21 is 131 days.

[1] I have not included the division by 11. I do not know of any astrologers who use the aspect derived by dividing 360 by 11 (32.727727273….. degrees).

ter all, they result from a division of the circle by integers, just as the other major aspects do. Perhaps astrologers don't use them as much not only because they find them more difficult to see on the horoscope, but also because they represent energies that people in our culture have a more difficult time grasping, articulating, or even recognizing; perhaps because of this they don't get the *demonstrably* accurate results with the septile and quintile that they do with the others.

This brings us to a hypothesis: that the Mayan time-measurements, and the Mayan Long Count as a whole, represent an approach to historical development and human awareness that arises from a habitual pattern of mind quite different from ours, an awareness that registers the phenomenal world differently, that encourages a perception shaped by different ideas or assumptions. That we should find profound differences shouldn't surprise us, for the notion that people in markedly different cultures register the phenomenal world differently has arisen in many other studies;[1] here, we will try to see these differences through a study of what we might call "comparative astrologies."

Space Into Time

We can begin this comparison by translating the above-listed aspect measures into time periods by using the common astrological practice called "directions," starting with the degree-for-a-year method and then the *solar arc* method, the latter being a slightly more precise version of the former.[2] When using the degree-for-a-year method, the astrologer moves each planet forward by 1 degree for each year in a person's life. So in 72 calendar years, each planet or position will move forward 72 degrees, forming a quintile aspect after 72 years and a septile aspect after 51.4285 years. Many astrologers consider these degree-per-year measurements as "quick and dirty" approximations of the more widely-used solar-arc directions, in which the astrologer moves each planet or position by the "solar arc" increment each year: each planet moves the same distance that the sun moves in a day, a little less than a degree: on an average, 360/365 degrees, with, in any particular analysis, some variation depending on the time of year from which one draws the measurement. (The sun moves more slowly when in Cancer and most quickly in Capricorn, the rate varying from 57'/day to 1d01'/day.)

By solar-arc direction, in a Calendar Round of 52 calendar years, a planet would move, not 52 degrees as in the degree/year method, but rather 52x(360/365)=51.28767123... degrees, a mea-

---

[1] Consider, for example, the writings of Owen Barfield, Edward Sapir, and Benjamin Lee Whorf.
[2] When astrologers do time-analysis for a horoscope, they often use not only *transits* (the positions of the planets in the sky for any particular moment or day), but also various types of *progressions*, in which each period of time in the ephemeris represents a different period of time in a person's life, and *directions*, in which each planet or position moves forward by a specific increment for each time period. We will focus, here, on directions. However, in our time analysis of the Long Count horoscope (chapter 4), we will make considerable use of secondary progressions and transits.

sure very close to the septile aspect.[1] Also, if we take 73, a number that we will see popping up in our various calculations, and multiply it by 360/365, we get precisely 72. To this we can add that in the precessional system used in Western astrology to calculate the Ages, the equinoctial point moves 1 degree every 72 years.

So we can see that these Mayan numbers translate, via the techniques we call "directions," almost exactly into our septile and quintile aspects: the 52 year period correlates with planets moving into a septile aspect; the 72 year period correlates with planets moving into a quintile aspect via degree/year measurements. If we then use the figure 365, the number of days in a year, and divide by 5 and 7 respectively, we end up with 51.142857.... and 73 days. These figures represent the number of days it takes for any planet or position in a horoscope to "direct" forward to a septile and quintile aspect respectively.[2]

Now that we have the time-correlations in hand, we can inquire into their meaning, noting as we do what I say in the introduction to this book: that the Maya would not necessarily have agreed with any of these speculations. They had their own language, their own conceptual system, and it probably did not include the ideas I've derived from *my* language and *my* conceptual system. Nevertheless, because, as I said earlier, much of what we know of the Maya comes from inference, we might get farther by examining their measurements and asking not what *they* made of them, but what *we* can make of them using our own, proven system of interpretation. And just as a novel may offer many meanings of which the author remains unaware or dimly aware, so the Maya in offering their time measurements may not have known of all their implications.[3]

We can find this meaning by inquiring into the meanings of the septile and quintile aspects. What do these aspect-measures signify, either in a natal horoscope or in what we might loosely call "collective matters"? Once we've looked into that, we can ask what it means to base a civilization upon the ideas implied by these measurements.

The Septile

The septile aspect measures 51.42857143 . . . degrees. One-seventh of a year is 52.14285 . . . days, the time it would take for a planet to move through a septile aspect if traveling at the sun's mean speed: the average number of years a planet will take to form a septile aspect by solar arc direction.

---

[1] 360/7=51.4285....
[2] 365/5 = 73; 73x360/365=72. 365/7=52.142857....
[3] I think we can feel fairly certain, though not positive (given the Mayan proclivity for precision and, apparently, inquiry) that no Maya astronomer-priest (a term many have applied to some Maya purportedly observing the heavens from their various pyramids) said, "Let us create 52 year periods because they come so close to the solar-arc movement of a planet through a septile aspect"!

The septile has to do with inspiration within a form. Those with strong 7th harmonic charts[1] (e.g. John Coltrane) seem to have a special ability to give inspired interpretations of given themes within a designated form. It seems that the septile (and the number 7, and the 7th harmonic generally) have to do with imagination, particularly when the imagination has to do with a collective ordering within a given structure. For example, the Bible tells us that God created the world in seven days even though what we know as "the universe" probably took a good deal longer than that to come together—and even though the idea of a "day" couldn't have existed until creatures created higher order abstractions. The importance of the number seven in the myth tells us that we have to do, here, with creation within a formal structure, for the thing created ended up having what humans take as discernible laws. (Perhaps notable here are the various disputes we see that involve the relationship between creation and laws. Some hold that because we see laws, we must discern a creator; others hold that the laws merely give us the structural elements of the "thing" created.)

Millions of humans use the number seven as part of their attempt to give order to their lives and their conceptions of the universe: we give seven days to our week; for millennia, humans spoke of the "seven planets"; we have the seven deadly sins, seven virtues, the seven wise men of Greece, the "Seven Wonders of the World," the "Seven Against Thebes,"[2] and others. Quite possibly some of these derive from the fact that with the unaided eye, humans can easily discern in the heavens seven "wandering"[3] bodies (the seven traditional planets). From this, via the insights of astrology, came the realization, no doubt unconscious at first, that these seven bodies symbolized the creative capacities or interactive modes consciously available to human beings. Thus human creativity seemed to have an association with the form given by these seven bodies. Thus too, humans "saw" the sevens in myriad aspects of experience. We have, finally, the notion, put into practice by many astrologers, that we can gain insight into a person's life by dividing it up into seven-year periods.[4]

So humans often give order by using the number seven, and astrologers see Libra, the seventh sign, as the first one pertaining to the external order and having much to do with law, fairness, and legal regulations. So though some will say that seven is the number of cosmic law, we would do better to say it represents the number that people often refer to when they impose what they see as "laws" on the cosmos. The seventh planet, Saturn has to do with ordering, structuring, scaffolding, underpinning, and regulation—words describing acts that people do, not qualities of the cosmos per se. Astrologers posit Saturn, the seventh planet, as the exalted ruler of Li-

---

[1] When we cast a 7th harmonic chart, all septiles emerge as conjunctions; the chart brings out, we might say, the "7-ness" from the horoscope, serving as a visual aid so that we might see that 7-ness more clearly. (See page 43, footnote 1 for a brief technical explanation of harmonic charts.)
[2] Nicholas de Vore, *Encyclopedia of Astrology* (New York: Philosophical Library, 1947), 349.
[3] Ancient sky-watchers apparently noticed that the planets do not move in fixed patterns but seem to "wander" through the zodiac. (See page 47, footnote 2.)
[4] See Alexander Ruperti's *Cycles of Becoming* (Reno: CRCS Publications, 1978).

bra, the seventh sign, reiterating the connection between seven and established (as distinguished from so-called cosmic) order. As the main planetary ruler of created forms, Saturn has to do with creative work of any sort that reaches form, so we should not feel surprised when an artist like Coltrane, who on the surface seems to create in quasi-formless ways, follows quite strict forms in much of his work—what we would expect for one with a powerful seventh harmonic chart.[1] As we will see, Saturn plays an important role in the Long Count horoscope.

The septile has to do with projections, not onto specific people, but onto the world in general: coming up with a version of "how things are" or of what laws pertain in that world and then acting on that interpretation. This aspect symbolizes the accepting of a certain structure and then improvising either within or on the basis of that structure. Though sometimes the structure has to do with what we take as *standard*, at other times it has to do with what we take as *real* and what we reject as *unreal*. Thus Saturn, the seventh planet, has a close relation to what we call the "reality principle," the principles we posit about reality. These principles both limit and promote our creative inspirations: they *limit* because they tell us of the formal limitations within which we must work, as a painter may recognize the limits of paint or someone like Coltrane the limits of his instrument; they *promote* because they make it possible to give form to creative impulse (for, despite the limits of his horn, Coltrane probably wouldn't have made music without it).[2]

Therefore the aspect has much to do with making significant, though not necessarily valuable, contributions to the collective situation, to the world outside of oneself, the world *about* which one has formed ideas and *to* which one offers something definite. The aspect has to do with imagination and inspiration, but not just of the type we find in specific works of imagination. Rather, it has to do with imagination that imposes itself upon the world outside by accepting a certain structural matrix. We may take this as an extreme limitation on inspiration's power, but we can also take it as the empowerment *of* that inspiration. (Consider, as an example, James Joyce's *Ulysses*, a novel that arguably gains in power not by refusing to accept a structure, but by accepting and exploring a very specific structure (the myth of Ulysses/Odysseus, the structure of which Joyce imposed, we might say, on the day in Leopold Bloom's life). I would categorize Joyce's 7th harmonic horoscope—with its two interlocked yods—as a strong one.)

Because many of our versions of reality arise from the assumptions current in the society in which we live, we can see how the septile has a close relationship with one's ability, willing-

---

[1] We derive the harmonic charts by "unfolding" each degree-measure into 360 degrees. So when we cast a 7th harmonic chart, we unfold every 51.42857…. degrees into a 360 degree horoscope. When we do this, all septiles appear as conjunctions, all semi-septiles as oppositions, and so forth. We might say that such a horoscope brings out the "seven-ness" (a term I think I've borrowed from David Hamblin's *Harmonic Charts: A New Dimension in Astrology*, published in 1984 by Aquarian Press)—often what we might call the "*hidden* seven-ness"—in the natal horoscope.

[2] Two more examples: both Woodrow Wilson and Adolph Hitler, two figures who attempted to impose their own order onto the rest of the world and who apparently saw in their personal vision some kind of universal significance, had strong 7th harmonic charts.

ness, and desire to make a contribution to the prevailing collective situation. Because, too, many of these versions arise through a particular language with its particular metaphysical assumptions, we can see how the septile has a close relationship to the way a particular group orders its meaningful symbols, whether that ordering take place through language, astrology, or some other means.[1]

On the positive side, the septile has to do with making a valued contribution to the collective. On the more problematic side, it has to do with making a contribution that one *sees* as valuable but which will have little value for others. We see the more problematic side in the 7th harmonic chart of George W. Bush, where we find the Sun, Saturn, Mercury, and Venus involved in a grand square in cardinal signs, plus a Mars-Neptune opposition forming, with Jupiter, a t-square in fixed signs.[2] Helena Blavatsky, Adolph Hitler, Woodrow Wilson, Israel (and therefore the Palestinian refugees), Herman Melville, James Joyce, and (as noted) John Coltrane all have strong 7th harmonic charts, and all, in their different ways, imposed their own order on the world, seeing that order as universal, yet worked within an established form.

When measured from 0 Aries in either direction through the zodiac, the septile extends to Taurus and Aquarius, suggesting social (Aquarius) value (Taurus) and fixed social principles, a connection between the earthy values suggested by Taurus and the social values suggested by Aquarius, two fixed signs. And it suggests, too, the differences between these signs—differences crucial to the Long Count period itself, a period in which human social and technical development (Aquarius) has threatened the health of earth (Taurus). The Taurus-Aquarius connection hidden in the septile might remind us of the Taurus-Aquarius connection discussed in the previous chapter: the Long Count began in the middle of the Age of Taurus and will end at the cusp of the Age of Aquarius. Civilization as we know it began in the Age of Taurus; its fate seems uncertain as we enter the Age of Aquarius.[3]

---

[1] Edward Sapir, the pioneering linguist, wrote, "The fact of the matter is that the 'real world' is to a large extent unconsciously built up on the language habits of the group…We see and hear and otherwise experience largely as we do because the language habits of our community predispose certain choices of interpretation." The quotation comes from "The Status of Linguistics as a Science," an essay that first appeared in *Language, vol. 5* (1929) and was read at a joint meeting of the Linguistic Society of America, the American Anthropological Association, and Sections H and L of the American Association for the Advancement of Science, New York City, December 28, 1928. The essay also appears in *Culture, Language, and Personality* (Berkeley: University of California Press, 1956), a collection of Sapir's essays.
[2] Interpretation: overexpansion and deluded action (the t-square) resulting from disparate impetuses (grand square in cardinals) in which one cannot escape one's overly-solidified convictions regarding the laws that purportedly rule the world. The t-square to Jupiter suggests delusory action based on misunderstood religious or philosophical principles; the grand square suggests misguided ideas about authority; the quincunx from Jupiter to Saturn suggests a misalignment between principle and authority. All of this in the 7th harmonic: it tells us about the way Bush attempts to impose his own "romantic" vision (David Hamblin's term) upon the world. The Moon in Capricorn suggests ambition.
[3] I owe to Bil Tierney (*Dynamics of Aspect Analysis*; see footnote 25) the principles of aspect analysis used here.

Citing Dane Rudhyar, Bil Tierney[1] also connects the 7th harmonic with anti-social tendencies, tendencies we see in so many creative artists (and, one might argue, in Woodrow Wilson and Adolph Hitler) and, in a curious way, in the various developments that took place around the beginning of the Long Count, when human beings developed social structures that in many ways did not serve the needs of the human beings who lived within them: what we might call anti-social social structures, for whereas *social* has to do with companionship and with joining together, the social structures that developed in the 4th millennium BC severed the social bonds evident in the Neolithic village.

The tension between individual and collective values, between the value of earth and the value of society, the tension suggested by Taurus and Aquarius, often produces marked creativity. The septile adds the element of universal law, or at least the search for it: creativity imbued with or following principles put forth or seen as universal. Thus in 3114 BC we see new forms of social organization purportedly imbued with divine sanction through the rulers' ability to inspire awe and make predictions. Inspiration arises within and because of a form believed to accurately symbolize universal law. That this has to do with rulers, and thus with both Leo (the fifth sign) and the Sun (its ruler), brings to mind the fiveness connected with the quintile; as we will see, Leo plays a central role in the Long Count horoscope.

In an individual chart, the septile often indicates that the person has a strong desire to make a creative contribution to collective trends or that he sees individual creativity as an expression of universal principles. This can obviously lead to benefit, as in John Coltrane's music: in many interviews, Coltrane referred to his inspiration as "spiritual," and even if we don't quite know what that term meant for him, we can acknowledge the uplifting power of the music he created. Similarly, whatever we think of George W. Bush and his activities, we can't deny either that he saw himself as acting on behalf of universal principles, or that his actions had a powerful effect on the collective.

When we move from individuals to collectivities, though, things get more knotted, for if we have a social ordering purportedly linked to cosmic principles, we often see marked excesses, as with Hitler and Wilson (and even in Melville's Ahab, who constantly attempted to impose his own order on the "dead blank wall" of the world that "butts all inquiring heads at last"—all of which seems to reflect Melville's challenging 7th harmonic chart). Many historians have pointed to the emphasis on human sacrifice in Mayan culture, one purportedly oriented toward cosmic principles; we can also see the destructiveness wrought by the United States, a nation purportedly under the direction of God. We also see the destructive element in the first civilizations, for there the priests called upon the gods of the sky (i.e. knowledge of planetary motions) to get the people to serve more readily. The social order developed as a mirror for the

---

[1] Bil Tierney, *Dynamics of Aspects Analysis* (Reno: CRCS Publications, 1983), 51.

heavenly order as perceived by the people who came to dominance in the Tigris-Euphrates valley.[1]

We perhaps find something similar in Mayan society, for though many have idealized the Maya and seen their society as a counterpoint to the more cruel and militaristic Aztecs, investigations of some scholars suggest that, whatever brilliance manifested through the Maya's various time measurements and astronomical knowledge, in the society itself (or, socie*ties*, as it seems that Mayadom consisted of many cities, not necessarily coordinated into a whole) we see top-down hierarchies, human sacrifice, and slavery. Lewis Mumford tells us that among the cultivated Maya, "slaves were even sacrificed at an upper-class feast, merely to give it a properly genteel elegance." Some important connections suggest themselves: in the septile we see the ordering of social life according to purportedly higher principles, and those in power see fit to sacrifice individuals to that principle. As Mumford points out, we still experience the dark side of the practice of human sacrifice:

> . . . as so often happens, this particular mutation, quantitatively restricted in the culture where it originated, dominated and debased the urban civilization that grew out of it, by taking another collective form: the collective sacrifice of war, the negative counterpart of the life-promoting rituals of domestication.[2]

The emphasis on the septile, revealed through the recurring 52's in the Long Count and other Mayan measurements, reflect an emphasis on collective trends as distinguished from individual initiative. We see this emphasis in the Calendar Round, the customs associated with which show the sacrifice of the individual to the collective and the emphasis on collective cohesion. And just as the 52-year period marked a collective cycle, so does the 5200 tun/5125 year cycle of the Long Count. From what we know of Mayan society, it seems to reflect the same notions as we see in the calendar, and when we examine the Long Count horoscope, we will see how accurately it measures collective trends. In Mayan society, if an individual wanted to make a creative contribution, he had to do with within a powerful, perhaps oppressive, collective situation.

As we have seen, however, the septile also indicates that the individual will wish to make his contribution based on what he sees as universal laws rather than simply as a mark of individual initiative. The emphasis on the septile and related multiples suggests not so much that we see less creativity within Mayan society as that the creativity took place in relation to the prevailing emphasis on what were seen as universal laws. Further, the septile suggests and points to the difficulties that arise when the individual misconstrues those universal laws, as individuals so of-

---

[1] The 7th harmonic chart derived from the Long Count horoscope has a dominating grand square, suggesting extreme tension in the drive for the formal expression of higher principles.
[2] Lewis Mumford, *Technics and Human Development* (New York: Harcourt Brace Jovanovich, 1967), 150.

ten will (for, as noted, we should probably refer to such "universal laws" as *laws that people take as universal*). From what we can surmise, Mayan society seemed obsessed with a search for universal law. We should distinguish this conclusion from another: that the Maya had discerned universal law accurately. The septile suggests the former, not the latter, though as we will see, the accuracy of the Long Count measurements suggests that the Maya had a strong connection to collective karma.

Certainly the emphasis on what we interpret as septile-measurements[1] suggests a society emphasizing pervasive connections to what was perceived as universal law or pattern, or the human interpretation of universal law, the inspiration people drew from what they saw as a connection to cosmic or universal law. Certainly many of those who have developed expertise in Mayan calendrics have emphasized this connection: terms like *cosmic, universal, prophetic, galactic* keep appearing in works on the Long Count. From all of this we might conclude that Mayan calendrics direct our attention to the relationship between "cosmic law" and individual inspiration—to matters connected to septile symbolism. The septile suggests the domination of the universal; the quintile, discussed below in connection with 72 and 73, suggests the emphasis on the individual, albeit working within the pervasive collective formalism.

According to some "occultists," the number seven symbolizes the number of steps spirit goes through as it incarnates into matter. We may not know exactly what this refers to (for what, after all, do we mean by "spirit"? a special type of intelligence? a capacity for empathy? for insight? for prophecy? some non-physical quality for which we have no better name?). However, whatever its merit, the theory deals with the relationship between individual action or inspiration and something more encompassing, whether we refer to it as "the collective" or "the cosmos," or "spirit."

Several writers have connected the septile aspect with fate, with submission to a transpersonal power. When astronomers and astrologers recognized only seven planets,[2] human societies generally had rather rigid demarcations, and one's birth-situation (particularly regarding social class) largely determined one's lot in life. Thus we see a kind of social fatedness. And, of course, astrologers have long referred to Saturn (the seventh planet) as "the planet of karma," a planet connected with the demands of tangible responsibility and the need to connect directly to the limits of the physical world and the limitations associated with one's "station in life."

When we speak of karma, we don't mean "fate," the former seeming more malleable than the latter. If we see a person as "fated" to do something, we imply that he has no choice. On the other hand, we can work actively with our karma, particularly because, as Buddhist teachers have

---

[1] 52 years = 51+ degrees by solar arc direction.
[2] With the Sun and Moon considered as planets: Sun, Moon, Mercury, Venus, Mars, Jupiter, Saturn—the "seven traditional planets."

said, karma arises most evidently in the mind-stream, in the thoughts, in our convictions about the way the world "is." So if we want to cut through our karma, we need to cut through the thought-stream that keeps reproducing or reiterating that karma. So when we speak of karma, we don't refer primarily to an external fate, but to habits of mind that we continually cement into patterns of behavior because we think we know "the way things are." These patterns often prove problematic because of the difference between the way the world really functions and our *versions* of how it functions.[1] Thus the number seven suggests delusion if we take our versions of the world *as* the world.

Septiles point to an impetus to act as if we do know "the way things are," and they point to the power that results from a connection to this purported knowledge. Mayan society may well have had, in large part, a "septile orientation," an orientation to what Maya priests saw as cosmic law. And if the Maya were indeed obsessed by time, as different writers have claimed, this might explain their abandonment of their cities, for possibly they abandoned them because "the time had come" to do so according to "the way things were." (On the other hand, of course, they perhaps abandoned those cities because of the ecological degradation of the surrounding areas: because of karmic law, cause-and-effect, which we might see as a universal principle. And perhaps the ecological degradation coincided with the time-indicators of their calendar.)

In the end the septile brings a paradox, one connected with inspiration. Though inspiration often leads us astray, particularly when we think we've captured truth within a particular conceptual structure, it also enables us to approach closer to truth. One may delude oneself if one thinks one has been "breathed into" by the gods, but it seems as if without this kind of feeling, without the sense of something beyond ourselves or beyond our ability to express, we wouldn't have a spiritual life worth mentioning. With the septile, we attempt to draw our ideas about universals down into the particular and to use the particular to work toward or express the universal.

The Quintile

Dividing the 360 degrees of the circle by 5 gives 72 degrees, the quintile; it takes 73 days for a planet moving at the Sun's mean rate of speed to move into a quintile aspect with its original position.[2] The Long Count, which consists of 5200 tun, or 5125 years, also consists of 7200 tzolkins, or Sacred Calendar periods, each of 260 days. If we double 260, we get 520, so again we see the interweaving of 72 and 52 in the Mayan measurements.[3]

---

[1] The limitations associated with Saturn appear to have much to do with language: not only with the limitations we continually reiterate by how we talk to ourselves and conceptualize the world, but also through the limitations inherent in whatever language we speak.
[2] 365/5= 73
[3] These connections may suggest that any individual creativity (quintile/72/73) takes place within a larger social context (septile/51/52), and that larger social contexts result from individual creativity.

The quintile has to do with power, with the ability to stand four-square in the center of one's world and from that central point to act creatively. The power emerges when the person sees that we all in some sense create the world we live in. We might also say[1] that the quintile suggests the creation of forms that further and assist the full expression of the energy the creator intends them to serve. An individual with a strong quintile (5th harmonic) emphasis often has a special ability to develop such forms. Miles Davis, with his genius for creating simple forms upon which jazz musicians could improvise, serves as an excellent example.[2]

Bil Tierney associates this aspect with the pentagram, the five-pointed star that symbolizes the power of light (when the pentagram points upward) or the power of darkness (when it points downward). This power has to do with the human mind, the human awareness, that which stands in the middle of the four directions of the material world. Whereas the septile has to do with the relationship between individual and collective, the quintile has more to do with the individual's creative stance within his own perceptual field. The septile has much to do with what seems to happen outside of the self, the quintile with what seems to happen within the self, though we shouldn't see this as a hard-and-fast distinction. Like the septile, the quintile has to do with work in the form-realm, though the septile's forms appear in the collective and particularly in the social order, whereas the quintile's have to do with the omnipresent pre-social form provided by the four elements and four directions, the space within which we find ourselves (four cardinal points plus the central point). To continue the jazz analogy begun above, the quintile has to do with the creation of vehicles for creation, and the septile has to do with the inspiration[3] that takes place within the vehicle. Though we again find a relationship between inner and outer world, with the quintile we find the individual in the central position, not yet subject to collective demand but in a position to exert influence.

Though the number five has a long association with the pentagram, a symbol of magic and power, magic does not seem to arise by itself or constitute an independent force external to the individual. Rather, the individual brings it about through actions in accord with the demands *of* or *within* a specific situation, creating a form (an action or series of actions) that have influence *on* (that have power in relation to) that situation. The individual accesses this power by remaining, we might say, in the center of his or her world, "on point" and completely present. The magic needn't involve any special kind of action; ordinary action, simply standing, or standing

---

[1] Borrowing, I think, from Rudhyar.

[2] In a series of articles, some years back, for (then) *American Astrology* magazine, I explored the creative relationship between Davis and Coltrane, the former with his genius for form, the latter with his genius for inspired improvisation within a form. Of course, both had strong 5th and 7th harmonic charts (for both men composed and both improvised), but in my view, Davis has a stronger 5th harmonic horoscope and Coltrane a stronger 7th harmonic horoscope. (Some might, pointing to Coltrane's composition "Giant Steps," question this conclusion; however, as I said, both men have strong 5th *and* 7th harmonic charts.)

[3] Inspiration comes from roots meaning breathed into by the god: the energy seems to come from outside of oneself. See Joseph T. Shipley's *Dictionary of Word Origins*.

simply, in the midst of experience—will often do the trick. Thus we see the emphasis on the four cardinal points with a fifth point in the center.

People with strong five-ness in the horoscope[1] (i.e. people with strong 5th harmonic charts) will often "have a way with form," but the individual *creates* the form, whereas with the septile, the form seems to present itself as something beyond the individual.[2] The quintile-process begins with simplicity: the individual standing in the center of his world, in the center of his experience and his field of awareness. In other words, the individual experiences magic and has power when he returns to the center, to the personal source or wellspring, instead of blindly involving himself in the events of the periphery, his own projections. By returning to the center, he gains power over the projections, and because those projections have a close relationship to the world we all experience, the person with magic can influence events. Thus the quintile has to do with what we might call spiritual or psychological power.

In the relationship between the septile and the quintile, we see the connection between individual creative power and the collective pattern. On the problematic side, the combination could point to negative power resulting from social forms, particularly when those in power see those forms as somehow representing the heavenly order instead of as merely humans' attempts to order their lives. The quintile-septile relationship also suggests the need to work within or in harmony with collective structures and the need to find sufficient self-identity to act powerfully on whatever situations arise within a social context. We see, too, the interweaving of collective presentation (septile) with personal creative responsibility (quintile), the human interpretation of cosmic law, and the power of the individual to affect the prevailing social order. In this last, we discern the individual's relationship to the various human attempts to capture what many call "cosmic principles" in created social forms, and the individual's simple and always-creative relationship to the four directions of space.

We might recall, here, the material from the previous chapter about the priests of Mesopotamia and their knowledge of patterns in the heavens: on the one hand, we see the relationship between individual creative power (quintile) and karma (septile); on the other, we have the relationship between individual and collective order. Individual artifice (quintile) joins with collective artifice (human interpretation of cosmic law). The priests, through their association with the kings, brought about a centralized social order reflecting both fiveness (center plus cardinal directions: personal power) and sevenness (the social order seen as a reflection of the cosmic order). All of this brings us to the *tzolkin*, the Mayan sacred calendar, where five-ness and seven-ness inter-

---

[1] I have borrowed the terms *five-ness* and *seven-ness* from David Hamblin. (See page 43, footnote 1.)
[2] Admittedly, the forms one creates often have currency in a larger social context. When Miles Davis created forms for improvisation, he did so with the western musical scale, often using forms (e.g. the 32-bar song-form) found in that tradition. As I say in an earlier footnote, fiveness and sevenness seem to intertwine.

weave. In that interweaving, though, the five-ness appears more readily, for the Long Count numbers 5125 solar years (i.e. by an evident measure) and 7200 tzolkin (a measurement devised by humans and not observable in natural cycles).

The Tzolkin and the Long Count: Sacred Calendar and Collective Karma

We can describe the *tzolkin*, the Mayan Sacred Calendar, as a device or technology that gives power (quintile) by referring the individual to a larger pattern (septile). We can consider it as a "sacred" measurement because it directs our gaze toward something ordinary and hidden yet extra-ordinary and evident—all of these at once. When we examine it, we find an underlying assumption about the importance of individual days, the temporal space in which people act. We can see this in two ways: first, the tzolkin has a primary use as a divinatory almanac; second, the Long Count (the collective patterning) consists of 7200 tzolkin.

The Maya apparently used the tzolkin for divination; contemporary astrologers have explored this use as well.[1] Thus we can consider it, as we consider the *I Ching* or any other divinatory system, as a device that gives power (quintile emphasis) to the individual. But any such device works only if it in some way aligns with some kind of at-least partly accurate understanding *of*, or relationship *to*, universal principles (septile), whether we consider those principles as residing in the mind or in the ongoing karmic (cause-and-effect) developments of the phenomenal world. We therefore find the tzolkin used not only by itself (in divination related to an individual, for example), but also in connection with the other measures that make up the Long Count, which we might see as a kind of collective divination.

Even if the tzolkin does not, by itself, offer us a precise or unambiguous measure of some astronomical cycle,[2] either it or its parts or multiples appear in various Mayan cycles and astronomical measures. For example, in order to account for the discrepancy between the 365-day solar year and the precisely measured year of 365.24 days, the Maya added *thirteen* days every *fifty two* years (mathematically equivalent to our practice of adding one day every four years). The number thirteen appears in the tzolkin (13 x 20 day signs = 260 days) and in the Long Count (consisting of 13 baktuns);[3] the number 52 (13x4) keeps reappearing in Mayan time divisions, not only in the Calendar Round, but also in the Long Count itself, which consists of 5200 periods of 360 days each, or 13 baktuns.[4]

That the tzolkin or any other such system does "work"—that is, that it gives demonstrably accurate results—suggests that it has some similarity in structure to the phenomenal world that it

---

[1] E.g. Bruce Scofield, in his *Day Signs: Native American Astrology From New Mexico*. See page 37, footnote 5.
[2] As noted in an earlier footnote, John Major Jenkins might question this assumption.
[3] A baktun consists of 400 tun, or 360-day periods, equivalent to 394.3 solar years.
[4] That is, 5200 tuns = 13 baktuns (13x400 = 5200).

measures. This idea of *similarity of structure* comes from Alfred Korzybski, founder of general semantics, who pointed out that any map that enables us to make accurate predictions must have this similarity in structure.[1] For example, if a map of the United States doesn't have the same structure as the territory of the United States—if, for example, it has New York City hundreds of miles west of the District of Columbia instead of hundreds of miles north—one cannot use the map as an aid; if you try to navigate using it, you end up well lost. Any accurate or useful map must have sufficient accurate information *and* the same structure as the territory. If it does, we can probably use it to make predictions about the territory it maps.

The same principle applies to verbal maps or the maps provided by divinatory systems such as the *I Ching* or the *tzolkin*. If such a system enables us to make predictions—if its predictions prove accurate—then we can hypothesize that it has the same structure as the territory it maps, at least in the matters that concern us. If we consider the tzolkin as a map, and if people have used that map to help them make predictions, then we will strongly suspect that the tzolkin must have a similarity in structure to the world of human experience. Further, we will intuit that similarity even if we have difficulty articulating the particulars of that structure. For example, we can notice the accuracy of many astrological predictions, an accuracy that suggests the above-mentioned similarity of structure, even if we don't know or can't articulate exactly why astrology "works."

Similarly with the *tzolkin*. The ideas *about* "cosmic law" that we find inherent in the tzolkin must have some basis in cosmic law *itself* as long as "cosmic law" refers to any operational statement about the cosmos, or even its parts, that gives accurate results when tested. We perhaps can't state the cosmic law, or any of the cosmic laws that make up some larger law, in the linear device we call language. However, divinatory systems that work give us insight into cosmic laws because they enable us to see them at work. Once we see these devices as working—as yielding accurate results—we can inquire into *why* they do so, and this inquiry can lead us ever closer to what we might, though with some trepidation, call "truth." Many have devoted much study to the *I Ching*, finding in it connections to all sorts of "scientific laws" of which the first writers of the *I Ching* possibly had no awareness; others have gone through the same process with our astrological system, a similar kind of technics insofar as it serves divinatory purposes. In this sense, of course, we can consider the *tzolkin* as part of Mayan science, not merely religion, noting as we say this that this distinction between science and religion comes from us, not from the Maya themselves.[2] In any case, we can consider it part of Mayan *artifice*.

---

[1] See Alfred Korzybski's *Science and Sanity*, published in 1933 by the Institute for General Semantics.
[2] When we use language to posit a distinction between *science* and *religion*, we draw a verbal map that may or may not have a close relationship to the territory. Notably, if a language does not have separate words for the items of experience (so to speak) to which *science* and *religion* purportedly refer, people speaking that language will possibly not see those items as distinct elements in the world.

Even if we consider the tzolkin as *artifice*, as something artificial or created, we don't thereby denigrate it. Of course, the word itself reminds us of *artificial*, which we associate with something misleading or even false. However, *artificial* also has a connection to *art*.[1] *Art* itself comes from the root *ars*, meaning "to fit"; the *ficial* part comes from the same root as "force," which itself comes from roots meaning "to make." Thus the etymological *artificial* (as distinguished from the term in popular usage) suggests *making things in a fit way*, or *to make fittingly*. If we see something as *artificial* in the etymological sense, as something connected with *artifice*, we see it as something made that fits. In the tzolkin we seem to have something artificial (the tzolkin) that fits at least some elements of "cosmic law"; and because it fits, it yields accurate results, enabling people to make predictions by using it. (We can say something similar about what we call the "laws of physics." They certainly qualify as artifice, as something made with some degree of fittingness, the last suggested by the resulting predictions. By using Kepler's laws and the formulae included in them, we can predict planetary positions. We might say that the artifice has a close connection to what we call "the real world" as it presents itself to our senses in a particular time and place, but insofar as scientific laws tell us about that "real world," they qualify as a map. Of course, insofar as we decide to study the laws themselves, they qualify as a *territory*, not merely as a *map*.)

According to the *Oxford Dictionary of English Etymology*, *artificial* also has etymological connections to craftsman (via *artificer*), a word that suggests care and skill, as well as some relation to lineage (because craftsmen generally began as apprentices). The craftsman has as close a relationship to the artist as to the manufacturer,[2] for he has a *craft*, a word that in the original Teutonic meant *strength*, but which came, in English, to mean *skill*, even a kind of deception (as in *crafty*). But the etymological roots of these words suggest not something deceptive or less valuable, but something of profound significance. *Artifice* suggests a connection not only to careful or fit making, but also to the lineage and tradition of the crafters.

Through the etymology, we can see the connection between artifice and both magic and power, for those who can do magic can do so, usually, because they have learned through lineage and because they make use of "artificial" items to effect change. One can do magic because one can "make carefully and fittingly" and because one has learned to do so through tradition. Humans have, since time immemorial, accessed their power by use of symbols and their relations—through *artifice*, through things made carefully. It makes sense, then, that the "artificial" tzolkin, associated with both the quintile and the septile, should help people measure and relate to "sacred time" (i.e. as a "sacred calendar"). From the Mayan point of view, this "sacred time" had to do with the gods (another artifice, it seems) and with one's under-

---

[1] Unless otherwise noted, the etymological material from Joseph Shipley's *Dictionary of Word Origins* (New York: Philosophical Library, 1945).
[2] However, the etymology of *manufacture* seems to suggest making (*fact-*) with the hands (*man-*), not in the mass-produced way we so readily associate with *manufacturing*.

standing of the moment, the energy of the day, of the present, of the place one stands in the phenomenal world (quintile).

The *tzolkin*, then, with its connection to both quintile and septile,[1] emphasizes the ways in which the individual can influence the collective, particularly when that latter term refers to the forms of social development which do so much to shape human behavior. The quintile suggests the power to influence the phenomenal world and all its processes by standing four-square in the center of that world and coming into an empowered relationship with it. The septile, by contrast, emphasizes the connection of the individual to the processes and laws that we call "the collective," or that we see as applying *to* the collective. Though both aspects speak to the relationship of individual to collectivity or phenomena, each has its particular emphasis and its particular danger: with the septile, the danger arises through the human tendency to take human creations like language and social formations as reflections of cosmic law instead of limited methods of interpreting the world or cementing our fears and limitations into rigid forms; with the quintile, the danger arises through the human tendency to think that if the ego gains enough power, it can make valuable contributions—or that a person can make his most important contributions by strengthening his ego.

I would speculate that the tzolkin, through its close connection to the quintile,[2] emphasizes individual responsibility. The divinatory almanac guides the individual in his relationship to the gods: to the collective and to some kind of applicable universal principle, generally taken as cosmic law even though that taking has more to do with the septile, as explained above. The emphasis on five suggests that the tzolkin helped (and, according to some, can still help) the individual to deal with the ongoing flux of the collective, whether worshipped, consciously eschewed, or creatively investigated. The interweaving of the 5-series with the 7-series that we see in the Long Count may symbolize the need to include in any spiritual path, for individual or group (however large), the recognition of both collective karma and individual initiative, what we often call fate and personal responsibility. Certainly the Long Count tells us of a collective karmic development, but its inner components suggest that it tells us about the relationship between individual potential and what might seem a collective inevitability. That the tzolkin repeats throughout the Long Count strongly suggests, though, that we should not accept collective karma as inevitable. Both 73/72 and 52/51 bring us to the borderline between

---

[1] But more evidently to the quintile. Just as the Long Count and other measures connected with 52 or 51+ seem more evidently associated with the septile, with the quintile connection remaining more hidden, so the Tzolkin and other measures connected with 72 or 73 seem more evidently connected with the quintile, with the septile connection remaining more hidden.

[2] The fifty-two tun calendar round consists of 72 tzolkin: 72x260=52x360=18720 days. Notably, these calculations include the Mayan *tun*, not the more precise solar year of 365 days. Again we see the use of artifice, of careful making. We see the number 52 connected to the collective cycle and the number 72 connected with the individual cycle. (18720/365=51.28, close to the number of degrees of the septile, so we see in the Calendar Round the emphasis on collective mixed with the emphasis on the individual.)

individual and collective, internal and external, but they seem to stand on opposite sides of the border. The Long Count, and Mayan calendrics generally, seems to emphasize what happens there.

If we accept the notion that the Maya based their time measurements largely on five and seven—on what David Hamblin refers to as fiveness and sevenness—then we would suspect that the Maya emphasized something quite different from what we emphasize with our astrology. In our system, five and seven play minor roles compared to two and three, numbers that, with their multiples (four, six, and eight) give us the most commonly used "major aspects" in our system. Many astrologers consider the septile and quintile as "minor" aspects, and even when they consider them as "major aspects," they generally use them less often or less readily than the others. Many astrology texts barely mention these two aspects; some don't mention them at all, or give them very scant and vague interpretations.

If we take numbers to symbolize types of processes or energetic frequencies, then we would speculate that the Maya attuned themselves differently than we do—and not surprisingly, as they came from a completely different cultural tradition. Though the relationship between individual creative power and collective karma seems central to any awareness of the world, our system doesn't bring it into as a clear a focus as the Mayan system does. Most of our astrology texts assume a different dualism: that between so-called "hard" and so-called "easy aspects," or between benefics and malefics. Many contemporary astrologers speak of "flowing aspects" and "challenging aspects," and see the influence of the collective largely in terms of the movements of the outer planets and of the equinoctial point (as in the Ages, discussed in chapter one), not primarily through aspects.

These various terms—*malefic* and *benefic*, hard aspects and easy aspects, challenge and flow—emphasize difficulties encountered or advantages experienced within action, not the larger modalities behind the action itself. The Maya, with the emphasis on fiveness and sevenness, seem to have taken a different vantage, one that we will keep in view as we look at the horoscope for the Long Count, a period that tells us, in the symbolic language of our astrology, much about collective movements (septile) and their relationship to individual initiative (quintile). We should remember, finally, that according to some scholars the Maya counted five major aeons in the precessional cycle, whereas we count twelve: in the Mayan count, we see the emphasis on the quintile; in our count, we see the emphasis of the square and trine ("hard" and "easy": 4x3=12). The quintile may suggest the power of human creativity or the blind power of ego: the Aztec Calendar Stone has the sun in the center, suggesting both.

The Mayan Calendar Stone, Ollin, and the Outer Planets

Ollin, the glyph associated with the current Mayan age, emphasizes two-ness: two processes intertwined; the interplay of opposites. We see this glyph prominently inscribed on the Aztec Calendar

Stone, as the central figure in the stone's design and thus central to a proper understanding of the current Long Count, the Sun of Ollin. And yet this apparent two-ness generates five-ness: included in *ollin* we find the symbols for the previous four Suns (Jaguar Sun, Winds Sun, Rain of Fire Sun, Water Sun) plus the present one. Thus Nahual Ollin, "Earthquake Sun," includes the other four.

The glyph for Ollin consists of two intertwined lines. Frank Waters offers his interpretation of it:

> The hieroglyph is basically simple, consisting of two entwined lines. There are many variations. The lines may be straight or curved, thin or blocked. One may be colored red, the other blue. One version is that of a serpent and centipede entwined. But simple as the hieroglyph is, its meaning is profound. It symbolized the interlocked polarities of the cosmic dualities: earth and sky, light and darkness, male and female, good and evil. The tension between them was what gave movement to life, to man and the universe.[1]

At the center of ollin, we find a sun-disk, suggesting completion and consciousness. At present, we approach the end of the Sun of Ollin, which the Maya said would end with earthquakes, and thus again movement—power (five-ness)—generated from duality (as in two earth-plates). According to some Mayan scholars, the end of the Sun of Movement also brings us to the end of the longer cycle, consisting of all five Mayan Suns. Ollin, the fifth, brings us back to the number five, to the quintile, and to the importance of the individual even when we have to do with what seems a collective destiny with roots far in the past and an apparently unstoppable momentum here in the present.[2]

We have spoken, above, of dualisms, of polarity, particularly the one between individual and collective. To that we can add another: awareness and phenomena (mind and world). As we approach the end of the Sun of Ollin, both of these polarities have come to center stage. The first has done so through the increasingly negative effects of collectivities on individuals and the environment, a development central to the coming Age of Aquarius, for as we have seen, Aquarius generally emphasizes the group instead of the individual, whereas its polar opposite, Leo (the fifth sign, often associated with personal dramatism and self-concern), generally does the opposite. So we can see that the coming Aquarius-Leo Age will emphasize the relationship between individual and collective, and, because we have to do with barren signs, we can expect ecological crisis. Questions related to the second dualism (the relationship between mind and world) have arisen through the many teachings (ranging from Buddhism to quantum physics to Jungian psychology to general semantics) that call into question the facile distinctions we make between

---

[1]Frank Waters, *Mountain Dialogues* (Chicago: Swallow Press, 1999), 109.
[2]Notably, in our system, the Sun rules Leo, the fifth sign; both Leo and the Sun play important roles in the Long Count horoscope. See chapter 3.

the two terms describing the polarity. Of course, from this distinction arises the edifice of Newtonian science and much modern technology, and to say that we must investigate the dualism doesn't mean that we can find no difference between mind and phenomena, for on a relative level we surely can. Nevertheless, the solution to what we might call the modern problem seems to hinge on our ability to release creative power by investigating this apparent polarity.

Because of its importance, we should look at this second polarity a bit more. Nagarjuna, back in 5th century India, argued (in *Fundamental Wisdom of the Middle Way*) that we should consider many of our ideas about the world, in particular our idea that the world arises outside of the mind and independent of it, as mere conceptual impositions. Nearly two thousand years later, Carl Jung and quantum physicists articulated a similar message, but perhaps in more familiar language (though without the meditative practices connected with Nagarjuna). According to the Heisenberg Uncertainty Principle, one cannot perform an objective experiment upon phenomena because the act of observation alters what one observes. On the one hand, the questions one asks determine the answers that one receives; on the other, matter itself doesn't seem anything definite, but something describable only through probabilities. We may not wish to conclude that the distinction between mind and phenomena arises largely because our language suggests it; on the other hand, we may not wish to conclude that the phrase "mind and phenomena" provides an accurate map of the relevant territory.

Jung wrote that the upheaval in the world and the upheaval in the mind are the same. From a Jungian point of view, that which one rejects from the inner world appears in the external world as an event or series of events. We can add to this that if this process takes place in only one person, we have to do with an individual projection, whereas if millions of people reject the same material, we have to do with collective projections, the sum total of which amounts to the world everyone experiences in common. These collective projections will often present people with problems simply because the projections themselves represent energies that people have rejected, that they have "negativized." We can consider the "world problematique" as consisting largely of these problematic projections, the rejected elements of the human psychic potential.[1]

Astrologers recognize these rejected elements in the energies symbolized by the outermost planets. We have realized for some time that the outer planets measure collective developments, and we also say that they symbolize the various stages of personal transformation, the various elements of the unconscious, and the psychological potentials or capacities that most people find difficult to integrate into the ego-complex. But ego always resists this transformation simply because ego itself represents and depends upon a psychological status quo; ego resists

---

[1] I have discussed these matters in *Astrology Beyond Ego* (Quest Books, 1986; republication by the American Federation of Astrologers, 2010). The term "world problematique" comes from *The Limits to Growth*. See the introduction of that text.

change because change undermines ego's cherished stability. People generally resist personal transformation because they wish to maintain the personal status quo, which we call ego. Even if someone appears to live for change (so to speak), we generally find that such a self-conception reinforces ego's security. So we tend to reject the outermost planets and therefore to project them into the environment.

We therefore meet these energies in their more problematic forms: not as agents of transformation and change, but as powerful and problematic collective forces and developments. Ego, with its insistence on maintaining the psychological status quo, rejects the demands of suddenly arising insight (Uranus), yearning, empathy, and boundary-lessness (Neptune), and empowered action, ego death, and phenomena-mind fusion (Pluto). Furthermore, ego rejects the basic suffering (Saturn) and sense of woundedness (Chiron) that one must recognize and accept if one wishes to walk the transformative path. (Thus the Buddha spoke of suffering as the First Noble Truth; in his Second Noble Truth, he added that people suffer because they develop attachments in a world that changes constantly. Similarly, Gurdjieff spoke of the need to take on "intentional sufferings" in order to walk the path of insight.)

Once people reject suffering (Saturn) and the demands of insight (Uranus), they generally meet the energies of the outer planets as projections through which the same energy takes on a more problematic appearance: powerful new technologies (Uranus) in the hands of deluded people (Neptune) leading to destructive power build-ups and toxic waste (Pluto), all in the hands of people in a highly stratified, hierarchical status-quo structure (Saturn), resulting in a wounded world (Chiron).[1] We find a negative and deluded use of technical power because we have not looked carefully at the mind that gave birth to the technology, to the delusion, and to the search for power itself.

Of course, power has to do with change: we have power if we can bring about change, the amount of power having to do with the rate of change. And so we find ourselves back with *ollin*: change related to polarity. *Ollin* seems to have many similarities to the energy that astrologers describe as "Pluto," the need for transformation and change, demands that we block by insisting too much, in our speech and thinking as well as in our actions, on the status quo. Pluto symbolizes the need, obsession, or instinct to investigate the dualistic projection altogether; it also symbolizes the need to transform perception through an examination of the conceptual approaches that shape it. These energies lie at the root of the modern problem; if we don't look into them more thoroughly, we probably will not deal effectively with the difficulties we face.

Notably, astronomers discovered Pluto right around the time that quantum physicists made their major advances and that Jung, in *Modern Man in Search of a Soul*, made the observations men-

---

[1] Chiron is the son of Saturn, the grandson of Uranus, and the half-brother of Neptune and Pluto (and Jupiter).

tioned above. Pluto symbolizes death and rebirth processes, control drives, and transformation: we get transformation by controlled chain reactions, whether in the plutonium bomb or in the psychological patterning of individuals (where the "control" arises, positively as discipline, or negatively as an exclusionary rigidity in mental attitudes); psychologically, we go through this transformation only when we go through symbolic death and rebirth processes.

Pluto also symbolizes the fusion of opposed polarities and the power that results. We see this fusion in the fusion bomb, certainly, but also in the mind. There, a person cannot transform himself unless he steps beyond dualism: beyond self and other; beyond good and bad; beyond sacred and profane; beyond mind and world. All of this seems implied in the Mayan symbol *ollin*, though I can't say whether the Maya themselves would have offered such notions.

Ollin symbolizes a process through which opposed polarities generate movement and change. That *ollin* rules the Long Count suggests that our major issues now have to do with such opposed polarities and that if we don't work wisely with them—black and white, rich and poor, "mine" and "not mine," inner and outer, powerful and powerless, and so on and on—we will find ourselves mired in opposition and therefore not in any movement except toward catastrophe. Such oppositions create enormous creative energy but often generate seemingly insurmountable problems at the same time, as occurred back in the Age of Gemini, when hunters and farmers sometimes worked in symbiosis but sometimes in opposition. As we have seen, the split became more and more egregious, so that it eventually appeared in a basic split in the civilizations that developed, with hunters coming to a dominance they have held ever since, as the descendants of the hunters took control over the descendents of the farmers through hierarchy and regimentation, leading eventually to a decimation of both people (through wars) and environment. Furthermore, a boundary line appeared, at least in the minds of many people, between a purportedly civilized "us" and a purportedly non-civilized "them."

We must grapple with the resulting problems today, as witness the ongoing difficulties arising between the so-called developed world and the so-called developing world. The clash at the borderlines has much to do with the "world problematique."[1] And if we consider that *problematique* as a projection of an inner crisis, we will find ourselves looking again at the mind's tendency toward dualistic thinking. The Age of Pisces arrived one quarter of a Great Year after the Age of Gemini (because the two signs lie ninety degrees apart), so we would expect that developments in the earlier period would present major challenges in the latter age.

---

[1] Some months after I drafted this, the Copenhagen climate meetings took place. The so-called "developing" nations presented to the dominant industrial powers a demand for reparations related to climate. The former reasoned that because the latter had caused the gathering climate catastrophe and because the developing nations would suffer the most egregious consequences, the richer countries should pay reparations. The industrial powers refused, reiterating the problems mentioned in this paragraph.

This doesn't seem surprising, as Gemini and Pisces both suggest, in their glyphs (♊, ♓) the need to join polarities. Gemini, an air sign and thus having much to do with thought, suggests distinctions that arise through concept and language. Pisces, a water sign and thus having much to do with feeling and absorption, suggests not only the dissolving of such distinctions, but also 1) the resulting inundation that has arisen from them, and 2) the problems resulting from absorption, whether into the oceans or the atmosphere, of particulates (Gemini) developed from the use of the substance of earth (as in metallurgy, developed during the Age of Gemini). As Jung has suggested, Pisces also has to do with the duality between sacred and profane, Christ and Anti-Christ, yearning for the absolute and reasoning about the relative. The straight lines of Gemini's glyph point to the rigidity of concept; the curved lines of Pisces' glyph suggest the receptive qualities of feeling. Gemini suggests clarity within duality, whereas Pisces may lose itself in emotion, devotion, or obfuscation. As humans have discovered as they have grappled with delusions during the Piscean era, human beings have a great capacity to avoid problems until the point of inundation.

Many of these difficulties have to do with language. We saw in the previous chapter that writing developed during the Age of Gemini and took on a more-or-less organized form during the succeeding Age of Taurus: humans began to shift from oral language into less malleable written languages. Humans have generally built their languages, albeit unconsciously, on the assumption that we can locate a world outside of ourselves that we hope our language can somehow address, describe, or refer to accurately. Humans first used written language not to record inner states of being, but to record sums and other information related to evident social organization. Thus, on the surface at least, written language seems to reinforce the dualism that we see between inner and outer worlds.

However, through the dualism of Gemini and Pisces, some humans have come to question the dualism itself; and it seems that they have done so at least partly through the use of written language. This search, which we can trace back at least as far as the Buddha and Plato (both of whom lived in the so-called Axis Age, the Long Count's midpoint; see Chapter Four), reached a critical point toward the end of the Age of Pisces, around the time of the discovery of Pluto in 1930, with the development of quantum physics, analytical psychology, general semantics, and other investigations.

Despite these developments, though, for most people language reinforces the notion that we have an inner mind making objective readings of an external territory. With this assumption, we generally conclude that if we wish to alleviate the difficulties we encounter in our dealings with that external territory, we would best develop strategies in the inner world that enable us to act effectively in the outer one. We generally do not think that we can alter the external world simply by altering or somehow cutting through the idea-structure that posits the original separation. Certainly language played a vital, perhaps indispensable, role in early humans' increasingly successful attempts to bring the external world under apparent control through well-considered actions, but in some ways it may hinder the search for a resolution of the resulting problems.

In groups not touched by "civilization" or by writing, it seems that many people did not always draw a clear boundary between inner and outer, even in pragmatic matters. (Thus, for example, the notion, apparently widespread among Native American groups, that one's attitude played an important role in hunting.) However, as "civilization" developed with its ever-increasing emphasis on increasingly complex external dealings of ever-increasing variety (connected to the "bigness" discussed in the introduction), people probably lost the original unity and developed a more dualistic—or, as some have said, "differentiated"—consciousness. As I have suggested above, this process seemed to reach a critical point as the Neptune-Pluto conjunctions began their long series in Gemini. Now, at the end of the Piscean Age, after two such conjunctions, we have begun to see the very practical difficulties that arise from this insistence on basic dualism: from assuming, first, that the world of mind exists independently of the phenomenal world (and vice versa), and second, that the mind, connected to the world via the senses, merely records events that have a purely "objective reality."

Language, it seems, shapes conception, and conception seems to shape perception, at least for most people most of the time; and if we take our perceptions as accurate representations of things "as they really are," we often generate problems. All of this suggests, as does *ollin*, that to deal with the "world problematique," we will have to depart from a dualistic utilitarianism and develop an approach that not only sees the utilitarian value of increased awareness, but that calls into question our ongoing assumption about the nature of mind and the nature of phenomena. More on this as we proceed. For now, we can simply note that *ollin* points to the intertwined nature of all dualities, including mind and world, and that we will not solve the problems that beset us until we take this into consideration.

The Venus Cycle

The Maya added another cycle to their calendric mix: the 584 day synodic cycle of Venus. Not surprisingly, they knew quite well that the cycle didn't take exactly 584 days. They had measured it as 583.92 days and kept track of the accumulated discrepancy in their time-measurements, adding extra days as necessary. They combined this Venus calendar with the solar calendar and the tzolkin. The three coincided every 104 years: two Calendar Rounds, 104 solar years, 146 tzolkins, the last two numbers returning us again to 52 and 72/3 (104 = 52x2; 146 = 73x2.). The Maya referred to the day on which the three calendars coincided as the *lub*, "the resting place," a time when the gods lay down their burdens of time, the day when Sacred and Solar calendars coincided with the rising of Venus as morning star. We might understand this "resting" by linking our understanding of Venus to that of the Maya.

For us, Venus joins things. We know her as the goddess and planet of love—or what Robert Hand refers to as non-coercive bonding, an energy that brings different but potentially complementary energies together to form a higher whole.[1] The joining may have to do with people, with artistic elements (Venus having much to do with artistic technique, for the artist brings together different artistic elements to form a higher whole), with principles like Heaven and Earth—or, for the Maya, perhaps the joining of sacred and non-sacred calendars, of a divinatory almanac emphasizing the individual with the solar-related calendar emphasizing the collective pattern.

The Maya knew Venus as Kukkulkan, better known to us through his Aztec name, Quetzalcoatl, the Plumed Serpent, a symbol that in itself unites above and below, sacred and profane, and which seems more akin to Scorpio than to Venus-ruled Libra, a correspondence which might recall to us that Ptolemy refers to Libra as the "Claws of the Scorpion," suggesting, at least to a contemporary mind, that the underworld grasps its prey through love, beauty, aesthetics, and law, that these serve as gateways to the underworld.

Two principle myths relate to Quetzalcoatl.[2] In one, he ruled the Toltec capital city but was deposed because of his opposition to human sacrifice. He subsequently sailed away to the east, prophesying his return in the year Ce Atatl, the year that Cortez arrived in Mexico, where many people took him as Quetzalcoatl returning to his lost brethren. This Quetzalcoatl seems based on a historical figure. The second story has some parallels to the first, though it seems to have its origins not in historical events but in astronomical ones and their connection to unconscious patterns. In this story, Quetzalcoatl ruled the city of the gods and the land of the dead. He begins chaste, wise, and pure, but through subtlety, his rival and antithesis, Tezcatlipoca brings about his downfall, first by showing him a mirror, then by offering him intoxicating drink, and finally, when he was drunk, by inducing him to have sexual relations with his own sister. Quetzalcoatl wakes in shame, orders people to build his casket, and journeys for eight days to the land of the dead. After that, he rises again as the morning star.

We can see in this myth the astronomical pattern of Venus' synodic cycle: Quetzalcoatl rises as evening star, and slowly, night by night, rises closer and closer to the Sun. Venus' light fades as he drops, day by day, toward the horizon, into the earth, into the underworld. He remains invisible—in the underworld—for eight days (the number of days that Venus remains invisible at the latitude of Mexico) before rising again as the morning star, transformed, like Quetzalcoatl, from evening star to Lord of the Dawn. We might see this as the fall of spirit into matter, with Quetzalcoatl at first representing spirit and then getting touched by the material world and thus descending. We might also see in the myth a process in which one begins with a one-sided

---

[1] Robert Hand, *Horoscope Symbols* (Rockport, Massachusetts: Para Research, 1981), 58-9.
[2] In these descriptions of MesoAmerican myths, I have borrowed liberally from Frank Waters' *Mexico Mystique*. See pages 122-126.

purity but then, through a process of self-reflection and spiritual intoxication, goes through the consummation of a sacred marriage or higher unity.

Though the Maya and the Aztecs saw Venus as a male deity, that figure, like our female Venus, unites apparent opposites: life and death, light and darkness, morning and evening. In the "esoteric" astrology of Alice Bailey, Venus rules Gemini, the sign of the twins, of opposites emerging from the same source; in our astrology, she has exalted rulership over Pisces. In any case, we see in both traditions the same theme reiterated. This should remind us that we see in Venus herself a unity of opposites, for she arises as the male *anima* and thus combines male and female elements within herself. Considering our previous speculations about Mayan calendrics, we should not feel surprised that those measurements emphasize the movements of a planet whose mythology stresses such union.

But what can we say about the "laying down" that occurs every 104 years? If we again change the Mayan years into our degrees, we come up with the bi-septile aspect of approximately 104 degrees, the exact measure being 102.857.... degrees, and a planet directed via the solar arc method will cover that number of degrees in 104 years. If we take this measure from 1 Aries and the cusp of the first house and move both ways from that point, we find ourselves in the second decanate of Cancer and of Sagittarius respectively.[1] Cancer suggests the needs and demands of the feminine: of the earth, of nurturing, of the kinship unit and the need for a harmonious, integrated relationship with the natural world. Sagittarius suggests the needs and demands of the masculine: of expansion, abstract philosophy, abstract ideas (e.g. *truth, faith*), religion, travel, accumulation, and meaning. These two signs quincunx each other, suggesting a hidden tension. (As we will see in the next chapter, the quincunx aspect plays a central role in the Long Count horoscope of 3114 BC.)

If we combine the symbolism of Cancer with that of Sagittarius, we confront the curious idea of religion and meaning applied to maternal containment, or of religious ideas related to the feminine, to the demands of earth and the unconscious; or we find, simply put, the relationship between expansion (as of the industrial state) and mother earth. As the gods lay down their burden of time onto the earth, everything rested; all was, for a time, contained with in the Great Round of birth and death, the realm of the Great Goddess.

If we add the meaning of the decanates, ruled by Scorpio and Aries respectively, we find the message repeated, but in what we might call a different key. Here, in signs again in a quincunx relationship, we have to do with death (Scorpio, the time of year in which organic life dies) and rebirth (Aries, the spring equinox, the time of year in which seeds sprout anew), departure and return, the mythic pattern of Quetzalcaotl (and Jesus, with whom Quetzalcaotl has much in

---

[1] Students of the United States horoscope may find it curious that the United States has its Sun in the second decanate of Cancer and its Ascendant in the second decanate of Sagittarius.

common). Altogether, the symbolism suggests the union of the Great Mother energy in two different forms—what Erich Neumann[1] called the containing (suggesting Cancer) and the transformative (suggesting Scorpio)—with the patriarchal spirit of external action (Aries) and abstract philosophy (Sagittarius), or of action and expansion. Like Cancer and Sagittarius, Aries and Scorpio have a quincunx relationship, a relationship crucial to an understanding of the Long Count horoscope, as we will see in the next chapter.

These decanates also bring in the Martian influence, for in the traditional system of western astrology, Mars ruled both Aries and Scorpio. (Most astrologers maintain that Mars still has an important connection to both signs even if they consider Pluto as the new ruler of Scorpio.) Perhaps we see in this symbolism the rise of militarism as an attempt of rulers and subjects to reconcile the inner tension (quincunx) that we have just described in astrological terms. Certainly the civilizations born at the time of the Long Count's beginning initiated a pattern of ecological destruction, expanded military conflict, and hierarchical dominance that has increasingly threatened the health of Mother Earth. Just as certainly, the Maya conquered many of the groups around them: that they measured time for ages into the past and future does not mean that they didn't attempt to dominate others, and many historians have speculated that Mayan civilization fell due to ecological considerations—considerations reflecting, again, the quincunx, a matter explained more fully in the next chapter. But that they perhaps didn't practice what their symbols seem to preach doesn't mean we should not attend to the preaching.

Synthesis

The most famous of Mayan time-measurements—the Long Count, a period of 5125 years beginning in 3114 BC and ending in 2012 AD—might seem to measure the destruction of the Great Mother energies (the Earth, for example) by a series of increasingly paternalistic civilizations that began back in Sumeria right about the beginning of the Long Count, for as Lewis Mumford informs us, the masculine gods returned to dominance around that time. We might also say that the Long Count measures the birth, development, and death of civilization as humans have known it. However, to see the Long Count only from this fatalistic point of view is to see only its apparent emphasis on the septile (5125 years; 5200 tun) and not on the quintile (7200 tzolkin), the former emphasizing the pervasive presence of the collective, what may appear as a collective fate, and the latter emphasizing the power of the individual.

The term "collective fate" suggests victimization, but only at the hands of our own creations—or at the hands, we might say, of our own projections, projections that we take as the substance of the phenomenal world, a substance arising from the unconscious and never separate from it. Ollin again suggests movement resulting from such opposites. We find ourselves

[2]Erich Neumann, *The Great Mother: An Analysis of the Archetype* (Princeton: Princeton University Press, 1963).

dealing with the karma of Ollin: the results of our insistence on seeing phenomena as existing apart from our awareness of them even though we have no knowledge of those phenomena except through the purportedly separate awareness. If we take "collective fate" as a collective projection, and if we see the collective projection as resulting from uncountable individual projections, we will see the intertwining of individual and collective. The *world problematique* has seemed increasingly impenetrable with the discovery of the Neptune in 1845 and of Pluto in 1930, the two planets whose interaction symbolizes, through their conjunctions, shifts in types of inspiration and delusion that dominate the collective awareness in the dominant societies of the modern era.

Ollin suggests that we bring dualities together, finding individual initiative in harmony with our understanding of "cosmic law," despite the admitted limits of the latter. This means taking responsibility for personal creative power, for if we don't, if we remain subservient to the collective karma, we will project even that personal power into the collective. The Mayan time-measurements point us toward the unity we seek, for though at first glance the Long Count seems to emphasize the septile (5200 tun, 5125 solar years), it also contains, in a more hidden way, the potential of the quintile (7200 tzolkin). The septile-quality seems to dominate appearances, and so we hear that the Long Count will end in great destruction (earthquakes, according to some texts) affecting the collective. This might incline us to a fatalistic viewpoint—and particularly if we accept the argument that the present Long Count was the final one in a cycle of five, those five taken together making up the entire precessional cycle. It would seem that if we approach the end of at cycle of nearly 26,000 years, we would find ourselves enmeshed in some rather obdurate karma. In such enormously long cycles, do we see any relevance for the individual?

However, when we look at the Long Count as 7200 tzolkin, we find ourselves looking at a hidden, "sacred" influence that enables and encourages individual initiative, the need to find creative freedom by "molding materials into forms that are true to the idea they are meant to express."[1] As we have seen, the quintile puts us in contact with the creative or destructive powers that link different elements of our world. When we emphasize the quintile, we see that the purported battle between inner and outer takes place not simply in the outer world, but within each person as well. We can come to this conclusion because the quintile adds, to the four cardinal points, a fifth point as the unifying center. That the Mayans count five ages, suggesting the quintile influence, in the development of collective karma and as an expression of purportedly universal law (septile), shows us again that the principle of *ollin* pervades their numerology.

Another quintile-related measurement contained in the Long Count has to do with the katuns. A katun consists of 20 tuns (360 day periods) and had much to do with "the social and political life of the community."[2] The Long Count consists of 260 (13x20) katuns. Thus we find, again, the

---

[1] Dane Rudhyar, *The Astrology of Personality* (New York: Doubleday, 1970), 374.
[2] Scofield, 16.

relationship between the life of the collective (the katun plus the Long Count with its 5200 tun) and the "sacred" development of the individual (7200 tzolkin). That the Long Count consists of 260 katuns suggests, in itself, a union of inner and outer, for the katun points to the collective, whereas the 260 day Tzolkin points to the individual (and, perhaps less directly, to the collective: 260x2= 520 = 10x52). On the one hand, we see the ongoing power of the collective; on the other, we see what we might call "sacred" power that remains hidden but that nevertheless does its work to maintain the balance of life—and the more so if, despite the prejudices of our age, we take seriously the notion that collective developments arise inseparably with individual awareness.

Power—the rate at which we do work (i.e. bring about change)—manifests when we withdraw our projections. When we withdraw our projections, we re-collect[1] our potential from the world. If we limit our view of our potentials, potency, or power, we reject these energies and experience them as an external fate related to the number seven; if we withdraw these projections and accept these energies as potentials, we find ourselves empowered in a way related to the number five. Our experience combines these two patterns.

The septile, based on seven, brings the danger of collectively induced blindness, and this blindness often comes from a limited view or limited appreciation of human nature. If we take on this limited view, we project out whatever doesn't accord with it. So, for example, if a person sees himself as merely a breadwinner, as a person of such-and-such occupation (as in "I am a teacher"), then, by succumbing to that limitation (often indicated verbally by the presence of "to be" and "should," the favorite verbs of Saturn, the seventh traditional planet and ruler of the seventh sign), in accepting that we "are" and "should be" such-and-such within the constraints of collective structure, we will likely project anything that does not fit within those constraints.

In our traditional astrological system (the one used before the discovery of the trans-Saturnian planets), astrologers recognized seven planets: the Sun and Moon, (considered as planets, though special ones, given the name "Lights") plus Mercury, Venus, Mars, Jupiter, and Saturn. And if we count seven signs, we come to Libra, with Saturn as its exalted ruler, a sign associated with the acceptance or need for a "socially accepted standard weight"[2] and that often accepts the status quo arrangements. This traditional system of rulerships has stability and balance.[3] With the discovery of Uranus, Neptune, Pluto, Chiron, and a host of other orbiting bodies, the stability broke down. This breakdown appeared in the world as well, not surprisingly, as we can consider the world as a projection of mental energies. In that world, as the old

---

[1] I have borrowed this term from Marie Louise von Franz. See her *Projection and Re-collection in Jungian Psychology* (London: Open Court, 1987).
[2] Dane Rudhyar, *Astrological Signs: The Pulse of Life* (Boulder: Shambhala, 1978), 85.
[3] Again recalling Libra, the seventh sign, symbolized by the scales.

order breaks down, chaos seems to creep in, a chaos that we can call "the new order" even though it often seems more chaotic than orderly. Yet this breakdown seems quite appropriate for the final phase of any cycle and thus seems part of a larger order; and if the cycle encompasses all that we refer to as "civilization" and that seems connected to what Lewis Mumford calls "the power system," then we will see rather pervasive breakdowns in order to create space for the cycle to come. The more obdurate, blind, and pervasive the prevailing structures, the more complete the breakdown.

The traditional seven planets ruled all of the twelve signs, with the Sun and Moon ruling one each and the other planets ruling two each, yielding a balanced arrangement suggesting stasis. (See Appendix for rulership systems.) The understanding of human nature symbolized by the seven traditional planets and their balanced rulership-scheme (in which each planet ruled two signs, a "day" sign and a "night" sign) yields a psychology lending itself to materialistic advancement connected with Saturnian ambition; a person defines himself by his function within the established order. Saturn functions, here, as the great trickster, his trick having to do with what we might call the bureaucracy of ego, connected with and nurturing external bureaucracies, ego in projected form. Stable societies, it turns out, *produce* a lot more; the hierarchical societies that arose around 3114 BC and their heirs have had little difficulty out-producing and decimating their competitors. The new order of 3114 BC has remained with us to this day, and now we must deal with the results.

Psychologically, Saturn represents our tendency to label the world and to think that we know it as it really is. From this assurance, however deceptive, we begin to build all sorts of social and psychological structures that tend to deny or obstruct the lunar-based organic energies necessary to life. We might therefore refer to Saturn as the deceptive bureaucracy of ego and of all that reflects ego in the external world: mostly things humans have built, though not necessarily consciously (e.g. hierarchies).

So although we might say, as do some occultists, that seven is the number showing the development of wisdom or the basic steps in the evolution of the soul, we might also call it the number of deception, for through these seven planetary steps, humans convince themselves that they "are" such and such, that the world "is" such and such. In short, we can see it as a number associated with collective delusion cemented into social forms, and what has had a more destructive influence than social forms that cement delusion?

Once we have the Saturnian ego, we generally develop ideas about what "is true" and what "is delusion," for our view of what "is true" in the world "out there" supports the assumption of what "is true" in the inner world. And once we have those convictions, we generate projections of all sorts, generally problematic ones. In this sense, seven can suggest the blind collective acceptance of status quo arrangements in both psychological and social worlds. Five, on the other hand, suggests the energies hidden within the Long Count: in the 7200 tzolkin that make it up, or in the precessional measure (72 years/degree) in which, according to some investigators (such as John Major Jenkins), the Maya took such an interest. Seven generally symbolizes working *within* a form resulting from powers beyond oneself or powers of which one remains unconscious; five generally indicates the creation *of* form from a central point.

We should not conclude from this that the septile represents a negative energy and the quintile a positive one. The septile also points to the inspiration necessary to make a contribution to the collective, to deal with a collective need or express a feeling necessary to the collective. The quintile, while it points to creative power, also points to destructive power, as we know from the traditional association of the pentagram with negative magic. The main point, here, has to do not with the nature of these aspects or the numbers from which they derive, but with the palpable fact that when we look at the Long Count time-measurements, we non-Maya notice the septile-influence and don't immediately notice the quintile-influence, just as we see, in the presented historical record, much more emphasis on large social formations than on individual creativity. Of course, that one keeps a historical record—a record, after all, that consists mostly of the development of collective forms—may itself suggest that one has an orientation toward 7-ness and not 5-ness.

The septile influence has to do most directly with solar years (5125 solar years in the Long Count), which we can experience directly through our senses and which measures movements (e.g. the Sun and Earth) over which humans have no power or influence, whereas the quintile-influence has to do with the tzolkin, which we don't experience directly through our senses but which has so much to do with human power and influence and which arose from human artifice.[1] The decimation of the Great Mother, the earth itself, has resulted from the blind power of collective trends, measured on the surface of the Long Count; the attempt to transform ourselves in such a way as to stave off the disasters predicted for the Long Count's conclusion—this has to do with the hidden emphases of the Long Count. At the same time, any viable solutions must retain a connection to natural law and natural rhythm, to forces that humans cannot control but must channel into creative outlets.[2]

---

[1] Some will say, correctly, that the tzolkin's 260 days approximates the nine months during which the fetus grows in the mother's womb. Because of this, some will say that people can have a direct experience of the tzolkin. But even this explanation points to a power developing within, not readily visible.

[2] Again, I should stress that these views come not from the Maya or any literal reading of their stone texts, but from an application of our astrological and numerical principles to Mayan measurements. I make no claim whatsoever that the Maya shamans would have seen or phrased things as I have. However, as I said earlier, any work of art lends itself to many interpretations, many of which may not have occurred to the creator(s) of that work. We find things in *Moby Dick* or *Finnegan's Wake* that the authors may not have intended, thought of, or would approve if told. Besides, the Maya, with their vastly different language and culture, would surely start with different assumptions, proceed via different symbols, and explain with a differently structured language than I do.

When we seek for causes for our present predicament, we can point first and foremost to fear and the resultant acceptance of collective delusion, both connected with Saturn, the seventh planet. Fearing our basic nature—or, fearing that if we look within we will find only voidness—we seek support through social structuring, augmenting those structures as we go, not because we need more structure in order to survive, but because the structures we build never seem to keep back the fear. So we build more and more of them. Thus we have ended up surrounded and beset by structures built because of constriction and fear and that therefore redouble them. Fear rejects the "outlaws" (those outside of the "laws" by which ego, or a centralized society, lives) beyond the protective walls, outlaws symbolized astrologically by Uranus, Neptune, and Pluto (and Chiron).[1] And thus we have the collective projections, the "external situation," that seems so destructive.

On the other hand, of course, if we look within, if we gather our inner power (quintile), we can work more effectively with these projections, for they represent transformative energies. The Maya apparently took a pessimistic attitude, assuming that the Long Count would end in destruction. If they felt this way, we can perhaps see their conclusion as one resulting from an insufficient consideration of projection, for we can interpret the prophesied destruction as a negative collective projection, and thus as something humans can recall, or "re-collect."[2] Yet if, as some have suggested, the Maya saw the Long Count not merely as a measure of collective fate but of inner transformation, then we find ourselves looking at the hidden emphasis on the quintile, suggesting individual magic.

In our era, individual magic and power must lie at the base of any transformative effort. We know this partly because we can see clearly that the external situation resists solutions based purely on external manipulation or alteration. If we look honestly, we can see that little change will occur on that level unless something happens in the hidden world first.

Finally, to conclude this section, a word on imprecision. There are 73 tzolkin to a Calendar Round, yet only 72 degrees in a quintile. Similarly, there are 52 years to a Calendar Round, but only 51.4285 degrees in a septile. The imprecision need not disturb us, even though, situated as we are at the end of an eon of apparent masculine dominance that has brought an emphasis on mechanical precision, we may wish for exactness. If we do, we should remember what Rudhyar referred to as a "coefficient of indeterminacy":

> . . . there is always in Nature a value of indeterminacy where two fundamental polarities are to be interpreted in terms of one another.[3]

---

[1] And, one supposes, by the various newly discovered trans-Plutonians, but I have not investigated the workings of these bodies enough, at this point, to comment on them.
[2] See Marie Louise von Franz, *Projection and Re-collection in Jungian Psychology* (London: Open Court, 1987).
[3] Dane Rudhyar, *The Astrology of Personality* (New York: Doubleday, 1970), 313

We may consider these "polarities" as masculine and feminine, external karma and internal development, Mayan and Western astrologies, collectivities and individuals, or some other pairing. The point remains: if we wish to bring together the wisdoms of the "Old" and "New" worlds, we will find this indeterminacy.

We may wish for precision, for we may wish to have our world conceptually intact, to feel, in a Saturnian way, that we have everything in neat and orderly boxes. But the world will always resist such efforts. Our various maps, whether verbal, mathematical, or astrological, never coincide exactly with the territory.[1] We may wish to plug all the leaks, but we probably won't succeed, for the map never maps with complete accuracy or completeness. And a good thing, too, for in the uncertainty or imprecision we find creative possibilities. In our thoughts, we want precision, but we probably won't find wisdom in thought alone. Perhaps the uncertainty suggests that we cannot completely explain Mayan astrology in our own terms (and vice-versa, presumably). Some mystery remains, some fundamental difference that resists our efforts to weave everything into a perfectly balanced and completely explained world.

Further Connections

1. Time as a Burden of the Gods

The makers of the Mayan calendar considered time as a burden carried by the Gods. The Maya depicted this quite literally: on stone stelae throughout Mayadom, we find carvings showing deities carrying the burden of time on their backs. Leon de Portilla writes:

> Their [the gods'] arrival at the end of a journey (*lub*, as termination or complete count in various Maya languages) is precisely the moment of the "weariness" of the gods. *Lub* also means "to become tired" in the various languages of the family. The new deities who in the same moment will take over the burden of time will carry it on their backs until, overcome by fatigue, they arrive at another place of rest which is the completion of one cycle and the beginning of another…These are unending series of periods with moments that are once ends and beginnings.[2]

We might at first find this concept strange, embodied in an alien set of symbols; however, if we consider it more closely and put it beside our own ideas and practices, we find a striking similarity. For our own planetary "gods" also move in cycles, and as they go through these cycles—cycles by which we, like the Maya, measure time—they accumulate karma, a development most evident in Saturn cycles but also in any other planetary cycle, the final phase of which, whether through the houses of a horoscope or in relation to any particular position (e.g. Saturn's cycle to his own posi-

---

[1] Students of General Semantics will recognize Korzybski's influence here.
[2] Miguel Leon-Portilla, *Time and Reality in the Thought of the Maya* (Norman: University of Oklahoma Press, 1990), 51.

tion), seems a time of endings and beginnings, a time when the energy of the cycle has worn down, when the karmic burden restricts further development and must be at least partly set down. During that final period, seeds from the old cycle fall into the fertile soil of the new. Dane Rudhyar describes the final phase of the soli-lunar cycle—and, by extension, of any interplanetary cycle—as

> ... a time of crucial disintegration, a breakdown of the "tone" of relationship. This tone is a sustaining factor throughout the cycle, and in any case its energy gradually exhausts itself during the waning fortnight of the moon. . . . [1]

So we see that the theme of exhaustion, the need for rest, an idea so important to the Maya, also has an important place in our astrological practice, for our planetary gods go through various cycles (and, like the Maya priests, our astrologers measure many different cycles and look for the ways in which those cycles interact and interweave), each one of which exhausts itself and passes on, giving way to a new cycle that arises with renewed energy.

As we approach the end of the Long Count, we find ourselves in such a final phase. Thus the "crucial disintegration" we see all around us; thus, too, the arising of problems that resist one-dimensional solutions but that seem solvable only by some kind of radical reorientation of priorities and values. Humanity as a whole carries a tremendous burden, one taken up back around the Long Count's birth-date. We might refer to this burden as civilization's set of discontents, or the burden of social forms that seem to have outlived their usefulness.

2. Living Numbers

To the Maya, "numbers and glyphs were not abstract entities, but the faces of supernatural personifications of the good and bad forces unceasingly interacting in the world."[2] In the words of Eric Thompson, one of the earliest interpreters of Mayan thought:

> The days are alive; they are personified powers, to whom the Maya address their devotions, and their influences pervade every activity and every walk of life; they are, in truth, very gods.[3]

Again we find ourselves in familiar territory, for we, too, have days and hours named after gods: our days of the week represent the seven major heavenly bodies recognized in our traditional astrological system, and we have planetary rulers for the hours of the day.[4] And like the Maya, we

---

[1] Dane Rudhyar, *The Lunation Cycle* (Boulder: Shambhala, 1974), 33.
[2] Portilla, 36.
[3] Qtd. in Portilla, 36.
[4] Our days: Sun-day, Moon-Day/Monday, Tues-day (in French: Mardi, Mars-day), Wednesday (Wotan's day; Mercury's day: French Mercredi); Thors' day/Thursday (French: Jeudi: Jupiter's day), Friday (French: Vendredi: Venus' day), and Saturnday:Saturday (Saturn's day). The hours: one hour ruled by each planet, though by "hour" here we do not mean 60 minutes.

see these gods as pervading our activities. Though we no longer formalize our homages to the degree that, or as consistently as, the Maya apparently did, we still go out on the town on Venus' day (Vendredi: Friday), and we often stay home from work on Saturn's day (Saturday), performing informal Saturnalias, and many people devote the day of the Sun-God to worship in churches apparently devoted to solar deities.

3. The Sacred Calendar and Our Numerical Cycles

Though not all scholars of things-Mayan agree with him, Carl Johan Calleman argues that Mayan calendrics did not generally accord with specific astronomical measurements.[1] In particular, many scholars argue, the *tzolkin* did not seem to measure any specific cycle,[2] but arose from a kind of applied numerology not linked to planetary cycles. We certainly seem to see this in other Mayan measurements, most particularly the 360 day *tun*, which only approximates the solar year and which permeates the Long Count. The Maya also counted 20-day cycles (360/18=20) that don't seem to have precise astronomical referents.

We find a similar numerological emphasis in Chinese astrology, where we find 12 symbolic animals (the ones you often find on placemats at Chinese restaurants) intercalated with the 5 elements recognized by Chinese astrologers (earth, fire, wood, metal, air) to generate a sixty-year cycle. Thus the Chinese (and Tibetans, and others) will speak of a certain year (beginning with a New Year that does not correspond with ours) as, for example, the Year of the Fire Pig, or the Year of the Earth Dog, and so forth, the cycle not corresponding to any specific astronomical cycle and yet seeming to have meaning to those who live in a society that uses it. And lest we think that this cycle has no "spiritual" or practical significance, we should recall the Chinese healing practices that refer to the five elements that form the basis of the calendar and to the *I Ching* in which these five elements play a crucial divinatory role.

In our society, we have similar practices. Most obviously, we have our seven-day week, a human imposition, but one that allows us to make a vast number of accurate predictions as long as we operate within a cultural framework in which people recognize and "live by" the week. For example, we can predict that Christian Churches will fill up rather early on Sundays, that the highways will fill up on Monday mornings, and that the bars will fill up on Friday nights.

But we can go further—and many astrologers do. We can divide life up into precise seven-year periods, birthday-to-birthday, and recognize the demands not only of each year within a particular seven-year cycle, but also of the seven-year periods themselves. And though we might say that this cycle corresponds to the movements of Saturn, which makes its quadrature approximately every seven years, or of Uranus, which spends about seven years in each sign of the tropical zodiac, Saturn does not travel exactly 90 degrees in exactly seven years, and Uranus does

---

[1] See his website.
[2] Again, scholars don't seem to agree on this point.

not spend exactly seven years in a sign. Still, many astrologers use this seven-year pattern in predictive work.

In his *Cycles of Becoming*, Alexander Ruperti (drawing from Rudhyar) connects these cycles roughly with the Saturn cycle but more profoundly with the age-factor of the individual, saying that the

> . . . context of meaning is directly related to and dependent on the age of that individual at the time of the event—for age is the "container" in which life's experiences are held. The exact same event occurring at different times in a life would have a totally different meaning.[1]

And age, though we correlate it with an important astronomical cycle (the Earth's movement around the Sun, plus other planetary cycles), does not have an exact correspondence with any other cycle: the Uranus return does not occur precisely on the eighty-fourth birthday, nor does the Saturn return occur precisely on the twenty-eighth; the mid-life Neptune square won't always take place within a year of the forty-second birthday, and the Pluto-Pluto square may not take place at "mid-life" at all. And yet we can recognize an important 7-year cycle, within which each year has a particular significance:

> First year: The new impulse is felt; feeling one's way toward a new condition of being. Experimentation.

> Second year: Resistance of past, in the form of memories, complexes, fears, social inertia. But the new impulse arouses the depths of the nature.

> Seventh year: Seed period. Culmination of whole seven-year trend, either in fulfillment or in defeat. Inner preparation for new cycle to follow, or sense of inadequacy in face of family or social pressures.[2]

Further, when we measure longer periods, we do not refer to astronomical cycles. Consider our *century* and our *millennium*, not to mention our *month* (not precisely calibrated to the Moon's cycle, of course).

4. Interpenetrating Cycles

As we have seen, from their 365+-day solar calendar, 360-day *tun*, 260 day tzolkin, and 584 day Venus calendar, the Maya created a wide variety of more extensive time periods, the most basic being the 52 year Calendar Round and the 104 year *lub,* after which the gods rested (laid down

---
[1] Ruperti, 25.
[2] Ruperti, 48.

their burdens). And from these and other measurements (e.g. the 360 day tun), they generated the Long Count, apparently built (so to speak) from many interpenetrating cycles.

We, too, measure time by interpenetrating cycles. For example astrologers work extensively with the Sun-Moon cycle (the lunation cycle), the Sun-Mercury cycle (which gives us Mercury-retrograde periods), the Sun-Venus and Sun-Mars cycles, the Jupiter-Saturn cycle, and others. We call these "synodic" cycles and measure them from one conjunction between two bodies to the next. The lengths vary, but astronomers have established mean values. Some examples of more extensive cycles:

Jupiter-Saturn	19.859 years
Saturn-Uranus	45.363 years
Uranus-Neptune	171.403 years
Uranus-Pluto	127.279 years
Neptune-Pluto	492.328 years

We will have more to say on the last cycle of this group when we come to the time-analysis of the Long Count.

So though the Maya looked at cycles whose lengths differ from our own, their practice has many similarities with our ours; and, like the Maya, we look not only at what we might call personal issues, but also at collective ones, such as the one measured by the Neptune-Pluto cycle.[1] Like the Maya, we symbolize these cycles as interactions between or among gods.

The material presented in this chapter can serve as a ground for the material in later chapters. It suggests that when we deal with Mayan calendrics, we don't enter a world to which we have no tie. Though the symbolism may seem alien, it has many parallels to our own, once we cut through cultural trappings. This doesn't mean that we should ignore significant differences, but it gives us good reason to think that we can learn a lot by applying our interpretive principles to Mayan time-measurements. And to that endeavor we turn next.

---

[1] A brief example might help. The previous two conjunctions took place in Gemini, one back at the time of the Renaissance (1398-1399, three geocentric conjunctions due to retrograde movements), one at the end of the 19th century (1891-1892). In Europe, the first marked a major shift in the perception of the phenomenal world, a time in which Europeans attempted to "see the world objectively" and to deal with it as an objective set of phenomena (not as something made by God, for example; not as a place in which to test humans or as an ante-room to the afterlife); the second marked a natural consequence of that development, as Americans destroyed the final remnants of significant Native American resistance to an onslaught resulting ineluctably from developments nearly 500 years earlier. I dealt with this some years back in an article in *Welcome to Planet Earth*. See chapter four for the significance of this cycle in the span of the Long Count.

Chapter Three

The Long Count Natal Horoscope

Preliminaries

In casting a natal horoscope for the Mayan Long Count, I enter, whether I want to do so or not, into a dispute having to do with the Long Count birth-date. Though most scholars on the subject seem to have settled on a date in August 3114 BC, with August 11 getting the most votes, John Calleman, often considered a significant figure in the debate, argues for June 17 3115 BC. As we might expect, the horoscopes from these two dates gives rather different messages—and, perhaps as importantly, give very different results when we progress them forward in time.[1] Not considering myself an expert in Mayan history, and not capable of reading the Mayan hieroglyphs for myself, I have decided to accept the near-consensus of those who know more than I. What follows, then, interprets a horoscope cast for August 11, 3114 BC.[2] I have chosen midnight for the time-of-birth: a somewhat arbitrary choice, so I do not include the angles or houses in the interpretation that follows.

We should have some caution, as we proceed, in regard to the high level abstractions or generalizations that we will apply to an extremely long period of time. Though considering the subject matter I can see no way around using such terms as *military*, *hierarchy*, *authority*, *ecological change*, and so forth, we should still have the aforementioned caution. If we take a period of over 5000 years, we can apply to it any series of abstractions or descriptive modifiers and then

---
[1] For example, June 17, 3115 BC would, when translated into solar arc directions, give a difference of about 420 years, as solar arc directions move about a degree a year.
[2] All dates refer to the Gregorian Calendar.

find events that seem to correspond with or "fit" those modifiers, for we have so many events to choose from. Furthermore, the astrological symbols themselves also exist as high level abstractions, so we have a great deal of what we might call "wiggle room" in discussing them. The combination of the long time period with the high level abstractions should remind us, if we need reminding, that sometimes when we think we've said everything, we've really said nothing, particularly if we don't tie the symbols to some kind of verifiable reality.

These difficulties notwithstanding, I hope to show that the defining symbols of the Long Count horoscope offer apt descriptive symbols and metaphors for the major cultural developments that have taken place during the Long Count's duration. Further, we will see in the next chapter that as we progress the Long Count horoscope,[1] we see some rather striking correlations between historical developments and astrological ones. To accomplish all this, I will begin by showing what kinds of large-scale or collective activities one would expect from the planets, signs, aspects, and larger configurations that we find in the Long Count horoscope. I will try to describe not what the signs and planets "are," but what they *do*, for surely the planets symbolize operations and thus give us a sense of what sorts of agents perform those operations (while the signs modify, often acting like adverbs); once we do that, we can turn to the world and see if we find such operations in the historical record.

We should not assume that we will find for the Long Count a horoscope that we might categorize as "unusual and fascinating." On the one hand, we could probably refer to *any* horoscope as "unusual and fascinating"; on the other, we should recognize that many rather extraordinary people had horoscopes that do not at first glance strike us as either unusual or fascinating. No specific astrological configuration or set of symbols indicates, for example, greatness, spiritual insight, or even neurosis. We might want, in the Long Count horoscope, some rare combination of, say, t-squares, grand trines, mystic rectangles, grand sextiles, or what have you. But with the Long Count as with many a horoscope for a "famous and significant" person, we shouldn't feel disappointed if we don't find anything of the sort.

Remarkable people may not have what we facilely consider remarkable horoscopes, and if we look for a reason for this, we should remember that such qualities as wisdom, intelligence, and creativity[2] do not appear in the horoscope itself. We will not find the "level of consciousness" (whatever that phrase might mean) written into the astrological symbols. In any case, because this horoscope—and the Long Count itself—has so much to do with what we might call "social organization as we know it," we shouldn't expect to see anything striking or extraordi-

---

[1] That is, as we move it forward in time: as we use techniques known as progressions, directions, and transits.
[2] We might wonder, as we ponder these matters, what exactly these words refer to. We may think that we can isolate these curious "things" called "intelligence" or "creativity," but studies suggest that, IQ tests notwithstanding, we really can't do so. Interested readers might wish to consult Stephen Jay Gould's *The Mismeasure of Man*.

nary, for the horoscope symbolizes the development of what we see before us in the present era.

A final point: we should not take the date of the Long Count's birth as a day when something unprecedented sprang into being suddenly, like Pallas Athena from Zeus' head. If we had been alive on that date, we probably would not have noticed anything out of the ordinary. The mystery of the Long Count lies, in part, in the way the birth-date seems to encapsulate, in its astrological symbolism, unprecedented changes in social structures, changes that continue to affect us today. These changes took place, surely, over the centuries to either side of the birth-date; they had traceable characteristics that the birth horoscope rather precisely symbolizes.[1]

An Outline

Let's start our inquiry by considering the missing factors (always important in any interpretation) and elemental preponderances. After that, we can look at the dominant signs and their relationships, and then at planetary configurations:

1. Missing Factors and Element Issues.

   The horoscope has no oppositions (no aspects of 180 degrees) and no planets in air signs. It has four planets in fire (Leo), three in water (Scorpio and Pisces), and three in earth (Capricorn).

2. Important Signs.

   The horoscope has three signs dominant:
   - Leo, with four planets, including the Sun (in its dignity: Leo)[2]
   - Capricorn, with three planets, including the Moon (in its detriment)
   - Scorpio, with two planets in conjunction (Mars and Neptune, the former in its dignity)

3. Important Aspects and Configurations.

   Among the many aspect-relationships in the horoscope, the following seem the most important:
   - the quincunx between Saturn in Leo and Uranus (conjoined with Pluto) in Capricorn
   - the quincunx between Mercury and Venus in Leo and the Moon in Capricorn
   - the quincunx between Mercury and Venus in Leo and Jupiter in Pisces

---

[1] We can perhaps find a partial parallel in what we call the Renaissance and its connection (discussed below) to the Neptune-Pluto conjunction of 1398. That the conjunction tells us much about the Renaissance as a whole does not mean that anything earth-shaking took place on the precise day of the conjunction.
[2] See Appendix for a discussion of rulerships.

- the Yod formed by these back-to-back quincunxes[1]
- the squares between Mercury and Venus in Leo and Mars and Neptune in Scorpio
- the various conjunctions: Mercury with Venus; the Sun with Saturn; Mars with Neptune; Uranus with Pluto
- the quintile between Mars and Saturn

Note that I make no mention of the Ascendant or of anything having to do with house positions. We derive these positions from a precise time and place of birth, and here we have neither. I have set the horoscope for midnight not because some scholars say that the Maya apparently took that as the beginning of the day, but because it reminds the reader to consider the time as arbitrary. So though Venus rules Taurus, the ascending sign for the midnight horoscope, we should not take ascendant-related factors into consideration until we know for certain if the Mayan priests said unambiguously what time of day the Long Count began.[2]

Missing Factors: Oppositions and Air Signs

Millions of horoscopes lack an element or a type of aspect, so we shouldn't take such absences as unusual or as indicative of insurmountable problems. Nevertheless, the astrologer should take the missing element or aspect as indicating matters demanding attention, suggestive of problems, potentials, or both at once. The evidence strongly supports the following conclusion: in the horoscope of a human being, a missing factor will remain a difficulty in the personal life but will often arise as a *potential* in the professional life. Thus, for example, the physical issues often indicated by the lack of an element—for example, those with no important placements in water signs often have difficulty washing toxins from the body—will often appear quite clearly even as the person seems to express the missing element quite powerfully in the world. This much we can see through observation. After that, we can offer some inferences: for example, perhaps the person moves into work related to the missing factor because he or she generates so much compensatory energy that the personal life cannot contain it; thus it emerges in the person's work, often through vocation.[3]

---

[1] A yod to Mercury and Venus from the Moon-Jupiter sextile: two quincunxes (Mercury-Venus to a. Jupiter, and b. the Moon) plus one sextile (Moon to Jupiter); 150+150+60= 360).

[2] Furthermore, because the ascendant moves about a degree every 4 minutes (15 degrees an hour, or one sign every two hours, the entire zodiac in a twenty four hour period), we would want some exactitude in time. We should not accept a time that sounds rounded off. Even if we say "two o'clock in the morning," as one source recommends, we should realize that the Mayans had no mechanical clocks like ours, so that the apparent precision of any clocked birth time may represent an imposition from our culture to theirs.

[3] I will not present the evidence for these assertions here. I have, however, an unpublished manuscript that contains a good deal of empirical backing for them, so I feel that I can rest weight on them. Some years back, I presented this material in a series of articles for *American Astrology* magazine (a publication since absorbed into *Horoscope Guide*).

However, though we can see how a *person* might do the necessary compensatory work, cultivating through experience what he doesn't have as a "natural endowment," we may have more difficulty seeing how an *Age* could do the same, for unlike a period of time, an individual seems to have what we call a *will,* a center of volition from which to coordinate a creative or compensatory response. We can therefore expect that the aeon in question will manifest the more problematic side of the astrological symbolism. This seems generally true in horoscopes for collectivities, whether for aeons, nations, companies, or groups; we generally find that the collectivity expresses astrological challenges in a problematic way, often in *the* most problematic way. Our interpretation of these factors in the Long Count horoscope will therefore lean toward what some will call the negative.[1]

A lack of oppositions (as here) often points to a difficulty seeing one's own projections *as* projections. At the same time, the very lack seems to generate energy in the individual, as if, sensing the deficiency, the person moves to compensate for it. A person lacking oppositions will often gravitate toward work in which he must develop the ability to work with projections. Carl Jung, despite the lack of oppositions in his horoscope, articulated much of the view of projections that has informed psychologists and astrologers ever since.

The lack of oppositions points to a difficulty attaining objectivity. We generally come to what we call "objectivity" through our dealings with others. Those others serve as hooks for our various projections, and by dealing with those people, organizations, or entities in an open-minded way, we can gain much objective understanding about ourselves. Those without oppositions seem to have more difficulty recognizing the projection as such. Of course, an Age probably doesn't have the power to recognize projections in any case, but the lack of oppositions strongly suggests that people in this period who have the power to make lasting impact will often act as if they had not received the feedback that the world constantly sends (for whatever their personal dispensations, those people will often find themselves carried along by what we might call "the spirit of the Age," particularly when dealing with matters of collective import expressing that spirit).

---

[1] A close square in a person's horoscope will often point to great creative potential, and we will often see the person find a healthy, vibrant expression for that affliction. In a nation's horoscope, on the other hand, we will generally see a problematic manifestation of the same aspect. An in-depth discussion of this would take us too far afield. One example, however, may prove instructive: the Mars-Neptune square in the United States horoscope seems to arise, again and again, through an unfortunate combination of deception (Neptune) and aggression (Mars). Our government has deceived the people in order to facilitate entrance into one war after another, starting at least as far back as the Mexican War and extending in an unbroken line to the present. (Those who see World War II as an exception should consult *Perpetual War for Perpetual Peace*, published over five decades ago, edited by Harry Elmer Barnes.) In an individual's horoscope, the same aspect can indicate compassionate action, or perhaps involvement in dance or yoga.

When a person has an opposition, he will generally play the role of the planet closest to the sun and project onto others the role of the planet farthest from the sun.[1] If a person has a Sun-Saturn opposition, for example, he will often find himself blocked by authority figures or people who in some way judge him or find him wanting. This pattern will generally keep recurring until the person begins to withdraw the projection by recognizing the projected energy as part of his own potential. At some point, he will (hopefully) begin to recognize the pattern, and through this recognition come to greater objectivity regarding his experience in the world. Though at first he keeps finding himself in conflict with energies marked by Saturn, these experiences may eventually wake him up.

Those *without* oppositions have difficulty waking up as a result of feedback. Michael Meyer says that a person who lacks oppositions will be "completely responsible for the maintenance of his own equilibrium" and "needs to learn how to maintain an objective life perspective."[2] He won't get the assistance constantly provided by the oppositions, for the opposition indicates that one gets recognizable feedback of a consistent enough type that one eventually gets the message. Those lacking oppositions will find themselves just as enmeshed in their projections, but they will have more difficulty extricating themselves—and they have this difficulty, it seems, because the feedback doesn't seem to them to contain a clear message. Oppositions occurring through transits or projections generally arise through virulent projections: through what the person will take as objective events even though they clearly have a close connection to inner dispositions, a point to remember when we look at the transits and progressions to the Long Count horoscope, particularly those for the Long Count's end-date.

The lack of oppositions in the Long Count horoscope suggests that when acting through and within large social groupings (e.g. nation states), or when caught up in activities expressing the spirit of the Age, human beings will not often reorient themselves toward balance. Because, as we will see, the Long Count has much to do with authority hierarchies, those with important positions in those hierarchies will find themselves expressing that spirit. They will persist in behaviors that seem clearly negative no matter what results or what conflicts such behavior leads to. This perhaps accounts for the peculiar drive of "civilized man" (humans living in what we often refer to as "civilization") toward collective behaviors that not only lead to environmental ruin, but that do not even yield satisfaction in the short run.

People who lack air often have difficulty allowing enough space for communication to occur naturally. That they lack air does not at all indicate a lack of intelligence or an inability to communicate, for many people who lack air make extraordinary use of the intellect. However, because communication takes place through air, and because air separates one being from another,

---

[1] When I capitalize the "s," as in Sun, I refer to an astrological factor; when I leave the lower-case "s," I refer to an astronomical factor.
[2] Michael R. Meyer, *A Handbook for the Humanistic Astrologer* (New York: Anchor Books, 1974), 161.

those without air tend to have difficulty allowing enough space in their deliberations and thus may lack perspective. *People* lacking air often tend to cut others off, and as a result have more difficulty taking part in the free and open flow of ideas; they may therefore have a plethora of ideas but difficulty listening with interest to others. They may hear what others say and have an intellectual understanding of it, but they will often have difficulty resting within natural communication give-and-take.

This can obviously lead to problems of all sorts. They may develop particular communication styles that preclude what we might call vital interaction. Yet one often sees, in those who lack air, great mental gifts leading to intellectual achievements. One who lacks air will often take on work related to air, perhaps as an editor, a teacher, or someone else who must, as part of his work, communicate effectively with others. In the horoscope for an *aeon*, the lack of air will probably suggest these last-mentioned results: great achievements of intellect, probably accompanied by a tendency to exclude any ideas that do not fit into the dominant mode of the society, and a difficulty resting within the natural communication give-and-take that so often generates balance in human relations.

Dignity and Detriment

In order to understand the material involving dignities, readers need to know a bit about the astrological tradition related to this term. Those already familiar with this subject can skip to page 83.

In our astrological tradition, astrologers say that certain planets "rule" certain signs. In the traditional system, the Sun and Moon rule one planet each (Leo and Cancer respectively), and every other planet rules two signs, a day and a night sign, with Mercury ruling Gemini and Virgo, the two signs adjacent to Cancer and Leo, Venus ruling Taurus and Libra, the two signs adjacent to Mercury's dignities, Mars ruling Aries and Scorpio, the next two signs in either direction, Jupiter ruling Pisces and Sagittarius, the next two, and Saturn ruling Aquarius and Capricorn, the final two, signs standing opposed to Leo and Cancer. An orderly pattern resulted. (See Appendix.)

With the discovery of Uranus, Neptune, Pluto and Chiron, this orderly arrangement dissolved: astrologers now say that Uranus rules Aquarius, that Neptune rules Pisces, that Pluto rules Scorpio, and that Chiron rules Virgo.[1] Nevertheless, though the new rulerships clearly have importance, the old rulerships still seem to operate, influencing the astrologer's judgment of a how a planet will function in a certain sign. To put the matter briefly, we can say that a planet in its dignity generally operates more easily according to its own nature, while a planet in its detriment

---

[1] Some would say Sagittarius, though. I see Chiron as having his *exaltation* in Sagittarius.

(opposite the dignity) has difficulty operating that way but must make adjustments in functioning.

For example, the Moon in Capricorn, its detriment—and its position in the Long Count horoscope—finds emotional security (Moon) through structure and responsibility (Capricorn), an odd or challenging way to find security, for the Moon, ruler of organic life, wants physical contact of some sort, and structure often seems inimical to the free flow of feeling expressed through the body, though the person will often discipline the body or feelings and make great achievements, finding security in hierarchy. Despite the difficulties, we shouldn't see the detriment positions as bad or negative; sometimes they produce heightened awareness precisely because the person can't seem to function blindly or go on automatic pilot. (This awareness seems related to the opposition aspect: just as the opposition often indicates objective awareness, so the detriment, the sign opposite the dignity, seems to encourage heightened awareness.)

We find numerous instructive patterns among the various dignities and debilities. Because of the placements in the Long Count horoscope, one dignity-detriment pair deserves our attention: Leo, the Sun's dignity, quincunxes Capricorn, the Moon's detriment.[1] The quincunx-relationship[2] between the Long Count's Sun in Leo and Moon in Capricorn symbolizes a particular kind of tension that seems endemic to the Long Count as a whole, not only because a quincunx between the two "lights" suggests, by itself, a definite but hard-to-isolate kind of tension, but also because, as we will see, the horoscope has several other quincunx aspects of almost-equal importance.

Also notable: in the Long Count horoscope, we find a pattern in the dignities and detriments: we find the planets of primarily masculine orientation—the Sun, Mars, and Jupiter—all in their dignities; we find one of the planets primarily indicating the feminine, earth, and nurturance—the Moon—in detriment. This suggests, in a preliminary way, that the human drives that we generally see as feminine in orientation—nurturing, belonging, feeling, sensitive response, etc.—will not find ready avenues for expression but will have to function in ways not harmonious with their nature. Humans will have to express these drives through venues that don't seem entirely suitable, in this case through structure, order, and hierarchy (Capricorn). At the same

---

[1]These relationships derive from the pattern given above: the Moon's dignity sits adjacent to the Sun's (Cancer sits adjacent to Leo), and the Sun's detriment (Aquarius) falls 180 degrees from the Sun's dignity, or 150 degrees from Cancer, the sign adjacent to that dignity. Capricorn, the Moon's detriment, falls 150 degrees from Leo, the Sun's dignity, adjacent to Aquarius, the Sun's detriment. See Appendix.

[2]I use this term—quincunx relationship—to indicate merely that two planets tenant signs with a quincunx relationship: signs that begin 150 degrees from each other. Sometimes these planets will also have a close quincunx *aspect* between them. It seems unlikely that the Long Count Moon quincunxes the Long Count Sun; certainly it doesn't do so for any birth time close to the midnight time for which I have cast the horoscope. We do know that Leo and Capricorn, the signs in which we find the Sun and Moon respectively, lie 150 degrees from each other (i.e. in a quincunx relationship).

time, the so-called masculine operations—those involving radiation, assertion, expansion, and centrifugal expression—will find venues more appropriate to that expression. The symbolism suggests that the Long Count measures an era in which "masculine" drives appear more clearly and function more straightforwardly, generally forcing "feminine" drives to express themselves through masculine imperatives or through subservient positions. The historical record provides much evidence that this occurred.

Signs and Aspects: Leo, Capricorn, and the Quincunx: Imbalance[1]

Before discussing Leo and Capricorn in themselves, let's say a bit more about the quincunx aspect (150 degrees) that links them, an aspect symbolizing a type of imbalance linking two signs with very little in common. When we describe the qualities of Leo and Capricorn, we will see this imbalance or lack of connection quite clearly.

The quincunx links signs from incompatible elements and different modes.[2] The quincunx between Leo and Capricorn, for example, links a fixed fire sign (Leo) with a cardinal earth sign (Capricorn), with fire and earth generally considered as incompatible, as we can intuit from the phrase "scorched earth." If a person has an important quincunx, he may not register the imbalance consciously; however, the imbalance remains, operating unconsciously, which often means "through the body" or through what we can call a "life ritual" that paradoxically hides the imbalance from the conscious mind while ensuring that it permeates the person's behavior so pervasively that the person will not see it clearly. For example, the person may go into a kind of work or vocational enterprise that does not utilize one's talent fully or in which one plays a subservient role that belies one's capacity to lead. If, on the other hand, the aspect manifests through the body, the person may develop a chronic illness of some sort. Because the linked energies have so little in common, the rituals that link them often prove problematic, particularly when, as often happens, they go on for years or decades—or, for the Long Count, centuries or millennia.

---

[1]Though the quin*cunx* measures exactly 5 signs of 30 degrees each (5x30=150), it belongs to a different set of aspects than does the quin*tile* (72 degrees = 1/5 of 360) discussed in the previous chapter. The former belongs to the 12-series of aspects, the latter to the 5-series. Thus they have distinct meanings.

[2]Compare the quincunx with the square, generally considered one of the more difficult aspects in a horoscope (and one that also plays an important role in our study). Planets in a square share their modality, whether cardinal, fixed, or mutable (a planet in a specific degree of mutable Virgo will square one in the same degree of mutable Gemini.), whereas planets in a quincunx do not (a planet in a specific degree of fixed Leo will quincunx one in the same degree of cardinal Capricorn). Like planets in a square, though, planets in a quincunx fall in incompatible elements: a planet in a specific degree of Leo (fire) will square one in the same degree of Scorpio (water, generally seen as incompatible with fire); a planet in a specific degree of Leo (fire) will quincunx one in the same degree of Capricorn (earth, seen as incompatible with fire). Traditionally, astrologers have seen fire and air as compatible with one another but incompatible with earth and water; and they have seen earth and water as compatible. By "compatible," we mean *enhancing each other's function without creating friction.* Of course, friction can indicate dynamic creativity, but let's put that discussion aside for now.

Because so many illnesses result from the kinds of imbalances just suggested, astrologers often refer to the quincunx as an "illness aspect." Though we can see the quincunx as symbolizing a search *for* balance, the persistence *of* the imbalance can often prove harmful to the organism, particularly if the person remains unconscious of the tension. It seems that the quincunx symbolizes an imbalance requiring healing, and we often find that people with strong quincunxes work with the energy by moving into the healing professions, healing themselves by healing others, thus participating in the search for balance. Often enough, though, this search for balance begins with an awareness of the results *of* imbalance: with illness. In many cases, and in particular if they proceed without reflection, people will not see this imbalance, and thus will fail to work effectively with quincunxes, unless they either look carefully at the apparently meaningless details that make up the illness-producing pattern or go through some kind of emotional catharsis. Further, they often go through catharsis most effectively by paying attention to the details, perhaps by setting up a situation that facilitates that catharsis, as through some kind of counseling, or through breath-work or work in the arts. In either case, we see the presence of ritual, and to benefit from ritual, one must pay attention to the details that make it up.

We can see from the above that the quincunx suggests a potentially dynamic drive to integrate disparate energies. The aspect generally provokes activity, even if the activity often proceeds blindly or leads to illness. If one can express the quincunx consciously, it can produce positive service and an understanding of the place of ritual in human development, for in many rituals, understanding of the particulars yields insight into some higher truth. Humans often develop rituals in order to create some kind of link *to* this "higher truth," and when rituals fail to make this connection, the cause often lies in the person's inattention to the details, and the effect arises as ill-health either spiritual or physical. For example, if one takes part in the ritual that Catholics call *Mass*, one will gain no benefit and may even suffer harm if one doesn't study the meaning of the details. We could cite other examples of rituals that depend for their value on this understanding of details.

The quincunx symbolizes a search *for* balance, not the achievement *of* balance. If something achieves perfect balance, it may remain stationary unless influenced by outside factors. Though buildings have that kind of balance, most organic things don't: a man on a tightrope moves in order to main*tain* balance. Something (or some*one*) badly out of balance will generally either fall over or struggle to regain balance, the movement suggesting that the "balance" we see exists as a process of constantly finding the point *of* balance and then, because nothing remains stationary, losing it. So the term "imbalance" often suggests the movement and dynamism needed to gain or regain balance. The quincunx suggests an ongoing search for balance *and* the imbalance that leads to that search. Thus it has to do not only with illness, but also with transformation and the search for health; it has to do with changes happening as a response to developments in the environment. Thus we can see the quincunx as an aspect of *con-*

stant adjustment, or *ongoing reorientation* in a search for balance and health.[1] Reorientation to *what*, though?

As noted, the quincunx brings together energies that have little in common. The planets and signs involved seek some accommodation with each other, some way to work together with more awareness. The two signs find themselves (so to speak) in relationship within one organism, so they cannot ignore each other—or, we might say, if they *do* ignore each other, illness results, whereas if they don't ignore each other, we find a dynamic interaction, either a movement toward accommodation or a movement driven by unconscious impulses. And, of course, we can also see illness as a movement toward accommodation and adjustment.

When a person gets a fever or other inflammation, we suspect that the body has heated up in response to an intrusion or imbalance (stress). We can therefore see the inflammation as a movement toward balance. Some studies suggest that when surgeons give anti-inflammatory drugs to patients just after surgery, those drugs, in preventing the inflammatory response that we can interpret as an adjustment to the invasion of surgery, hinder the patient's healing responses. In the quincunx aspects of the Long Count horoscope, we can see a marked imbalance, a definite tendency toward illness and inflammation in the form of social organization we often call "civilization." We don't have to look far for the results, for the planet seems, as a result of this form of social organization, to have developed a severe illness, a kind of fever or inflammation (overheating) that we can attribute to some kind of imbalance.

Astrologers generally associate illness with the lower quincunx more than with the upper quincunx. We have the lower quincunx when the faster moving planet has moved 150 degrees ahead of the slower moving planet, as the Long Count Moon has done in relation to Venus and Mercury and as Venus and Mercury have done in relation to Jupiter in Pisces. So the Long Count's natal yod (consisting of Mercury-Venus plus the Moon and Jupiter) consists of two lower quincunxes, strongly suggesting illness. The horoscope also has an upper quincunx: Saturn, the faster moving planet, has moved 210 degrees ahead of Uranus and (more loosely) Pluto—or, we might say, it has come within 150 degrees of those planets (210 + 150 = 360). This aspect suggests transformation resulting from developed awareness. Thus, in the Long Count horoscope, we find both upper and lower quincunxes: on the one hand, illness hopefully producing more objectivity; on the other, the possibility of profound and powerful social changes resulting *from* that awareness.

---

[1] In the cycle between two planets, the 150-degree aspects both precede and follow from the opposition. If we see the opposition as an aspect suggesting a kind of balance—just as Libra, the sign opposite Aries, the first sign in the zodiac, has the scales as its symbol, as indicated by its French name: *La Balance*—then we can see that the quincunx symbolizes, first, the search for balance, and then the result of any stasis.

The quincunx symbolizes or points to a situation in which two energies do not work smoothly together but for reasons not obvious on the surface. They find themselves linked, but because the imbalance doesn't become immediately evident, and may not register consciously *as* an imbalance if it remains buried in the "thousand and one things" of life, the system's energy finds itself in constant adjustment and constantly driven. In the horoscope of a person, this imbalance will often arise as an unacknowledged tension between personality factors and energetic needs (as for example if a person stays for years in an unsatisfying job, ignoring creative inspiration because of unacknowledged security patterns). But whereas a quincunx in an individual's horoscope can often point to a creative combination of apparently disparate energies, in the horoscope for a period of time, we shouldn't expect any such creative combination, for time-periods have no central identity or awareness that might serve as the organizing center for creative effort.

What might "illness" mean when we apply the term to a period of time? To answer this question, we can return to material presented in the first chapter. The Long Count began at a time that saw the beginning of what we can call "civilization as we know it," a particular form of social organization that we perhaps take as the only possible one, and that millions of people apparently see as the *best* one, simply because it has achieved such dominance. This "civilization" seems to involve a marked imbalance that has resulted in illness for the planet considered as a living entity. The social organizations that arose in the 4th millennium BC initiated a cycle of environmental degradation that has continued to this day; during that period the dominant group conquered others in order to gain purportedly needed resources. As we approach the end of the Long Count, we face the possibly catastrophic consequences of resource depletion, global warming, water shortages, microbe mutations, the extinctions of numerous species, and on and on.

We can spot the imbalances in the developments of the 4th millennium BC; in the horoscope, they appear first in the relationship between Leo and Capricorn, signs in a quincunx relationship, each with three important natal planets. The middle of the 4th millennium BC brought the development of large-scale, top-down hierarchies with kings, under the auspices of the sun-god, at the central point: the hierarchies clearly suggest Capricorn; the influence of the sun-god strongly suggests Leo, along with its traditional ruler, the Sun. These quincunx relationships suggest tension between the regal mode and the hierarchical mode; they suggest that when these modes get entangled in the horoscope for the non-conscious entity we refer to as the Long Count, illhealth will likely result.

This may strike us as odd. We may think that a union of regal authority with a hierarchy or bureaucracy merely promotes powerful efficiency—and it often *does*, for the (lower) quincunx has a close symbolic relationship with Virgo, a sign associated with effective action, while the upper has a close symbolic connection with Scorpio, a sign associated with power and transformation. Some will point to the way many modern states enshrine the Leo-Capricorn union, with decisions emanating from a central point and the bureaucracy ensuring more effective development resulting from those decisions. However, that we see regality and bureaucracy as inseparable—a centralized ruling figure surrounded by a hierarchical bureaucracy to promote efficiency—probably reflects a simple fact: that this social form, developed in the 4th millennium BC, has come to dominate all others, so much so that we see the union of regality and hierarchy as natural, even inescapable.[1]

I said above that the quincunx presents a tension not always immediately evident. In many cases, one discerns the tension only through its results: either illness or obsessive activity, two ways of adjusting to the tension. We can see the contemporary environmental crisis as the resulting illness—or, we might say, as the symptoms of that illness, for the causal factors remain hidden, though accurately symbolized in the Long Count horoscope. To see those causal factors more clearly, we can look further at the relationship between Leo and Capricorn, between fixed fire and cardinal earth, between the centralized being who draws his power from on high (Leo) and a sense that ends justify means (Capricorn). In the Long Count horoscope, we see this imbalance in the series of quincunxes from Leo to Capricorn: the quincunxes from Mercury and Venus to the Moon; the even-closer quincunx from Saturn to Uranus, and (more loosely) to Pluto. The first series suggests an illness-producing imbalance between a set of values and ideas related to regality and a tendency to find security through one's place in a hierarchy; the second series, particularly the aspect from Saturn to Uranus, suggests that inventiveness will get co-opted by the forces of the status quo, thus augmenting the power of the latter in obsessive-compulsive activity, a kind of destructive ritual.

Speaking of developments late in the 4th millennium BC, around the time of the Long Count's birth-date, Lewis Mumford writes (in *Technics and Human Development*) of the importance of "a new kind of social organization, capable of raising the human potential and bringing about changes in every dimension of existence—changes that small, down-to-earth communities, on the early Neolithic scale, could hardly contemplate even in the imagination."[2] A bit further on, in one of the many passages that suggest the relationship between Leo and Capricorn (suggesting, in this context, kingship and hierarchy), Mumford continues:

> Out of the early Neolithic complex a different kind of social organization arose: no longer dispersed in small units, but unified in a large one; no longer 'democratic,'

---

[1] Some will point to the United States, arguably the dominant state at the end of the Long Count, as a clear exception, a country without a king and created in opposition to royal dictates. However, many historians have noted the development of what they call the "imperial Presidency," for the office of President in the United States has taken to itself more and more power over the years. Far from standing as an exception, the United States gives us additional evidence in support of the principle under discussion, for even in a country purportedly anti-royal, we see the development of royalist tendencies in combination with bureaucratic ones.
[2] Mumford, 163.

that is, based on neighborly intimacy, customary usage, and consent, but authoritarian, centrally directed, under the control of a dominant minority; no longer confined to a limited territory, but deliberately 'going out of bounds' to seize new raw materials and enslave helpless men, to exercise control, to exact tribute. This new culture was dedicated, not just to the enhancement of life, but to the expansion of collective power. By perfecting new instruments of coercion, the rulers of the society had, by the Third Millennium BC, organized industrial and military power on a scale that was never to be surpassed until our own time.[1]

Though the seeds for this transformation may have grown from the work of the astronomer priests, who perceived an order in the heavens, the resulting civilization developed in a distinctly non-heavenly way. Speaking of a transformation he sees as religious in nature, Mumford writes:

The earliest stages of this religious transformation antedates writing and can only be inferred from later documents. But there is general evidence of a shift in interest and authority from the gods of vegetation and animal fertility—subject to human weakness, to suffering, misfortune and death—to the gods of the sky: the moon, the sun and the planets, the lightning and the storm wind—powerful and implacable, awful and irresistible, not to be swayed from their course.[2]

And, he adds, though the older gods (the earth gods related to vegetation) and the new gods (the sky gods) "remained side by side in most cultures," and though the vegetation gods "continued to be more sympathetic, lovable, and popular, there was no doubt which were the more powerful."[3]

So we can see the shift, but where do we see the above-mentioned dynamic imbalance? Let's start from some facts and inferences accepted by various historians:[4] that human societies achieved an agricultural abundance; that "civilization" could not have formed without this surplus; and that the surplus gave birth (so to speak) to a hierarchy, to people who managed the surplus. Thus, the beginning of social classes, reflecting Capricorn, a sign associated with hierarchy and social stratification, not as an evil but as a method yielding greater efficiency. The surplus itself seems to reflect the Age of Taurus in which it first developed.[5]

One factor remains, a factor connected with Leo, the sign in which we find the Sun, Saturn, Mercury, and Venus on the Long Count birth-date. Together with the increase in the food supply (Taurus) and the new "set of institutional controls" (Capricorn), we find that "at the center of

---
[1]Mumford, 164.
[2]Mumford, 167.
[3]Mumford, 167.
[4]Lewis Mumford and Arnold Toynbee, to start with.
[5]See chapter one.

this whole development lay the new institution of kingship." Further, through the Middle Ages and even to this day, we see a strong connection between kingship and hunting—originally, in both Egypt and Assyria, the hunting of lions (Leo):

> This original connection between kingship and hunting has remained visible all throughout recorded history: from the stelae upon which both Egyptian and Assyrian kings boast their prowess as lion-hunters, to the preservation of vast hunting forests as the inviolable domains of kings in our own epoch. Benno Landsberger notes that with kings in the Assyrian empire, hunting and fighting were virtually interchangeable occupations. The unscrupulous use of the weapons of the hunt to control the political and economic activities of whole communities was one of the effective inventions of kingship. Out of that a whole series of subsidiary mechanical inventions eventually came.[1]

We should note, here, that when Mumford speaks of machines or mechanical devices, he does not restrict himself to things made of steel or with non-living moving parts. Rather, he includes those machines that had human beings as movable parts, such machines as built the pyramids and religious temples in Mesopotamia and Egypt thousands of years ago.

From this institution of kingship came, quickly and inevitably, "a kind of unrestrained cannibal lust in dwelling on the scope and power of the divine king. As pictured [in the most ancient pyramid text,] kingship was actually a man-eating device." Mumford then gives a translation of the text-in-question:

> He it is that eateth men; that liveth on Gods, that possesseth the carriers and despatcheth messages. . . . The Runner-with-all-Knives. . . he that strangleth them for him; he draweth out for him their entrails, he the messenger whom he sends death to. . . . He it is that eateth their magic and swalloweth their lordliness. Their great ones are for his morning meal, and the little ones for his night meal. . . .[2]

This provides us with a not-so-nice segue into a discussion of Leo, sign of regality and lordliness, in which we find four important planets, including the Long Count Sun, resting in the sign of his dignity.

Leo, the King, and the Solar Gods: Power in the Center

Obviously, not every entity, whether person or collectivity, with a strong Leo statement in the birth-chart will act as a devourer of human flesh. However, as suggested above, the signs and

---
[1] Mumford, 168-9.
[2] Mumford, 184.

the planets tend to take their most problematic manifestations when they play out on a collective scale, either in the horoscopes of nations, of centuries, of large institutions, or, here, of an aeon.

Astrologers have said for a long time that the Sun, sitting at the center of the solar system, rules Leo. Thus the Long Count's emphasis on centrality and confidence: we see the centrality in the central royal granary, generally housed in the temple of the city, itself the center of the realm; we see the confidence in the figure of the king himself, who from very early on saw himself as either a god or as one chosen *by* the gods. This confidence seems to stem from the relationship (discussed above) between kingship and hunting:

> As to the origin of the king's unconditional supremacy and his special technical facilities, there is no room for doubt: it was hunting that cultivated the initiative, the self-confidence, the ruthlessness that kings must exercise to achieve and retain command; and it was the hunter's weapons that backed up his commands, whether rational or irrational, with the ultimate authority of armed force: above all, the readiness to kill.[1]

Leo, the fifth sign, stands not only for what we might call the ruthless blindness of kings—the blindness resulting from the blazing light of self-concern and self-involvement that no doubt enveloped and radiated from the king as it would from any man who saw himself specially favored by the gods—but also for the illuminated self-consciousness that suggests not only the Sun (ruler of Leo, the fifth sign) but also the quintile aspect (resulting from division of the circle by five; see previous chapter). The number five suggests self-consciousness standing in the middle of the four directions of the world: the four directions plus the center from which self-consciousness radiates; thus the relationship to the quintile and to power, creative or destructive (and in this case both): on a personal level, ego and its world; on a collective level, the king and his realm. Thus, too, the relationship between creative power (quintile) and collective patterning (septile). And thus, by the end of the Long Count, what Mumford calls "the Pentagon of power," a subject taken up in the next chapter.

For an individual, Leo has to do with the radiation of self-awareness and/or ego. This awareness can blind even as it illuminates, for self-awareness can easily blind us to the demands of the rest of the world; and every creature with awareness has a particular *type* of awareness. Because those with self-awareness often forget that the awareness arises from a self that takes its own view as truth, Leo can easily suggest blindness as regards these other factors; it can easily put too much importance on itself, blinded by its own self-conceit. Similarly, though the sun illuminates, it can also blind. So though we speak of "self-consciousness" in connection with Leo, the term can mean either illuminated awareness or the blindness that comes from accepting limited awareness as total awareness.

---

[1] Mumford, 169.

So we have the central conundrum of Leo: how to create through one's illuminated self-consciousness and pride without succumbing to the blindness that often comes as part-and-parcel *of* that consciousness and pride. And some of this blindness involves the unconscious, for just as the Sun illuminates phenomena, it blots out the stars, symbols of unconscious processes and collective movements. So when we find Leo strong in a horoscope, we do well to ask whether we will find an awareness of those unconscious processes that have such an intimate and demonstrable connection to developments in the external world and to full self-awareness.

Kingship arose together with a regulated bureaucracy (Capricorn), beginning with the local priests and chieftains who developed the ability to discern regular movements in the night sky and thus augmented the power of the king. As we have seen, emphasis on earth gods shifted to an emphasis on sky deities, the sun preeminent among them, and as this took place, human beings more and more sought regularity. An important part of this regularity involved the demands of large-field agriculture and knowledge of the seasons, though the heavens proffered more information than that alone. In any case, with their knowledge of the solar calendar, astronomers, who perhaps also functioned as priests in the bureaucracy, provided invaluable information by looking to the sky and making decisions based on the regularity and order they found there. But more importantly, regularity in the skies served as a model for social regularity. Thus

> . . . regularity and order that had first come in with the Neolithic grinding and polishing and became visible in geometric patterns and decoration, now spread over the whole landscape: rectangles, triangles, pyramids, straight lines, bounded fields, testify to both astronomic order and strict human control. Standardization was the mark of the new royal economy in every department. Confucius was characterizing a much earlier achievement of this culture when he observed: "Now all over the empire carriages have wheels of the same size, all writing is with the same characters, and for conduct there are the same rules."[1]

We see in Mumford's description of regularity the influence (so to speak) of Saturn-ruled Capricorn, a sign associated with hierarchy and order of all sorts; and when we consider what was said above about kingship, hunting, and warfare, we see the link, in the historical record, between Capricorn and Leo. From their union, as a result of the tension between the two signs, came new social rituals and "a change in scale" from the village to the city, from the small household or village shrine to the "towering temple," invariably near the granary, holder of the surplus (Taurus). And with the city came walls, and projects—the city walls, the temples, the pyramids—requiring the coordination of thousands of humans under a rigid hierarchy (Capricorn) enforced by the ruling and warrior classes descended from Neolithic hunters (Leo). And that city stood not as the home of mere humans, but as the purported home of a god, for it stood

---

[1] Mumford, 167.

as "a replica of heaven,"[1] suggesting the regularity of the heavens symbolized primarily by the sun, taken as the Sun God that we so closely associate with Leo.

As we saw in chapter one, the development of the surplus reflects the Age of Taurus. The Long Count horoscope describes with great specificity the kinds of social developments that took place in connection with that surplus. For, after all, though human beings developed the kinds of social systems described above, and though we might see this choice as dictated by the natural, even evolutionary, developments of the Age of Taurus, humans could have made many other choices than the ones they did. Further, Taurus does not generally emphasize either regality or hierarchy and so cannot account for the specific types of social development that took place towards the end of the 4th millennium BC.

(A bit further on, we will discuss a terra cotta plaque depicting the solar eagle devouring the bull of the Moon. Astrologers consider the Moon as the exalted ruler of Taurus. By itself, Taurus suggests abundance, particularly from the natural yield of the earth, a yield that augments naturally, like so many living things. The solar eagle, here, could suggest the way that civilizations under the partial dominance of Leo devoured the fertility of the earth. The plaque still has relevance today, as preponderant solar power devours the earth's fecundity through overheating. The dominant country in that process has the eagle as one of its primary symbols. Also, as some people have connected eagle symbolism to Scorpio, we might take the solar eagle as a representative of both Leo *and* Scorpio, two signs that play an important role in the Long Count horoscope.)

The change in scale and emphasis required what Mumford calls a "highly efficient type of social organization," a type of organization that arose many centuries before the development of metal necessary to make efficient tools. People of that age built pyramids with "only small, modest, mechanically primitive instruments: chisels, saws, mallets, ropes." So to what do we attribute these developments? To, it seems, what Mumford calls the "megamachine." Before looking into this, though, let's return to our discussion of Leo and kingship, for this symbolism seems integral to the kinds of developments under discussion.

Leo has to do with regality. One takes on the role of king not because one has demonstrated an ability to rule or judge accurately, but because of blood lineage, appropriate for an institution ruled by Leo, for Leo rules the heart, which pumps the blood throughout the system. Leo rules by divine right, by an inner sense, not necessarily accurate, that one "is meant" to do so. (As we will see, this contrasts sharply with Capricorn's notion of leadership, for Capricorn becomes a leader through hard work and competence—or, negatively, by acquiring an ability to manipulate forces within a hierarchy.) We might remember, here, that we consider the lion as the "king of beasts" not because of any physical attributes. Elephants have more strength, cheetahs more

---

[1]Mumford, 167-8.

speed, and tigers, larger and as mobile, may well prove better fighters, while leopards move with greater stealth and jaguars with more grace. Yet we call the lion *king* because of what seems its attitude and bearing: we seem to see in the lion a notion that it "is meant" to rule and intends to do so simply by exerting its presence. We might say that this rulership results from natural dramatic display, from a natural sense of being, not from any desire to serve the people. Though one would hope that Leo (regality) would develop into service (Virgo), too often Leo's self-insistence leads to inequality (Virgo again) instead.

We also see this connection to blood-lineage in Leo's connection to children. Astrologers have often noted this connection, for though Cancer has more to do with the process of gestating, giving birth, and feeding, Leo has more to do with seeing children as one's own creation or reflection. Thus we have, for example, a "pride of lions," a family group of lions, a group including children. Thus, pride in one's children, in one's creations, for they carry what Leo sees as the essence of his own importance. (Thus astrologers' long-standing connection of the Leo-ruled fifth house with the person's first child.)

Many consider Leo a "creative" sign, even though it doesn't have any better reputation for creative work than any other sign. However, Leo creates its own world, or thinks that he does, through natural radiation. The Sun illuminates, and thus creates, unstintingly, giving birth to the world each morning. The Sun also dries up moisture, and, interestingly, as we come to the end of the Mayan aeon in which Leo plays such an important role, we confront three Leo-related problems (not *only* these three, of course): a proliferating population (more and more children, connected to the Leo-ruled fifth house), a need for clean water (connected to evaporation, and therefore to the sun), and overheating (obviously connected with the sun). We might attribute these problems to the incoming Age of Aquarius-Leo, but they also seem connected to the strong Leo-statement in the Long Count horoscope, for in that horoscope we find Leo tenanted by the Sun (in its dignity), Mercury and Venus (focal planets of the natal yod; see below), and Saturn (symbolizing structure and limits).

We have seen that Leo can easily generate ego-driven blindness that one mistakes for awareness. Though many astrologers have with good reason connected Leo with what Carl Jung (with his natal Sun in Leo) called the *self*, Jung himself often sounded a warning about the way people often mistake the ego for the self. The ego, he says, generally "lacks any critical approach to the unconscious" and thus may find itself overwhelmed or taken over by unconscious contents instead of assimilating them. When we take ego inflation for individuation, Jung tells us, we at the very least isolate ourselves from the world and the feedback it gives, courting real psychic danger in the process.[1] In these discussions, Jung seems to touch on a central problem for Leo: how

---

[1] Jung discusses these matters in various writings. See, for example, the chapter entitled "The Self" in *Aion* (Princeton: Princeton University Press, 1959), from *The Collected Works of C.G. Jung*, Volume 9, Part II.

to fully pour forth the creative energies of this sign without blinding oneself with self-involvement. How will one achieve or take part in individuation without developing an overly egocentric point of view? The egocentric point of view leads to barrenness, both individually and collectively. In the Long Count horoscope, the self-centeredness has to do not only with the individual, but with the state and its rulers as well, for late in the 4th millennium BC, we see the first growth of what we now know as the state. This hardly seems surprising, particularly if we include the symbolism of Aquarius, Leo's polar opposite, for Leo has to do with regality and Aquarius with group-orientation.

All of this seems particularly germane to humanity as we approach the Age of Aquarius, for Aquarius opposes Leo and with it comprises one of the six bi-polar signs of the zodiac. (As discussed earlier, we see this bi-polarity in the development of the astrological ages: the symbolism of the ruling sign seems to define the age, but it does so in tandem with the slightly-less-visible symbolism of its polar opposite.) We might therefore speak more accurately if we spoke of the Age of Aquarius-Leo. We should expect problems to arise that reflect the Leo-Aquarius polarity: problems related to regality on the part of dominant nation states (groups: Aquarius), those that have adopted the practices developed in Mesopotamia and Egypt five millennia ago and have used them to dominate any society that did not develop those practices. For though Aquarius has much to do with the needs of the group, Leo has much to do with the ego or king making demands; and when we turn to the community of nations, we can see quite clearly that the egocentricity (so to speak) of nation-states and their leaders continually blocks the kinds of developments needed in the present era.

But though we see the result of these problems now as we reach the cusp of the Age of Aquarius-Leo, we see the seeds back before 3000 BC. For with kingship came earlier versions of most of the problems that beset us today and that seem so unsolvable and intransigent. Perhaps they seem so because they have such deep roots, because we cannot envisage civilization without the patterns that took definite form back in Mesopotamia and Egypt, and because we have never seen a civilization without these patterns. Mumford tells us that the "whole development" of new creative energy and new institutional patterns had kingship at the center; and, he notes, we see the same pattern continuing today, for though recently some historians have "swung to the opposite extreme and belittled the part that kings and institutions derived from kingship have actually played," the "massing of centralized economic and political power in every modern state, totalitarian or quasi-totalitarian, has cast a fresh light on the earliest similar assemblages."[1]

The hunting connected to the Paleolithic hunting chief (Leo) has remained with us, not only in the private hunting domains of so many kings, but also in the practice of warfare, where we see the "unscrupulous use of the weapons of the hunt to control the political and economic activities

---

[1] Mumford, 169.

of whole communities."[1] The increased capacity for food production combined with the capacity to control populations to give the king heretofore unequalled power.[2] Not only did the king require a surplus of grain—stored in the royal granary that stood side by side with the temple in the center of the city—he required a people prone to a methodical life, for which Neolithic farming prepared them admirably.

And, of course, kingship received sanction from the local deities. As we have seen, the astronomer priests brought the sanction of the heavenly bodies, seen as celestial deities, which through their orderly movement made the predictions of the astronomer-priests possible. Many of these predictions played a crucial role in the large-scale agriculture that sustained the community and, by leading to a surplus, made possible the centralized and hierarchical social order that emerged. So the hunting chief metamorphosed into the king partly because he had weapons, partly because he had a population prone to docility, and partly because of what seemed a divine sanction that, in turn, induced further docility:

> .. divine kingship ... was the product of a coalition between the tribute-exacting hunting chieftain and the keepers of an important religious shrine. Without that combination, without that sanction, without that luminous elevation, the claims that the new rulers made to unconditional obedience to the king's superior will, could not have been established: it took extra, supernatural authority, derived from a god or a group of gods, to make kingship prevail through a large society. Arms and armed men, specialists in homicide, were essential; but force alone was not enough.[3]

The archeological record demonstrates the connection between the surplus and the divine sanction:

> Even before the written record becomes available, the ruins from the earliest pre-dynastic al'Ubaid period of Ur indicate that the transformation had already been effected: here, as elsewhere, Leonard Woolley found a temple, within a sacred enclosure, where the royal granary, at once a food storehouse and a bank, would likewise be placed. The authority, priestly or royal, that collected, stored, and allocated the grain, held the means of controlling a large, dependent population—provided the granary was constantly guarded by walls and warriors.[4]

---

[1] Mumford, 169.
[2] This control took many forms, not limited to military aggression. The king's army guarded the granary and thus controlled life-giving power. See below.
[3] Mumford, 170.
[4] Mumford, 170.

The king served as high priest, effecting a union between sacred and temporal realms, a union that released

> . . . an immense explosion of latent energy, as in a nuclear reaction. At the same time it created a new institutional form, for which there is no evidence in the simple Neolithic village or the Paleolithic cave: an enclave of power, dominated by an elite who were supported in grandiose style by tribute and taxes forcibly drawn from the whole community.[1]

In sum, then, the efficacy of kingship, all through history

> [r]ests precisely on this alliance between the hunter's predatory prowess and gift of command, on one hand, and priestly access to astronomical lore and divine guidance.[2]

The king gave commands and ruled a kingdom with hitherto unthinkable "functional efficiency"; the priests observed the rhythms of natural phenomena, particularly heavenly bodies, and interpreted various omens. From all of this grew the impersonal order that we call "civilization," and the shift took place right around the time that the Mayans placed the birth-date of the Long Count. We should not, of course, expect a precise, to-the-day timing for a process that took many centuries. However, it seems that the new form truly crystallized at the end of the 4th millennium BC. Instead of asking that history give us a precise date for this development, we might wonder how the Mayans chose a date with a horoscope that so precisely describes it.

Leo to Capricorn

The science that developed during this period, crucial to the new order, reflects both Leo and Capricorn: Leo because of its connection with the sun and thus with the king; Capricorn because of the emphasis on measurable order and because the king maintained his supremacy not only by purportedly supernatural forces, but also because of the bureaucracy that surrounded him. Mumford tells us that the new order could not have developed without "a new kind of science, different from the close observations and intimate association that fostered domestication." This new kind of science offered "an abstract, impersonal order: counting, measurement, exact notation—attributes without whose early development no such consummate monuments as the pyramids could have been built." The priestly cast oversaw the counting of days, the noting of lunar months, and the establishment of the solar year, developments that "were effectively symbolized . . . by the establishment of the first Egyptian solar calendar":

---

[1] Mumford, 170.
[2] Mumford, 171.

> [w]ithout this widely shared reverence for undeviating cosmic order, the great technical achievements of early civilization would have lacked the mathematical precision and physical mastery they actually showed.[1]

The power-mandated form of social organization reached completion because by

> ... identifying the person of the king with the impersonal, above all implacable, order of the heavens, royal power received an immense supercharge of energy: the king's political authority, based on weapons and military exertion, was vastly augmented by the inordinate supernatural powers he wielded.[2]

We might add, as a final note before moving to the Capricorn complex of symbols, that this period also saw the seeds of what we now call *astrology*:

> Eventually, the Babylonians introduced the same concept of predetermined order into the seemingly irregular events of daily life: they plotted the course and positions of the planets and associated this with the hour of a person's birth in order to predict the entire course of his life. The biographic data needed for such plotting was based on systematic observation. Thus scientific determinism not less than mechanical regimentation had their inception in the institution of divine kingship. Long before the Ionian scientists of the 6th century BC, the fundamental mathematical and scientific foundations had been laid in astronomy.[3]

Capricorn, Regimentation, and Hierarchy: the Organization of the World

Leo has to do with the development of a centralized authority and central point of reference, Capricorn with regimentation, with the building of social structures and bureaucracies. Leo emphasizes authority maintained through blood-lineage; Capricorn maintains authority through hierarchical modes of activity, through various social skills instead of blood. To maintain its central role, Leo refers to the larger, "sacred" order of the heavens and the divine fire, Capricorn to the apparently non-sacred orders of earth and the ability to organize effectively.

As with Leo, we will speak of the Capricorn "complex of symbols": just as the Leo complex of symbols includes both a sign (Leo) and a ruling planet (the Sun), so with Capricorn, ruled by Saturn.[4] When we consider this complex of symbols, we will see the interweaving of the two signs, for in the Long Count horoscope we find Saturn, ruler of Capricorn, in Leo, conjoining

---

[1] Mumford, 173.
[2] Mumford, 173.
[3] Mumford, 174.
[4] If we had a birth-time, we would also speak of houses: the fifth in connection with Leo; the tenth in connection with Capricorn.

the Long Count Leo Sun, a Sun dignified in its own sign (Leo). Saturn forms a very close (17' orb of aspect[1]) quincunx with Uranus in Capricorn, and a slightly looser quincunx with Pluto, in the same sign and conjoined with Uranus.[2] Further, both Mercury and Venus in Leo quincunx (though not quite so closely for the midnight horoscope)[3] the Moon in Capricorn. These various factors draw the two signs together, telling us of the importance of the relationship between them in the Long Count horoscope and the era it measures. Of the ten planets in the horoscope, seven fall in either Leo or Capricorn; all but one of the Leo planets (the Sun) makes an aspect to a planet in Capricorn, and vice-versa. Later on August 11, the Moon in Capricorn quincunxed the Sun in Leo. So, not surprisingly, the events taking place at the beginning of the Long Count give abundant evidence of the two signs in relationship.

Around the central figure of the King and the centralized enclosure of temple and granary developed an extensive bureaucratic structure and an emphasis on social order based in rules, walls, and limits. On the most obvious level, we find around the granary guards who derived their weapons from age-old hunting practices and who took their position from the more newly formed bureaucracy. Here we see, first and foremost, limits, associated with Capricorn and, even more particularly, Saturn: the guards limited the people's access to food. The very presence of guards reminds us that we have, for the first time, a hierarchy of clearly delineated social classes. People found their place in society not because of kinship ties or because of the need for voluntary cooperation, but because of functions divorced from the rest of life. They found themselves performing those functions because they found themselves in a hierarchy, working for goals not of their own devising, goals that those at the top of the hierarchy presented as worthwhile. All of this again suggests Capricorn, a sign associated with an often-problematic relationship between ends and means—and, of course, those connected with hierarchy.

We might associate Leo, through its connection to kingship, with hierarchy, for clearly the king reigned over all and occupied the central and highest position. Most of the kings whose names have come down to us have maintained their own bureaucracies, but this doesn't mean that we should see kingship and bureaucracy as inseparable. Leo symbolizes strength and potency that, at least in theory, does not need such supports as bureaucracy; Capricorn symbolizes the development of bureaucracies and hierarchies that often end up divorced from their original guiding purpose. Though Leo wants to rule by natural right, Capricorn wants to maintain its authoritative position through an organized system of defined social relations of the kind that pervaded the civilizations of Mesopotamia and Egypt so long ago. In the former, "an orderly world" was "unthinkable without a superior authority to impose his will"; in the latter, a document entitled

---

[1] In other words, the aspect is within 17' of arc of a precise quincunx. Astrologers would consider this an extremely narrow orb and would therefore see the aspect as a strong one.
[2] In astrological terms, Saturn disposits both of these planets, and the Moon, also in Capricorn.
[3] The orb would narrow if we moved the horoscope back to the previous evening.

Satire on the Trades tells us that "[t]here is no profession free of a boss."[1] Though Leo symbolizes a centralized royal figure, Capricorn symbolizes the bureaucratic structures through which that figure maintained "an orderly world" through the workings of authority.

Mumford tells us that we find rudimentary forms of kingship (Leo) even in communities in which we don't find social stratification. However, at a certain point, public lands, held in common by the community, metamorphosed into private property owned by the king, and "gross inequalities, as between slaves, freemen, nobles, which attended the growth of private property, all too soon crept in."[2] At first this change can be called "state-administered communism," and Mumford speculates that because it grew out of very ancient customs (e.g. of communal ownership, suggesting practices probably developed during the Age of Cancer[3]), people perhaps didn't object right away. And, most likely, by the time the inequality had "crept in," the change seemed natural—or, perhaps, it seemed no change at all, for it didn't happen all at once.

From the king who ruled by divine right came the separation of king from the people, a separation enforced not only by physical walls but also by customs, most particularly the custom of self-abasement enforced on the people. This, too, broke from ancient customs of egalitarianism; it "had the effect of turning human beings into 'things,' who could be galvanized into a regimented kind of cooperation by royal command, to perform special tasks he assigned them, however stultifying to their family life and incompatible with normal village routines."[4] As we will see, the Long Count's Capricorn Moon suggests a tendency to place work and "responsibility" ahead of the home or emotional satisfaction. The Capricorn drive toward hierarchical order will naturally oppose the Moon's (and Cancer's) drive toward home-enclaves emphasizing emotional ties. If sacred regality reflects Leo, the task-oriented regimentation that stultified family life and village routine surely reflects Capricorn, for Capricorn stands opposed to Cancer in the zodiac and demands of people kinds of activities and mental attitudes that too-often restrict, and eventually starve, the Cancer-based community.[5]

The Neolithic village of the Age of Cancer gave way to king-ruled communities reflecting Leo, the next sign in the zodiac. As the Neolithic villages of the Age of Cancer developed into the cit-

---

[1] Mumford, 179.
[2] Mumford, 181.
[3] Capricorn's polar opposite, ruled by the Moon, which in the Long Count horoscope we find in Capricorn, its detriment: people increasingly found security (Moon) through or within hierarchy (Capricorn). Later in the Long Count, even those who chose to live apart from "civilization" found it impossible to do so, for the representatives of that civilization sought them out and either killed or enslaved them.
[4] Mumford, 183.
[5] American history gives us a gruesome and literal example of this starvation, as the United States Army killed many thousands of buffalo in order to starve Native Americans who depended on them for food and shelter.

ies of the Age of Taurus, we see the cohering of the new social order that we now call "civilization." Whereas the abundance associated with Taurus meshes nicely with Cancer's emphasis on security, it meshes less well with things Leonine (Taurus sextiles Cancer but squares Leo). Thus the immense tension visible in the new structures that arose in the Leonine kingdoms associated with the Long Count. When we see the interaction of two signs that square each other—here, the fixed signs Taurus and Leo—we often find the development of a new structure. For an individual, this can point to creative, structure-building activities that serve as a venue to bring the disparate energies together. In the horoscope for an aeon, we can expect the development of new and dominant social forms.

This shift in social form occurred first in the period around 3114 BC, then later in one place after another throughout the world. Today, even those who would prefer to live in what we would call a Neolithic village find themselves having to deal with the organized hierarchies of the nation states and the international ruling bodies (e.g. IMF, the Foreign Relations Committee, etc.) that have arisen as their offspring. Throughout the Long Count, then, we see the Capricorn emphasis. Mumford cites as new developments in the 4th millennium BC.

> ... the centralization of political power, the separation of classes, the lifetime division of labor, the mechanization of production, the magnification of military power, the economic exploitation of the weak, and the universal introduction of slavery and forced labor for both industrial and military purposes.[1]

Mumford refers, here, to the development of what he calls "the megamachine," the presence of which we can see in the building of the pyramids and other monumental physical structures that we find not only in Egypt, but in Mesopotamia, in Central America (a bit later), and in other places as well. Mumford calls this the "archetypal machine," and it had for movable parts not iron, steel, or any other inorganic substance, but human beings regimented to such a degree that, together, they performed like a machine. Without this invention, impossible without the king and his bureaucracy, the "huge engineering tasks" of five thousand years ago would not have taken place. To make this happen, the rulers had to reduce people to bare functions (Capricorn) related to subordination.

This subordination suggests both Capricorn and Virgo: Capricorn because of its connection to hierarchy; Virgo because of its connection with service and inequality. As the sixth sign of the zodiac, beginning 150 degrees from 1 Aries, Virgo has a close connection to the quincunx aspect, as does Scorpio, which begins 150 degrees from 1 Aries moving in the opposite direction. Thus in the quincunxes between Leo planets and Capricorn planets—quincunxes from Mercury-Venus to the Moon, Saturn to Uranus and Pluto, as well as from Mercury-Venus to Jupi-

---

[1] Mumford, 186.

ter—we see subordination (Virgo) and power (Scorpio) manifesting through and because of hierarchy (Capricorn) under the auspices of royal power (Leo).[1]

Both Leo and Capricorn have to do with authority; the tension arises because they have to do with very different types or approaches to authority: Leo has to do with authority emanating from the conviction that one derives one's powers from the gods; Capricorn has to do with authority arising in systematic form through clearly delineated hierarchies. At the Long Count's beginning, we find the two signs enmeshed in the quincunxes that symbolize the resulting tension that continues to this day in ritualized structural arrangements promoting inequality and power, the inequality coming from the lower quincunx (as between the Moon and Mercury-Venus and between Mercury-Venus and Jupiter) and the power from the upper (as between Saturn and Uranus). Taken together, the signs and aspects tell us much about Mumford's megamachine, a mode of social ordering based in rigid order and hierarchy (Capricorn) under the direction of a king purportedly quasi-divine (Leo), meshed together in forms emphasizing inequality or subordination (lower quincunx) and power (upper quincunx), particularly of one group over another. We see in all this the kind of social ordering that has prevailed from the 4th millennium BC to the present.

This megamachine had as its functional parts the thousands of people forced to labor in the construction of the monolithic structures that suddenly arose in that period, particularly the pyramids, structures strongly suggesting the hierarchies associated with Capricorn, built with slave labor associated with Virgo, serving as tombs associated with Scorpio (of which more below), all done at the behest of the Leonine king. The military protected the central granary and forced laborers to become functional units in a larger, mechanical ordering that served to protect the king's inner sanctum and enabled him to conquer other peoples, thus furthering the inequality in power-relations. However, when not at work on such projects, the megamachine dissolved away, for it consisted of human parts and appeared clearly only when the rulers assembled those human parts to perform a function. It stood as the model for all later machines and has resurrected itself in the modern age.

We will return to this resurrection when we discuss transits and progressions (chapter four); for now, we should consider Mumford's injunction that to understand the point of the machine's origin and its line of descent "is to have a fresh insight into . . . the origins of our present over-mechanized culture," the results of which have so much to do with the Long Count's conclusion, and "the fate and destiny of modern man," which, I suggest, we find reflected so dramatically in the Long Count's horoscope. When we discuss that fate and destiny, we will find "that the original myth of the machine projected the extravagant hopes and wishes that have

---

[1] This doesn't mean that an individual with a quincunx aspect will always act in a subordinate role or manifest negative power. The person might serve an apprenticeship as training for a role in which he takes on positive power.

come to abundant fulfillment in our own age" and that it "imposed restrictions, abstentions, and compulsions and servilities that, both directly and as a result of the counter-reactions they produced, today threaten even more mischievous consequences than they did in the Pyramid Age."[1] We will return to these developments in chapter four.

We can see the marks of Saturn and Capricorn not only in the regimentation necessary for the megamachine, but also in the appearance in the environment of "strict boundaries and geometric shapes" that reflect "a cosmic order and an inflexible human will."[2] We see Saturn also in the work of "governors, generals, bureaucrats, taskmasters" through whom—or, through the systematic working of whom (or *of which*, if we consider these terms indicators of function and not of personalities)—the royal will worked itself out through society.

We can discern the quincunxes in the new emphasis on effectiveness, for the quincunx suggests both effective work and rebirth (popularly called "transformation"), and we see both of these in high definition during the period in question. The quincunxes also suggest inequality (lower) and the values or power of others (upper): thus, the introduction of slaves who worked at the behest of those in power. The tension of the quincunx generally doesn't appear directly; it appears, rather, in *activity*, generally of a somewhat compulsive nature, that gets ritualized into various forms of habit. So, here, we see the ongoing tension between Leo and Capricorn. Whatever its drawbacks in terms of human suffering, the megamachine certainly proved effective, as slave-labor effected a complete transformation not only of the way people lived, but of the external environment as well. At the end of the Long Count, we can see quite clearly the long-term effects of these developments.

In the intervening centuries, the megamachine spread side-by-side with kingship, so that the two sometimes seem inseparable, as if taking part in the same ritual (quincunx). Mumford tells us that one form of the megamachine—the army—transmitted the "standard model of the megamachine" from culture to culture. We see this in the square from Mercury and Venus in Leo over to Mars in Scorpio, a matter discussed below.

To close this section, we can look at Mumford's observations about the megamachine's need to give commands at a distance. Writing served admirably well to fulfill this need:

> If one single invention was necessary to make this larger mechanism operative for constructive tasks as well as for coercion, it was probably the invention of writing. This method of transplanting speech into graphic record not merely made it possible to transmit impulses and messages throughout the system, but to fix accountability when written orders were not carried out. Accountability and the written

---

[1] Mumford, 189.
[2] Mumford, 190.

word both went along historically with the control of large numbers; and it is no accident that the earliest uses of writing were not to convey ideas, religious or otherwise, but to keep temple records of grain, cattle, pottery, fabricated goods, stored and distributed.[1]

We see here an appropriate description of the Mercury-Venus-Moon quincunx: effectiveness in transmitting (Mercury) the commands of the king (Leo), rooted in communications based on value or money (Mercury-Venus), in a tense linkage with the rigidity of social forms (Moon in Capricorn). Thus we can better understand the document from Egypt's New Kingdom: "The scribe, he directeth every work that is in this land."[2] Messengers reported to central headquarters, the *centrality* reminding us again of Leo, the sign in which we find Mercury.

Mars and Neptune in Scorpio

The Leo-Capricorn material relates directly to what Mumford calls the work army, and indirectly to the military army (though the one readily transformed into the other) for which the Mars-Neptune conjunction stands as an apt symbol, suggesting as it does a union of aggression (Mars), delusion (Neptune) and power (Scorpio). The square from Mars-Neptune in Scorpio to Mercury-Venus in Leo suggests the tense and energetic union, through specific social structures, of the aggressive drive with the ideational one: the power seeking military (Mars in Scorpio) driven by delusion (Neptune), on the one hand; the royal scribe (Mercury in Leo) who deals with money (Venus) on the other. The delusions of power and strength (Neptune and Mars in Scorpio) arose in connection with ideas (Mercury) about the god-king (Leo). As the closest hard aspect in the horoscope, the Mercury-Mars square has a dominant effect, marking the "vocation"[3] of the Long Count, apparently one in which thought unites with aggression: thinking in terms dictated by the central power led to military aggression.

Scorpio probably qualifies as the most maligned sign in the zodiac, and we can certainly challenge some of the negative interpretations that we hear about it, particularly when applied to individuals. Nevertheless, we have good reason to expect problems when we see afflicted planets in Scorpio in the horoscope for a collectivity—or, here, for an aeon—for, as noted above, in such horoscopes, we usually find the most problematic manifestation of any astrological configuration. So though in the horoscope for an individual a Mars-Neptune conjunction in Scorpio might suggest highly idealistic and transformative actions, for the Long Count we should expect obsessive aggression based on delusions and driven by unconscious factors.

---

[1] Mumford, 192.
[2] Qtd. in Mumford, 192.
[3] I think this principle comes from Marc Edmund Jones, but I cannot remember the source. The principle, briefly stated: the closest challenging aspect in a horoscope has much to do with vocation.

Scorpio rules death and the underworld. Its traditional ruler, Mars, the god of war and thus connected to the military class, has a bad reputation in traditional astrology, one connected with the god Ares, the war-like god of Greek myth. The new ruler, Pluto, known as Hades (Aides) to the Greeks, rules the underworld and has obvious connections to plutonium. In psychological terms, Pluto has to do with unconscious complexes that drive behavior. Scorpio, symbolizing a time of year in which vegetation dies and gives nutrients back to the soil, has to do with death and rebirth processes that bring about change—what we call transformation, which for people often involves dealing with psychological complexes in some way. Astrologers have always considered Scorpio an immensely fruitful sign, yet a dangerous one as well, for the decrees of the underworld lord, arising from a realm not amenable to conscious control, do not alter.

The Mars-Neptune conjunction in Scorpio suggests obsessive aggression apparently driven by illusions, delusions, and ideals, yet really driven by the underworld gods. By itself, the aspect can indicate either compassionate action that transforms situations in need of transformation, or action based in confusion, deception, self-deception, or obfuscation. In Scorpio, and in a chart for a collectivity, we can expect action driven by the underworld gods toward what emerged along with civilization:

> With the ideas of submission and absolute obedience which were essential to the composition of a human machine, came, however, the possibilities of disobedience, treachery, and rebellion. To ensure that the heavenly sanctions of kingship were sufficiently respected, kingship in the end must be ready to fall back on force: not merely naked force, but force in ferocious, sadistic forms, repeatedly magnified into nightmarish extravaganzas of cruelty, as dehumanized as those we have witnessed in the last generation in the ingenious horrors perpetrated by 'civilized' governments in Warsaw, Auschwitz, Tokyo, and Vietnam.[1]

This describes one of the possibilities of a square from Mars-Neptune in Scorpio to planets in Leo, uniting the underworld demons associated with Scorpio, the delusions of Neptune, the aggression of Mars, and the demands of the Leonine king, particularly through his relationship with order (Capricorn planets). In collective matters, Mars symbolizes the military and Neptune symbolizes the dangers of delusion.

So we have a tense, energy-producing relationship (square) between the ideas and values associated with the king's divine right (Mercury and Venus in Leo), operating through an expansive bureaucracy (Jupiter sextile Moon in Capricorn, quincunx Mercury-Venus, forming a yod: see below), and the military. That we have close aspects and larger configurations among all these planets—Mercury and Venus square Mars and Neptune; Mercury-Venus quincunx both Jupiter

---

[1] Mumford, 184.

and Moon; Mars-Neptune trine Jupiter and sextile Moon—strongly suggests that all of these forces will arise together and have a pervasive influence on the horoscope. In other words, these characteristics will characterize the Long Count period, a statement that finds corroboration in Mumford, who tells us that "[f]rom the beginning, the balance of mechanized power seems to have fallen on the side of destruction" and that insofar as the megamachine was passed on intact to later civilizations, "it was in the negative form of the military machine—drilled, standardized, divided into specialized parts—that its continuity was assured."[1] And within the military machine we find the bureaucratic one, for the military machine required the passing forth of orders, the emphasis on function instead of choice, and the stripping of human qualities from action.

Mumford speaks of three machines: the "communication machine," the military machine, and the labor machine (that built the pyramids). He notes that bureaucratic regimentation was "part of the larger regimentation of life, introduced by this power-centered culture."[2] We can see these three machines reflected in the aspects and positions discussed so far: in Mercury (focal to the yod, square Mars-Neptune, quincunx the Capricorn Moon) we see the communication machine; in Mars (square Mercury, sextile the Moon, trine Jupiter) we see the military machine; in the Capricorn planets (Moon, Uranus, Pluto), and in the emphasized Saturn, we see the bureaucratic machine.

We see Scorpio in what Mumford calls the "destructive animus of the military machine," for, he tells us, the "mere increase of power"

> ... had the effect on the ruling classes of releasing the obstreperous fantasies of the unconscious and giving play to sadistic impulses that had hitherto had no collective outlet."[3]

But because the machine "was dependent for operation upon the weak, fallible, stupid, or stubborn human members," and therefore "liable to disintegrate," the leaders needed some way to keep it under control. They found the means of control in "a profound magico-religious faith in the system itself, as expressed in the cult of the gods."[4] Thus the presence of Neptune, apt symbol for magic, particularly in Scorpio: illusions, with "magical" overtones, induced people to give their lives to the military machine. It seems that, at least as regards the military, much has remained the same up to the present day.

Mumford points to the anxieties that must have arisen among people as civilization developed more complexity, as one group came in contact with others. "Under circumstances beyond local

---

[1] Mumford, 228.
[2] Mumford, 201.
[3] Mumford, 229.
[4] Mumford, 228.

control," he suggests, "neurotic anxiety probably grew." Thus arose the desire for magical sanction and control; thus we see evidence of the sacrifices of kings, or of citizens—or, perhaps more conveniently, of "captives from *other* communities."[1] In other words, human sacrifice as a means to decrease anxiety.

But it apparently didn't work very well. We can see why if we look at the pattern associated with war: first, you have the presence of a military machine, one capable of bringing destruction on a heretofore unimagined scale; second, behind this, you have the prostration of the individual before the "*mysterium tremendum*, some manifestation of god-head in its awful power and luminous glory" as a means to "call forth such excessive collective effort"; third, you have a military organization with the specific function of protecting the king, the local god, and the granary; and thus "the extension of military and political power became an end in itself, as the ultimate testimony to the power of the divinities that ruled the community, and to the supreme status of the king."[2]

The importance of Mars-Neptune to the Long Count and the megamachine appears quite clearly when we consider "the spread of war as a permanent fixture of 'civilization'" that "only widened the collective anxiety that the ritual of human sacrifice had sought to appease." Neptune stands, here, as a potent symbol for anxiety, collective sacrifice, and delusion; Mars represents aggression arising from that anxiety and the energy driving the sacrifice, for "as communal anxiety spread, it could no longer be overcome by symbolic disembowelment at the alter: that token payment had to be replaced by a collective surrender of life on a far wider scale."[3] This fear probably began as "man-hunting raids" and then escalated into ever-larger confrontations with "more effective weapons," all in a kind of ceremony in which "what was at first an incidental prelude to a token sacrifice itself became the 'supreme sacrifice,' performed *en masse*."

Mars, in its dignity in Scorpio and thus quite strong, symbolizes the motive power that sustained the megamachine for centuries, for the military remained the megamachine's most visible manifestation. Neptune symbolizes the paranoia and fear driving the military and the appeal to magic as a way to deal with the fear. Scorpio appears as the inner complexes now given social—that is, collective—expression. The Mercury-Mars square, the closest hard aspect in the horoscope and thus a vocational indicator, symbolizes what societies do: they generally think in terms of conquest and aggression. This obsession finds support in pervasive bureaucratic structures (Mars-Neptune sextile to Moon in Capricorn) that have a blinding effect because they *seem* so effective and valueless.

The quincunx from Saturn in Leo to Uranus in Capricorn has perhaps more strength than any of the others, partly because of its narrow orb or aspect. It strongly suggests the coöption of human

---

[1] Mumford, 219.
[2] Mumford, 220.
[3] Mumford, 220.

inventive brilliance (Uranus) by the demands of the status quo. Uranus in Capricorn by itself might suggest this; the quincunx to Saturn, ruler of Capricorn, restates the theme. Pluto, in conjunction with Uranus, suggests the power of the resulting order. Thus the revolutionary impulse finds itself directed back toward the very power-system it had intended to escape; thus inventiveness augments the power of the status quo.

The Finger of God

The Mars-Neptune conjunction connects with the important yod from Mercury-Venus up to the Moon-Jupiter sextile. This yod includes the two quincunxes from Mercury-Venus in Leo, the first going to the Moon, the second to Jupiter. The Moon-Jupiter sextile completes the configuration: a yod with Mercury and Venus focal. (It also has 7-8 degrees of Aquarius as the reaction point, the point directly across from the focal planets, a place of importance to the time-analysis.)

Jupiter symbolizes expansion; Mercury symbolizes thinking and the function of scribes to assist action-at-a-distance. Venus symbolizes value. Mercury-Venus in Leo suggests thinking about and valuing what Leo represents: strength, regality, the individual personality as embodied in someone purportedly blessed by the gods; the central precincts from which the strong ruler rules. The quincunxes to Jupiter, along with the trine from Mars to Jupiter discussed below, point to aggression (Mars-Neptune) driving a ritualistic (quincunx) expansion (Jupiter) of the entire system described above. Thus the megamachine did not remain in one place, but expanded, conquering one group after another.[1]

Taken together with the quincunx from Mercury-Venus to the Capricorn Moon, the quincunx to Jupiter forms a yod, sometimes called the Finger of God.[2] Consisting of back-to-back quincunxes plus a sextile, yods suggest the above-mentioned ritualization combined with intellectual curiosity and social application. However, whereas quincunxes easily move toward illness, yods often have more focus, while at the same time suggesting energies remaining in a state of potency for quite some time, perhaps hidden in a developing illness (though here a planetary one), before finding an outlet in a potent crisis or sense of reorientation, this reorientation often occurring when important transits or progressions activate the reaction point.[3] Yods

---

[1] As we will see in chapter four, transits and progressions at the end of the Long Count affect these positions in a dramatic and troubling way.
[2] Some will feel doubtful, here, that the horoscope has an effective yod. They will note that though the Moon remained in orb at midnight, after that it quickly moved on. True enough. However, about sixteen hours after midnight, the Moon made a precise quincunx to the Leo Sun, thus reiterating, though in a slightly different way, the Leo-Capricorn tension. That horoscope would have closely parallel quincunxes but not a yod. However, those quincunxes would give an even stronger suggestion of illness than does the yod.
[3] The reaction point lies directly across from the focal planets. Even those readers hesitant to accept that the horoscope has a functioning yod will see this point as important, as it opposes part of the Mercury-Ve-

channel energy in a specific direction that becomes apparent due to surrounding circumstance and inner compulsion. Mercury and Venus in Leo symbolize the direction: ideas and values colored by royalty: the tendency to think and value in terms of regality, either personal or otherwise. What needs reorienting here? The tendency, during the era measured by the Long Count, to think and value in terms of the centralized ruler (Leo) and the attendant bureaucracy (Capricorn), the tendency to expand (Jupiter) bureaucratic structures and to think (Mercury) in terms of the centralized power-system (Leo and Capricorn). In short, the configurations symbolize an aggregation of tendencies we tend to see as part-and-parcel of "civilization."

The reorientation associated with a yod often has the feel of coming to a fork in the road and having to make a decision about which direction to go. Though any transit or progression to the yod will bring this energy into play, the powerful progressions of 2012 AD to the reaction-point of the yod (chapter 4)[1] suggest possibly catastrophic changes—as long as we understand *catastrophe* in its original meaning as "turning over," which may involve new leaves as well as old social forms. Until the catastrophic process becomes visible, the quincunxes will tend to operate in hard-to-isolate ways making up a pervasive pattern of behavior that comes to a crisis when the yod activates (as it does in the last 500 years of the Long Count, a matter discussed in the next chapter). The tendency of quincunxes to develop in hard-to-discern ways explains why the megamachine didn't continue except through various militaries (for the most part) for many centuries—until it resurfaced in the modern era.[2] But though the megamachine in its pure form disappeared, the machine-making tendencies did not, so that the megamachine existed, we might say, hidden in the pervasive patterning. Thus Mumford writes of the "resurrection" of the megamachine from the 16th century onward, a resurrection he sees as the main evil associated with "mechanical invention and capitalistic organization."[3] We might add that Mumford's phrase—*mechanical invention and capitalistic organization*—seems an apt description of Uranus' position in Capricorn.

The strongly-placed Leo planets tell us that regality would remain during the entire period of the Long Count, always allied with hierarchical and bureaucratic forms of organization and with expansion. This union enabled tremendous expansion and multiple benefits, for the Moon-Jupi-

---

nus-Jupiter quincunx. Transits and progressions to it would still have importance, though the interpretation would turn more toward unbalanced illness than to a kind of fated result.

[1] Or, even without the yod, opposed to Mercury and Venus, and square Mars, thus creating a t-square. More on this later. As we will see, even without the yod, transits or progressions to those degrees turn the natal square (Mercury-Venus to Mars-Neptune) into a t-square.

[2] The megamachine re-emerged in a clearly defined form when, around the Renaissance, SP (secondary progressed) Pluto moved into its opposition with the Mercury-Venus conjunction: the "reaction point" of the yod, and the area that, once tenanted, makes a t-square out of the natal square from Mars-Neptune to Mercury-Venus. By the end of the Long Count, SP Saturn had joined SP Pluto in that area. The activated quincunxes suggest the activation of an illness long in incubation; the t-square suggests the danger of catastrophic obsessions related to the military. See the next chapter.

[3] Mumford, 293.

ter sextile suggests organized and benevolent social expansion mitigating security needs. However, the quincunxes suggest something else: through bureaucracies bent on expansion (Moon in Capricorn sextile Jupiter in its dignity, Pisces), regal dictates bring on collective health problems (i.e. environmental degradation: quincunxes) that reach the aforementioned crisis-point when progressed planets came to the "reaction point."

With Leo planets at the apex, the yod directs attention to the function of kingship,[1] particularly in its problematic manifestations, and to the resultant illness of the lunar function: the quincunx from Mercury and Venus to the Moon in its detriment in Capricorn, one side of the yod. These difficulties arose together with the continual expansion (Jupiter) of the regal imperative (Leo), also possibly a sign of illness. Leo, the most barren sign of the zodiac, suggests a developing barrenness of the ecosystem (the "sub-lunar realm") and of those social institutions that emphasize centralized authority supported by rigid social forms (Capricorn), even though this will occur inseparably with the expansion (Jupiter) of knowledge (Mercury) and of the social order generally. The cure or catharsis for the illness lies, not surprisingly, in the relationship between Leo and Aquarius, for at the end of the Long Count, SP Pluto and SP Saturn arrive at the above-mentioned "reaction point," in Aquarius, directly opposite Mercury and Venus (and square Mars)—at the one point in the horoscope that unites the yod (Mercury-Venus plus Jupiter and the Moon) with the square (Mercury-Venus to Mars-Neptune). This point falls in Aquarius and returns us to a matter discussed earlier in relation to our astrological ages: the relationship between Leo and Aquarius, important there because the incoming Age of Aquarius brings in Leo as a powerful sub-tone, important here because of aspects in the Long Count horoscope.

The Yod Plus the Leo-Scorpio Squares

In analyzing yods, astrologers often pay attention to the aforementioned "reaction point."[2] The Long Count's reaction point falls in either the eighth or ninth degree (7+ and 8+) of Aquarius, directly opposite Mercury and Venus, the two planets at the focal point. Squares, such as the one between Mars-Neptune and Mercury-Venus in the Long Count horoscope, become t-squares, considered tense and dynamic patterns, if we add a planet at a point opposite any of the planets in the square. In the Long Count horoscope, we find one such point directly opposite (again) Mercury and Venus. In the natal chart, no planet occupies those degrees; however, a transiting or progressed planet would simultaneously turn the square into a t-square and activate the yod: the former would bring a danger of destructive aggression based on delusion and confusion; the latter would bring into manifestation difficulties that had long remained hidden within the ongoing rituals of living. Either one alone would suggest a troubling conclusion to the Long Count; taken together, together, they seem worse than foreboding.

---

[1] Yod or no yod, the horoscope, with four important planets in Leo, has a strong emphasis on kingship.
[2] I've borrowed this term from Bil Tierney's *Dynamics of Aspect Analysis*. It refers, as noted, to the point directly opposite the focal planet(s).

To this we can add that important transiting or progressed planets opposite Mars and Neptune (i.e. planets in the eighth and twelfth degrees of Taurus) will also turn the square into a t-square, though without activating the yod. When this occurs, the empty leg of the t-square falls in (again) the eighth or ninth degree of Aquarius. The reader should keep these points in mind as we proceed, for we will see important transits opposite Mars-Neptune right around the middle of the Long Count, and even more important *progressions* at the even-more important points in Aquarius at the end of the Long Count. We could perhaps see these transits and progressions as encoded within the natal chart; we would also say that when they hit, pervasive changes will take place. Though I doubt that the so-called Mayan astronomer priests knew that secondary progressed Saturn and Pluto would come into this zone as the Long Count came to a close, *we* know it and can attempt to interpret it—and to prepare for it. We will return to this subject in the next chapter.[1]

Summary

The Long Count horoscope, with its powerful square involving Mars and Neptune, certainly suggests delusion-driven military aggression of an extreme sort, all in service to the king (Leo). The horoscope also suggests, through the yod to Mercury-Venus and the various Leo-Capricorn quincunxes,[2] a quasi-ritualistic union of kingship with bureaucracy, all resulting in excess (Jupiter). The powerful quincunx from Saturn to Uranus and Pluto, running parallel to the one from Mercury-Venus to the Moon, suggests the cooption of invention by the forces of the status quo—by, we might say, the king's bureaucracy (Saturn in Leo dispositing Uranus). This description takes into consideration all the planets in the horoscope.

The following quotation from Mumford sounds as if he had many of the above-mentioned astrological factors in mind (even though I feel almost certain that he didn't):

> The two poles of civilization, then, are mechanically organized work and mechanically organized destruction and extermination. Roughly the same forces and the same methods of operation were applicable to both areas. To some extent systematic daily work served to keep in check the licentious energies that were now available for turning mere dreams and wanton fantasies into actualities; but among the governing classes no such salutary check operated. Sated with leisure, war gave them 'something to do,' and by its incidental hardships, responsibilities, and mor-

---

[1] As we will see in that chapter, the term "end of the Long Count" doesn't refer only, or even primarily, to the specific end-date. Rather, it refers to the long period in which SP Pluto and SP Saturn move onto the reaction point and in which SP Uranus sextiles its own position.

[2] Again: the midnight horoscope has quincunxes from Saturn to Uranus (and loosely to Pluto) and from Mercury-Venus to the Moon. In the hours after midnight, the Moon departs from the quincunx to Mercury-Venus and begins to approach a quincunx with the Leo Sun. At any time on that day, Mercury and Venus quincunx Jupiter in Pisces.

tal risks, provided the equivalent of honorable labor. War became not merely the 'health of the state,' as Nietzsche called it: in addition, it was the cheapest form of mock-creativity, for in a few days it could produce visible results that undid the efforts of many lifetimes.[1]

We can see the astrological indicators quite clearly: Capricorn's love of regimentation; Mars in Scorpio's tendency toward wanton violence; Leo's alleged "creativity," love of regality, and tendency toward satiation with the pomps of kingship; Capricorn's emphasis on social structure; Scorpio's relationship with the underworld pantheon; the quincunx's connection to "mechanically organized work"; and an afflicted Mars' proclivity toward destruction.

We can add to this three facts: first, that Capricorn sextiles Scorpio, a relationship indicating mental advancement inducing movement and development; second, that Mars in Scorpio trines Jupiter in Pisces, suggesting expansive action, purportedly (and sometimes actually) based on principle and learning, though in this case too often an expansion driven by demands emanating from the divine king (challenging aspects to Leo planets from both Jupiter and Mars-Neptune); third, that Mars quintiles Saturn, suggesting a drive for organized power in which military imperatives combine with bureaucratic ones. Thus we see the development, visible right from the beginning, of order and more order: for "order of any kind, no matter how stringent, reduces the need for choice and therewith reduces anxiety." As a result, "[t]he rituals of sacrifice and the rituals of compulsion were . . . unified through the operation of the military machine."[2]

Small wonder, then, that we so often stare in wonder at the purported wonders of these ancient civilizations: the monuments that "abound in insensate boasts of power," the presence of kings portrayed as terrifying and all-powerful, the obsessive drive for power, augmented by the cult of kingship, a cult walled off from the population by the inner walls of the temple, given power by weapons, numbers, organization, and fear of the gods—a fear that the powerful have, for five thousand years, instilled in the powerless.

Summary of Long Count Planets, Signs, and Aspects

- Mercury in Leo: likely focal planet of a yod, certainly square Mars-Neptune and quincunx Jupiter. The importance of *communication* to the formation of the megamachine that the yod partly symbolizes.
- Venus in Leo, conjoining Mercury (and thus with the same series of aspects). The communication had to do with *values*, particularly those values (e.g. grain) connected to the king (Leo).
- Mars in Scorpio, conjoined to Neptune and square Mercury-Venus. *Aggression* on

---

[1] Mumford, 220.
[2] Mumford, 222.

behalf of the king and his *valuables*. The army. Aggression undertaken because of *delusion*. The importance of *communication* to the military effort.
- The connection of Mars-Neptune to the yod (via aspects to all planets in it: square to Mercury-Venus, sextile to Moon, trine to Jupiter). The importance of the military to the transmission of the mega-machine through the centuries. The Mercury-Mars square brings to mind the importance of scribes and communication to the more efficient workings of the war-machine (the megamachine in its military manifestation), for without precise communication of messages from the center, the machine wouldn't have operated so efficiently. Neptune symbolizes the quasi-magical rites associated with the military. That we find these planets in Scorpio suggests the cruelty and sadism accompanying military efforts.
- Moon in Capricorn, likely quincunx Mercury-Venus and sextile Jupiter; also sextile Mars-Neptune. (For a later birthtime: possibly quincunx the Sun or even conjoined to Pluto.) With the coming of civilization, people increasingly found *security* (Moon) through participation in the *hierarchy* (Capricorn). The *ritualistic* (quincunx) maintenance of security through *structural* connections to the ruler (Leo), particularly those connections related to social *class* (Capricorn).
- Jupiter in Pisces (its dignity), quincunx Mercury-Venus, sextile Moon; also trine Mars-Neptune *Expansion (*Jupiter) of the megamachine, often through *aggression* (Mars).
- Saturn in Leo quincunx Uranus, and, more loosely, Pluto. Saturn in Leo suggests the *bureaucracy* (Saturn) that throughout recorded history has always accompanied the king (Leo), though it apparently did not do so before the era of the Long Count's beginning. The quincunx to Uranus suggests the way *invention* and human *brilliance* has generally ended up co-opted by the status quo.
- Uranus-Pluto conjunction in Capricorn. *Transformation*, change, and *evolutionary growth* accompanied by *inventiveness* working through the ordered *hierarchies* (Capricorn) of society. The power of invention and the ongoing relationship between invention, power, and hierarchy.
- Sun in Leo (dignity) conjoined Saturn. The importance of *kingship* and centralized *rulership through hierarchy* to all that has transpired since the 4th millennium BC. The notion of the divine nature of kings. The conjunction to Saturn symbolizes the king-bureaucracy connection, so that even if we consider the king as a divine or quasi-divine being, he maintains his power through the maintenance of bureaucratic order. The conjunction suggests the centralized authority of kingship, with Saturn representing the king's ruling arm (the hierarchy).
- Quincunx and yod. The quincunx suggests an *imbalance* that does not result in the overt challenge or structure-building of the square. The imbalance appears in the innumerable details of life, a pattern of behavior embedded within those details. Whereas with a square a person will seek or create a specific structure or set of

discernible activities or projects in order to bring together disparate facets of personality, with a quincunx the person will generally *find himself acting* in a discernible way. The quincunx pattern brings things together, but it often results not from a conscious decision but from compulsions whose nature escapes notice. Because the impulse comes from the unconscious, it appears as a pattern of projection difficult to discern except in retrospect. In this sense, the quincunx differs from the opposition, for with the opposition one will generally confront the projection directly, whereas with the yod one more "finds oneself dealing with it," often not even recognizing the pattern for many years. (We might therefore call it a pervasive projection without a clear *hook*.[1])

Because of the largely unconscious nature of the quincunx, many astrologers refer to it as the illness aspect, for when we find quincunxes in an individual's horoscope, we know that the tension, unacknowledged for many years, will often manifest through the body.

The yod, which consists of back-to-back quincunxes united by a planet or planets at the focal point, generally has more focus or direction than the isolated quincunx. Thus astrologers often refer to a yod as "the finger of god." The yod seems to point to a kind of destiny resulting from the clear manifestation of illness or imbalance, often after decades (or, with the Long Count's horoscope, after many centuries). These inner drives often manifest at last in clear behavior, often driven by acute understanding (the sextile) of the inner energies involved. This manifestation-period generally coincides with important transits or progressions to the yod, particularly to its "reaction point" (the point directly opposite the focal planet(s)).

- The square. The ninety degree angles in a horoscope tell us where the individual needs to build new *structures* or *venues* through which to engage energies that otherwise will pull in different directions. Though in some cases we see that the energies do pull in different directions, in millions of others we see the person actively create the structure or venue in question. In the Long Count, the symbolism suggests the structural continuity of a military class in which the king's delusions, communicated throughout the realms, constantly drove the military to destruction.

---

[1] Carl Jung said that we hang projections on hooks just like we hang coats.

Chapter 4

Time Analysis

SINCE WE OBVIOUSLY CAN'T COVER all, or even *most*, of the important events or developments that have taken place during the Long Count's 5125 year span, we must pick our spots. In doing so, we should look for trends reflecting some of the important indicators in the natal chart:

1. The development of authority systems: for during the period of the Long Count's birth, human beings in specific locales developed a new kind of social organization, one based on rigid authority and manifesting through what Lewis Mumford calls the mega-machine. That original development had repercussions that should appear in the transits.

> *Main astrological indicators: Saturn, and therefore Uranus (through its close aspect to Saturn); any of the natal planets in Capricorn: Uranus, Pluto, and the Moon; any of the planets in the Leo-Capricorn quincunxes (because of the quincunx's connection to ritualistic forms of behavior, amenable to authority-dictates): Mercury and Venus, the Moon and Jupiter; planets in Leo (because of Leo's connection to kingship): the Sun (in conjunction with Saturn); the square from Mercury-Venus to Mars-Neptune (because the authority systems maintained their authority through the military).*

2. The progressive destruction of the eco-system: the emphasis on machine-like efficiency showed, even at the beginning, a marked ability to alter the eco-system, though at first only at a local level.

Main astrological indicators: any of the planets involved in close quincunxes (connected with illness): Mercury-Venus, Jupiter (expansion), the Moon; Saturn and Uranus.

3. The manifestation of aggression through war: the beginnings of the Long Count witnessed the first development of armies, part of the mega-machine.

Main astrological indicators: Mars and Neptune; Mercury and Venus (because of their square to Mars-Neptune); Pluto (because it disposits Mars and Neptune in Scorpio); the Sun (because it disposits Mercury and Venus in Leo); Saturn (because it disposits Pluto); Jupiter (imperialism).

4. The development of what we might call philosophy; the development of wisdom.

Main astrological indicators: Mercury, Jupiter, Neptune, Pluto; also the Moon (through its quincunx to Mercury) and Mars-Neptune (because of their squares to Mercury and trines to Jupiter). Also Uranus, because it has much to do with revolutionary breakthroughs that begin with a new insight and because it does not readily acquiesce to the dictates of the status quo.

5. The development of what we might call "intellect."

Main astrological indicators: Mercury, Jupiter, Uranus, Pluto.

6. The development demonstrating the assumed separation of so-called "wisdom" from so-called "intellect" (a distinction that may have its roots in words rather than in the experience to which the words refer), the development of languages that distinguish what we call "science" from what we call "spirituality."

Main astrological indicators: the square between Mercury-Venus and Mars-Neptune; the quincunx from Mercury-Venus to Jupiter.

Some Technical Notes

In doing time-analysis of a *person's* horoscope, we pay attention to transits, directions, and the secondary progressions of the inner planets. We emphasize these because all of these factors show appreciable development during the life-span of an individual human being. However, some of the factors that prove useful in analyzing a *person's* horoscope will *not* prove useful when we analyze a aeon, in this case one lasting 5125 years. For example, the secondary progressed (SP) Moon, moving about a degree per month, measures developments of such a short duration that, however indispensable we might find it when we work with a person, particularly a person going through a crisis, we can largely ignore it in our study of the Long Count. Similarly for the transits (TR) of all inner planets, and even for those of Jupiter and Saturn, so important in natal counseling, though some of these may function as catalysts for longer-lasting influences.[1] Similarly, too, for most progressions of inner planets: they measure developments spanning at most a few years and thus seem of negligible importance in a discussion of a period of 5125 years. However, we may find such factors operating as triggers for most long-lasting influences.[2]

Though we must *ex*clude some factors that we use in our study of individuals, we can *in*clude some that seldom prove useful in natal horoscopy. Most importantly, we can use the secondary progressions of the outer planets, for though progressed Pluto (to take a prominent example) will generally move only a degree or so during a person's lifespan, it will move about 16 degrees during the Long Count, enough to form aspects (important ones, as we will see).[3] The other outer planets move even more during that period:

Neptune: 21 degrees   Uranus: 60 degrees
Saturn: 161 degrees   Jupiter: 433 degrees (1 cycle of 360 degrees plus 73 degrees)

In addition to the secondary progressions of these planets, we should consider the following:

- transiting Pluto, and to a lesser extent, transiting Neptune and Uranus
- the interplanetary cycles of these, especially the Neptune-Pluto cycle
- to a lesser extent, the solar arc Sun or any other solar arc direction (moving about a degree/year, making a complete cycle in about 360 years) operating as a trigger.

We may wish to introduce other factors as we proceed.

The dates:

    I. The period between 600 BC and 400 BC
    II. The "Renaissance"

---

[1] As Marc Edmund Jones pointed out years ago, for convenience of phrasing we often speak of the planets as causal factors even if, technically speaking, we don't consider them as *causing* anything.
[2] We often consider "triggering factors" in astrological practice. For example, as a person goes through a Pluto transit, which may take two or more years in all, various inner planets will make challenging aspects to natal positions. Some of these latter will serve to trigger the outer planet into specific manifestations. The specifics will vary from one horoscope to another. In discussing the Long Count and the secondary progressions of outer planets, the entire period of the progression may last centuries.
[3] I don't mean to indicate that we never look at secondary progressed (SP) Pluto—or, for that matter, secondary progressed Saturn, Uranus, or Neptune—in interpreting a person's horoscope. However, we generally look at such factors only when the SP planet changes direction. Those periods will often prove of great importance even if the secondary progressed planet barely moves during the lifetime.

III. 1891: the end of significant organized native resistance[1] to the depredations of industrial civilization
IV. 2012 A.D. The end of the Long Count

I. 600-400 BC: The "Axial" Period

1. Secondary progressed Uranus opposes natal Saturn
2. Secondary progressed Pluto enters Aquarius
3. Transiting Neptune-Pluto conjunction squares Mercury-Venus, opposes Mars-Neptune
4. Secondary progressed Saturn conjoins Mars and squares Mercury-Venus

Many historians see this period as marking the spiritual high point what we often call "civilization" (i.e. the form of social organization that has come to dominate the planet since around 3114 BC). During this period, some of the seminal figures in the history of philosophy taught, wrote, and left their mark: Aristotle, Socrates, Plato, Lao Tse, Buddha, Pythagoras, and others. The period also brought a sharp reaction against some of the more important tendencies indicated in the Long Count natal horoscope.

I have progressed the Long Count horoscope to 551 BC, the middle of the Long Count. The following developments characterize the period:

1. At 24 Aquarius, SP Uranus has reached its opposition with natal Saturn.
2. SP Pluto has just entered Aquarius, where he will stay, for the most part,[2] for the rest of the Long Count (eventually reaching 8 Aquarius, and an opposition to natal Mercury and Venus, a matter discussed below in connection with 1398, 1891, and 2012. Notably, Saturn and Uranus both rule Aquarius, so SP Pluto's entrance there highlights the relationship between these two bodies (a relationship well-depicted in myth, as we have seen, and also relevant to factor #1).
3. The positions of TR Neptune and TR Pluto suggest a recent conjunction between these bodies.[3] The exact conjunction took place in 578 BC at 9 Taurus 07, opposed to the natal Mars-Neptune conjunction, square the Mercury-Venus conjunction, forming a t-square with Mercury and Venus at the focal point and the natal yod's reaction-point at the "empty leg."

---

[1] I don't mean to indicate, here, that later uprisings, as occurred somewhat recently in southern Mexico, don't qualify as "significant," "organized," or "native." However, the events of the early 1890s involved native groups attempting to retain their aboriginal forms of social organization, whereas later resistance involved native people who to a large extent, and often against their wishes, found themselves absorbed in or surrounded by the dominant industrial and post-industrial forms of social organization.
[2] Secondary progressed planets go through retrograde periods. Thus SP Pluto will enter Aquarius, leave, and enter again over many centuries.
[3] By 551 BC we find Neptune about 30 degrees ahead of Pluto in the zodiac. This suggests the mentioned earlier conjunction.

4. SP Saturn conjoins the Mars-Neptune conjunction and squares Mercury-Venus, thus participating in the t-square mentioned in #3.

Secondary Progressed Uranus Opposes Natal Saturn

During the Long Count, SP Uranus moves forward almost exactly sixty degrees.[1] Here at the halfway point of the Long Count, he has moved half that distance. In doing so, he opposes natal Saturn. This aspect brings the natal quincunx forward into an opposition.[2] As we have discussed, the natal quincunx indicates a deeply rooted imbalance resulting in a ritualistic and not-generally-acknowledged connection between the forces that build the status quo (Saturn) and the inventive energies of the human mind (Uranus). The aspect points to the tension between naturally occurring inventiveness (Uranus) and the social order that absorbs or gives form *to* that inventiveness (Saturn).

We have encountered this imbalance already in our discussion of the megamachine, which we can surely see as a kind of invention, and it emerged within the established order, even seeming inseparable *from* that order, creating not only power (upper quincunx)[3] but also a tremendous tension that we still have with us today. We see in the pyramids an extraordinary example of the relationship between human brilliance (Uranus) and a restrictive social order (Saturn): Saturn's love of hierarchy combines with Uranus's inventiveness to create a kind of technical mastery never surpassed, but one involving the aforementioned tension. We see in the natal aspect a collective ritual—a pervasive social patterning—developing as a response to that tension. We see Saturnian order and hierarchy in the shape of the pyramids; we see Uranian brilliance in the technical inventiveness necessary to construct them; we see the quincunx in the slave labor part of the megamachine, that did the constructing.

From a further vantage, we can see our current ecological disaster as a further manifestation of the natal Saturn-Uranus quincunx, and of the related quincunxes between Mercury-Venus and

---

[1] Because we have to do, here, with a secondary progression, Uranus does not move steadily forward. Every 369.7 years, it enters a retrograde period lasting about 150 years. (We can find Uranus retrograde 41 percent of the time.)

[2] Many astrologers "read the transit or progression back into the natal chart," interpreting transits and progressions by integrating the natal positions of the planets involved: the progression indicates developments related to the natal factors. For example, if a person's natal horoscope has a Moon-Saturn square, any movement of or to those two planets will point to developments related to the natal tendency indicated *by* that aspect. Because such an aspect can indicate a lack of nurturance or support early in life, transits or progressions involving that square will show how one deals with the energy later, particularly in personal relationships (where one might have a tendency to choose partners who reiterate and reinforce the natal pattern). The mentioned practice reflects what we see in experience: that people often react to present circumstances in ways largely influenced by what may seem innate predispositions.

[3] In an upper quincunx, the faster moving planet (in this case Saturn) has moved 210 degrees ahead of (or, we might say, has reached a point 150 degrees behind) the slower-moving planet (in this case Uranus). 210 + 150 = 360 degrees. I have borrowed the terms *upper* and *lower* from Bil Tierney (*Dynamics of Aspect Analysis*).

both ends of the Moon-Jupiter sextile.[1] The authority-issues emerge when we consider the natal signs involved, for as we have seen, Leo and Capricorn connect to authority, though in different ways (Leo having to do with centralized control of the many by the one, Capricorn having to do with hierarchical social structures and their consequences). We see Leo in all autocratic regimes; we see Capricorn in all bureaucracies and hierarchies. That those living at the Long Count's conclusion so readily see these two as inseparable suggests the dynamics of the quincunx: a hidden-in-the-details social patterning. The imbalances so clearly marked in the natal horoscope appear more clearly at the Long Count's midpoint, when Uranus, one element of the imbalance, comes to its opposition with Saturn (the other element), and doing so in Aquarius, the sign co-ruled by those planets. With this aspect comes greater awareness and objectivity regarding the issues symbolized in the natal horoscope.

At the beginning of the Long Count, humankind (probably mostly the males, as suggested by the stellium in Leo including both the Sun and Saturn) developed, we might even say "invented," rigid hierarchies and social roles, and from these came the further invention of the megamachine that not only destroyed much of value from Neolithic cultures, but also began a process of accelerated environmental degradation and social inequality, both suggested by the quincunx. We would expect, given the position of SP Uranus around 500 BC, to find some greater awareness and evident tension (opposition) related to these matters. However, because SP Uranus remained within orb of an opposition to Saturn for hundreds of years,[2] the aspect does not mark a specific year, event, or individual lifetime. Rather, it marks a period spanning some hundreds of years and including the lifetimes of all of the individuals mentioned above.

Let's put this period into perspective by looking at the period from the 13th century BC to the Long Count's midpoint in the 6th century. Mumford notes that what some historians have called a lull in humankind's inventiveness for that period doesn't really qualify as a lull at all, for it brought multitudes of inventions. That these inventions had their locus in domestic life and not militaristic aggression perhaps accounts for the persistent notion that a "lull" occurred. Mumford discusses the resistance to the militarized system into which civilization had developed:

> So among the various conditions that help account for the slowness in enlarging the province of the megamachine, once the original spurt of constructive activity had reached an apex, something more than the negations of war must be taken into

---

[1] At the Long Count's midpoint, we find all the natal quincunxes expressed: Saturn-Uranus through SP Uranus' opposition to natal Saturn; the quincunxes in the yod through the Neptune-Pluto conjunction (forming, with natal Mars-Neptune and Mercury-Venus, a t-square with Venus focal). See below.
[2] If Uranus moves 60 degrees in 5125 years, then it will move about 0.01 degrees per year, or a degree every hundred years. We should consider this an approximate figure, as Uranus will turn retrograde once every 369.7 years and so does not move steadily forward. Nevertheless, the approximation (a degree every hundred years) will help us to see that this opposition marks a *period*, not a specific year or event. Thus in our discussion we can speak of people and events separated in time by centuries.

account: there was a recurrent disillusion with power and material wealth themselves when alienated from the purposeful and significant life-course of the community. This disillusion in time touched the exploiters as well as the exploited.[1]

Eventually, the disillusion resulted in a visible and wide-spread revolt:

> Between 3500 BC and 600 BC the physical shell of civilization had thickened; but the creature within it, he who had fabricated the shell, felt increasingly pinched and constricted, if not immediately threatened. The rewards of large-scale organization and mechanization were small in proportion to the sacrifices demanded. Only this increasing sense of disillusion can explain the popular revolt that began slowly between the ninth and 6th century BC: a revolt of the inner man against the outer man, of the spirit against the shell. Because this revolt did not depend upon physical weapons, it could not be put down by whips, truncheons, or shackles; and it quietly threatened to shatter the whole power system based on land monopoly, slavery, and the life-time division of labor.[2]

Mumford's analysis speaks directly to the gathering opposition between Saturn and Uranus, for astrologers have long taken Uranus as a symbol of individuality and rebellion, and Saturn as a symbol of form, order, walls, and limits (Mumford's "shell"). Uranus symbolizes brilliance, inventiveness, and iconoclastic tendencies springing from within; Saturn points to the structural work of the "outer man." The opposition suggests not only the resistance Mumford mentions, but also objective awareness, one of the hallmarks of the opposition aspect. It can suggest marriage, a union of complements, but just as often (and almost always when we apply astrological techniques to collectivities) as a visible split along some demarcation such as the one Mumford describes. Those representing the hierarchies (Saturn) would surely resist change (Uranus) and so would experience Uranus as a series of projections, for oppositions generally arise through projection, particularly if the transiting or progressed planet symbolizes an energy that the inner planet has difficulty accommodating: those within the hierarchies (Saturn) could not, so to speak, abide the figures who arose outside of them and spoke of freedom (Uranus) of the mind and spirit. So though the aspect could, in theory, emerge as a fruitful union between insight and discipline, and though it *did* so emerge in the teachings of Buddha, Lao Tse, and some others, we should expect something much less enlightened on a collective level, particularly on the part of those representing the status quo.[3]

---

[1] Lewis Mumford, *Technics and Human Development* (New York: Harcourt Brace Jovanovich, 1967), 257.
[2] Mumford, 257-8.
[3] We might wonder, here, whether we see in the Long Count progressed aspect something connected to the birth of our notions that Saturn and Uranus must stand opposed to each other. Perhaps this opposition reflects not the un-conditioned interaction of these energies within human beings, but an interaction conditioned by what we have come to call "civilization," where the status quo limits individual expression so drastically while at the same time offering specific forms for its expression.

New religions and philosophies arose at that time; both Mumford and Karl Jaspers[1] call them "axial," an interesting term for our study, as these religions and philosophies arose so close to the midpoint of the Long Count's 5125 year span. These developments challenged materialistic assumptions equating human welfare with "centralized power, military dominance, and economic exploitation," and the ones issuing the challenge generally lived far from the centers of power, out in villages or hinterlands. Those people emphasized "not power but, rather, righteousness . . . not snatching, seizing, and fighting, but sharing, cooperating, even loving; not pride, but humility; not limitless wealth, but a noble self-restricting poverty and chastity."[2] The names of these prophets remain with us: Amos, Hesiod, Lao Tzu, and the Buddha.

These ideas spread quickly from India and Persia, all the way to Palestine, Greece, and Rome, igniting in "a seemingly spontaneous combustion." From many teachers came an emphasis on modesty, not heroism; on morality, not might; on self-imposed restriction and discipline, not on unrestrained appetite—a turning away from civilization:

> What is important to note is that this new movement rejected the obvious goods and achievements of 'civilization' no less than its patent failures and evils. This was not merely a revolt against the system of regimentation that had elevated the ambitious and ruthless and depressed the cooperative and amiable: it was a revolt against all the pomps and vanities of worldly success, against ancient rituals that had become empty. . . .[3]

In astrological terms we can see this as a revolt (Uranus) against (opposition) the forms of civilization (Saturn), whether those forms emerged as cruelty or as meaninglessness, whether as evident evil or as the less-evident blinding of the status quo. Like the progression (SP) that carries its symbolism, it went on for centuries.

Secondary Progressed Pluto Into Aquarius

The second factor also involves a secondary progressed outer planet: SP Pluto's movement into Aquarius, another shift that took several centuries. Pluto begins the Long Count at 22 Capricorn and ends it at 8 Aquarius, a movement of 16 degrees. At the middle of this journey, he enters Aquarius, a sign traditionally ruled by Saturn, and, since 1781, by Uranus as well. In astrological terms, we would say that *natal* Pluto occupies Saturn's *night* sign and that around the Long Count's midpoint, *SP* Pluto enters Saturn's *day*-sign. Uranus' ruler-ship (of Aquarius) suggests a reiteration of the Saturn-Uranus issues just discussed: the relationship between individual freedom or insight, and the social structures through which that insight operated.

---

[1] The following owes much to Mumford. See p. 258ff.
[2] Mumford, 258.
[3] Mumford, 259.

So though we see Pluto as always under the influence (so to speak) of Saturn,[1] a shift took place at the Long Count's midpoint. Pluto in Capricorn emphasizes the power of hierarchy and organization *per se*. Pluto in Aquarius has more to do with the power of fixed ideas that arise from the hierarchical mode. In more contemporary terms, Capricorn has to do with order and one's relationship to hierarchy, while Aquarius has to do not only with the resulting ideas, but also with the forming of groups based on, and perhaps blinded by, those ideas. In Capricorn, Pluto empowered a civilization stressing limits, boundaries, and hierarchy. As he enters Aquarius, a sign ruled by both Saturn and Uranus, Pluto points to the kind of society that formed from Capricorn's emphases. Thus the development, around 500 B.C. of social critique: Plato's *Republic* (and other works), Aristotle's *Politics* (and other works), the development of the Buddhist *Vinaya*, and the social critiques of Lao Tse, to name just a few.

This development should come as no surprise to astrologers, for processes begin in cardinal signs (e.g. Capricorn) and develop rigidity or stable form in the fixed signs (e.g. Aquarius). We might note, as an example of this, the ongoing influence of Plato and Aristotle on European civilization that came to dominance some centuries later. (As we will see, by the time of the Renaissance, a period partly characterized by a renewed interest in some of the classics just mentioned, Pluto had moved to a significant point in Aquarius, showing the results of processes begun here at the Long Count's midpoint.)

Pluto in Aquarius points again to the battle between that sign's two rulers, rulers who want to go in very different directions, as we have seen in our discussion of SP Uranus' opposition to natal Saturn and our discussion of the natal quincunx between those planets. It also sets off Pluto's natal conjunction with Uranus. The relevant factors suggest once again the ongoing power-struggle between Saturn and Uranus that has played such a formative role in the development of our civilization, though the natal quincunx between those two bodies suggests that the battle would take place not through conscious engagement, but through a wide variety of pervasive social rituals and illnesses suggested by the quincunx. (The quincunx suggests an imbalance that will reach a crisis-point and that demands resolution. The crisis point comes at the end of the Long Count, when SP Uranus forms, along with natal Uranus and natal Saturn, a yod, the so-called "Finger of God," and when SP Pluto and Saturn reach their opposition to natal Mercury and Venus. But more on that later.[2])

Thus we see, throughout history, a constant tension, not always out in the open, between those who wish to maintain rigid social structures and those who would rebel against those structures,

---

[1] Why? Because we find natal Pluto in Capricorn, Saturn's sign.
[2] We will see, during that period, two yods, one natal and one formed by SP Uranus. In the former, we find Venus, Mercury, Jupiter, and the Moon; in the latter, we find natal Saturn and Uranus, plus SP Uranus. At the end of the Long Count, the former receives the powerful and dangerous progressions from Saturn and Pluto.

between so-called civilized people and so-called barbarous ones, between repressive form and possibly irresponsible anarchic trends. Pluto's movement into Aquarius suggests an empowerment of group endeavor. It suggests transformation arising through a union of discipline and insight. At the same time, it suggests power-struggles (Pluto) arising between the Saturnian and Uranian "sides" of Aquarius—that is, between human inventiveness and the social organizations that have co-opted the resulting inventions even if the actual invention took place not in the cities but out on the fringes. So Pluto's movement into Aquarius reiterates many of the themes already described in connection to SP Uranus' opposition to Saturn.

If we take Aquarius to indicate new ideas applied to the body social, then we can take Pluto as an "empowerer" of such ideas. Thus we see in Greece around 500 BC, and in the teachings of Buddha and Lao Tse, attempts to bring more enlightened principles to bear in the organizing of society. Though we must acknowledge that some of these ideas bear a clearly Saturnian stamp (e.g. those of Plato, emphasizing as they do the importance of order and the subordination of the individual to the dictates of society, ideas that remain with us to this day), we must acknowledge that Greek society differed from the societies around it not only in the sophistication of its art and science, but in the degree of freedom afforded its citizens—in, we might say, the radical idea of a citizen's freedom *per se*.

Though many Western scholars emphasize the importance of Greek ideas, if we look further east, we find ideas showing a clearer Uranian emphasis. Buddha, for example, emphasized the development of *prajna* (insight) and awareness, and though he also taught that one could not develop either without discipline (Saturn), he didn't see discipline or order as a goal. Lao Tse stated the basic principles of what we now call Taoism, a philosophy adopted by many who stood apart from the cities where "civilization" flourished. In chapter LXXX of *Tao Te Ching*, we find what we might take as a rather guarded view regarding the purported benefits of civilization:

> There might be boats and carriages, but no one would go in them; there might still be weapons of war but no one would drill with them…the people should have no use for any form of writing save knotted ropes, should be contented with their food, pleased with their clothing, satisfied with their homes, should take pleasure in their rustic tasks. The next place might be so near at hand that one could hear the cocks crowing in it, the dogs barking; but the people would grow old and die without ever having been there.[1]

If we interpret this passage as a harkening back to the earlier, gentler social order of the Neolithic village, we would see both a Saturnian emphasis on order and the past and a Uranian emphasis on rebellion or resistance.

---

[1] Arthur Waley, *The Way and Its Power: A Study of the Tao Te Ching and Its Place in Chinese Thought* (New York: Grove Press, 1958), 241-2.

Transits: Neptune, Pluto, and the Neptune-Pluto Cycle

The third factor has to do with transits, particularly those of Neptune and Pluto. The positions of these two planets at 551 BC tell us that they had gone through a conjunction not many years before: in 578 BC at 9 Taurus, opposite the natal Mars-Neptune conjunction and square Mercury and Venus. Because we will look at other Neptune-Pluto conjunctions as we proceed through the time-analysis, we should begin by asking what they indicate, beginning with a very literal interpretation of the planets' meanings.

The Neptune-Pluto conjunctions take place about every 500 years (see chart on page 128), initiating (conjunction) a new cycle of empowered (Pluto) illusions, delusions, ideals, or yearnings (Neptune). The conjunction can indicate the death of an older order of illusions and the rebirth of a new. Pluto transforms fixed ideas about the nature of reality or the world; Neptune symbolizes illusions, delusions, yearnings, or ideals that arise from that transformation.

This process need not seem esoteric or mysterious. Consider the conjunction of 1891, which coincided with the Massacre at Wounded Knee, a triumph of expansive capitalism over native and so-called "primitive" types of social organization. The fixed idea had to do with capitalism (or, perhaps, empire based *in* capitalism) and with the use of the world's resources for ends related to money and dominance. From these arose what seemed like ideals to those who promulgated them but which may seem more like dangerous delusions to others. Certainly the various elaborations of these ideals/delusions (capitalistic domination, industrial means of production, mass education, wealth accumulation, and the dominance of the nation-state) have had a disastrous effect on the ecosystem and on all traditional cultures. We will return to these matters in our discussion of the Renaissance and later periods, when we will see related astrological developments.

In its most general terms, the conjunction symbolizes a transformation and empowerment of what we might call the primary delusions of the period in question, delusions many people of the period will see as "reality" or "normalcy." Because Pluto transforms through failed attempts at control, the aspect can manifest as obsessions about a particular set of either ideals or delusions. Further, as Neptune dissolves boundaries and thus releases compassion, the conjunction can indicate the power of compassion and empathy.

Taking the more problematic indications first—the empowerment of delusion—we should note that though astrologers often (and not incorrectly) take Pluto as a symbol of the deep emotional blockages that we often call "complexes," it seems to have as much to do with concept: with ideas, about the world or about "reality," that lie beneath and support the complexes.[1] At Pluto's

---

[1] This linkage of complex with language would probably have pleased Alfred Korzybski, who spoke of the problematic nature of many "semantic relations" and who wrote his seminal works at the time of Pluto's discovery. Pluto, of course, symbolizes fusion, in this case the fusion of dominant idea and world.

discovery, scientists found themselves probing what we can call the "dualistic fixation" that seems to come so naturally to human beings as they perceive a world they take to be external to themselves. Those scientists—including Carl Jung, Alfred Korzybski, Edward Sapir, and Werner Heisenberg[1]—made discoveries that call into question our fixed ideas about ourselves and the world, insofar as we can separate that *world* from our *ideas* about it. In particular, those discoveries seemed to undermine our assumption that human beings operate as objective perceivers perceiving a world that exists independently of their ideas about it.

This understanding of Pluto leads us to see *how* Pluto transforms—when he does, of course. Because he doesn't always, or even usually, do so. More often, and probably *usually* when Pluto operates on a collective level, Pluto symbolizes fixed notions about the world in general, about what we often call "reality" (as distinguished, here, from Aquarius' fixed ideas, which generally have to do with social situations),[2] ideas to which we have strong emotional ties and which often emerge through the complexes. Though Pluto symbolizes transformation and evolution, he also symbolizes those blockages that prevent either (for Pluto fuses the neurotic with the wise). He (or *she*, for Pluto fuses gender as well) often arises as what we might call *control in search of a lack of control*: for when ego feels an impending transformation (so to speak), it will generally do what it can to prevent that transformation from occurring, because ego depends on stability. So Pluto often points to areas in which, because of our attachment to cherished points of view that seem to provide some semblance of emotional security, we resist transformation. Yet the very resistance suggests the energy *of* transformation.

Pluto, ruler of the fixed water sign Scorpio, symbolizes the process by which our fixed ideas about the world—about human experience generally and about ourselves and our own emotions—bring about emotional fixity. That emotional fixity then induces, hopefully, a transformation involving the root of the self, or the very idea-feeling[3] *of* a self and its place in society. (Pluto-ruled Scorpio squares (challenges) both Leo (self-concern) and Aquarius (social con-

---

[1] Sapir suggested in 1921 (*Speech*) and thereafter (with a seminal essay appearing in 1928) that our concepts do not "attain to individual and independent life" until they have "found a distinctive linguistic embodiment"; a few years later, Heisenberg wrote that one cannot do a completely objective experiment or attain complete objectivity about reality.

[2] The four fixed signs symbolizes fixity about different realms: Aquarius has to do with fixed mental patternings about social structure; Taurus has to do with fixed mental patternings about organic development or fixed abodes; Leo has to do with fixed mental patternings about self-identity; Pluto-ruled Scorpio has to do with fixed mental patternings about feelings. We might also say that the fixed signs symbolize patterns of fixity arising from four causes, or four kinds of desire: the desire for social stability (Aquarius); the desire for personal rootedness (Taurus); the desire for a fixed self-identity (Leo); the desire for fixed patterns of feeling (Scorpio).

[3] I've hyphenated this word, á la Alfred Korzybski, because what I have in mind qualifies as a fusion (Pluto) of idea and feeling. Korzybski, writing right around the time of Pluto's discovery, advocated using hyphenated words (e.g. thought-feelings) that join together items of experience that language articulates as separate but that may not arise separately in the non-language world.

cern).) We might ask how such fixity and control can lead to transformation. Pluto operates like plutonium: one needs a critical mass, which on an emotional level has to do with an emotional fixity that leads to an increase in emotional pressure; this pressure can then lead to a chain reaction appropriately called *transformation*. And though the emotions seem to supply the energy that empowers this transformation, the process begins with our ideas about the world, ideas that have a pervasive influence on our perception altogether. (Again we see Pluto's fusion, whether of spirit and flesh, intellect and emotion, male and female.)

We find corroboration for these ideas when we consider intellectual developments taking place about the time of Pluto's discovery, 1930. Right around then, Heisenberg said that one cannot do an objective experiment on the world because one's perception affects the world one perceives; Jung, clarifying his ideas about projection around that time, felt that whatever one rejects as part of the self will appear in the world either as an event or as what one perceives as properties of outer objects;[1] Korzybski pointed out (as had Edward Sapir and Benjamin Lee Whorf a few years earlier) that one's language-structure contains its own metaphysics and will color the perceptions of a person speaking that language. Pluto has to do, then, with the power of mind to affect perception—or we might say, of the power arising when we develop an awareness of the fusion of mind and phenomena. To a considerable extent, we perceive according to the concepts that we have available to us through the language that we speak. Through those concepts, we conclude that the world "is" such and such a kind of realm and that within that realm "this is this" and "that is that."[2] And thus we think that we control (Pluto) the world we experience.

Around middle of the Long Count, and thus under the influence of the Neptune-Pluto conjunction of 578 BC, Buddha taught what we now call the Mahayana teachings and did what Buddhists refer to as the Second Turning of the Wheel of Dharma. The later Madyamika teachings have their root in the Heart Sutra, spoken by Gautama Buddha during the period under investigation. These various teachings tell us that the world does not arise as we think it does, that if we see the world accurately, we see it as "empty" of the characteristics we generally attribute to it. We see analogous ideas, though perhaps less precisely worked out, in the writings of Lao Tse and Plato.

---

[1] Marie Louise von Franz, "Projection: Its Relationship to Illness and Psychic Maturation," in *Psychotherapy* (Boston: Shambhala, 1993), 256.

[2] Some readers may perceive, here, one of what people refer to as Aristotle's Laws of Thought: a thing is what it is; a thing in a certain category is a thing in a certain category. Aristotle, of course, lived in the Axis period, right around the Long Count's midpoint. Korzybski, whose ideas lurk behind some of what I say here—and who referred to his work as *non-Aristotelian*—published his major work just a few years after Pluto's discovery and thus very close to the end of the Long Count. Anyone who has tried to get university students to question these laws of thought will see how deep a root they have in the minds of contemporary people. We find it easy to see that "a horse is a horse," but much more difficulty to see the limitations in, and resulting from, that conceptual-linguistic schema.

So on the one hand, Pluto symbolizes the emotional fixity that empowers a pervasive perception of the world—a perception that people take for reality but which we should probably take as a delusion (Neptune). As a collective planet ruling a fixed sign, Pluto symbolizes collective mind and its fixations. Neptune symbolizes the deceptions or yearnings that arise *from* those fixations. On the other hand, Pluto suggests a transformation of that perception and a transformation of the emotional fixation that results from the habitual mode of perception, and Neptune suggests a dissolving of veils that separate us from a more encompassing truth. From what we might call the Plutonian point of view, the world arises as it does because of our concepts; this suggests that if we alter our concepts, we alter the world we see, or at least our seeing of it. (Let's put aside, at least for now, the question of whether "the world itself" actually changes, noting as we do that we might wish to question whether this "world itself" actually exists. If we ask, "But does the world change, or only one's perception of it?" we perhaps indicate that we have accepted the dualistic fixation under discussion.)

The Neptune-Pluto conjunctions usher in 500 year periods in which human beings give distinctive colorings to the world—to *their* world—colorings suggested by the sign in which the conjunction takes place (and other factors, but let's keep things somewhat simple for now).[1] These conjunctions move forward through the zodiac and measure shifts in the prevailing view of the world, the prevailing view of "what the phenomenal world *is*," and thus of resultant cultural developments.[2] The conjunction that took place in 3057-3056 BC, about 50 years after the Long Count birth date, occurred in the twenty-first and twenty-second degrees[3] of Pisces. The next three conjunctions took place in Aries, the next five took place in Taurus; the last two in the present Long Count took place in Gemini:

3057-56 BC	21st and 22nd degrees of Pisces
2561-69 BC	1st and 2nd degrees of Aries
2065-64 BC	11th and 10th degrees of Aries
1569-68 BC	21st and 20th degrees of Aries
1073 BC	1st degree of Taurus
0578 BC	10th degree of Taurus
084-083 BC	17th degree of Taurus
0411-0412 AD	23rd and 24th degrees of Taurus
0905 AD	29th degree of Taurus
1398-99 AD	4th and 3rd degrees of Gemini
1891-92 AD	9th and 8th degrees of Gemini

---

[1] Though we speak of "the" conjunction of two planets, often we find more than one. Though the 578 BC conjunction only occurred once, others occur more than once. See chart below.
[2] See, below, the discussion of the Renaissance.
[3] That is, 20+ and 21+ degrees.

As Neptune moves farther and farther ahead of Pluto in the zodiac in any particular Neptune-Pluto cycle, the ideals and delusions separate farther and farther from the original idea—or, we might say, the original assumption. The individual conjunctions in any sign show and measure the different permutations of this process. A series of conjunctions in a particular sign tells us about the root-delusions of the period (which, as we can see from the chart, may last many centuries) and about the root-potentials of the period, that which people must cultivate in order to evolve.

Now let's return to the symbolism of the Long Count's midpoint. That midpoint falls just twenty-seven years after the Neptune-Pluto conjunction in the tenth degree of Taurus (9+); the conjunction closely opposes the Mars-Neptune conjunction in Taurus, the opposition (transiting Neptune-Pluto opposing natal Mars-Neptune) forming a t-square to the important Mercury-Venus conjunction in Leo (and in a close trine with the natal Moon in Capricorn, but let's not get too many balls into the air at once). As we have seen in chapter two, the natal square between Mercury-Venus and Mars-Neptune suggests, among other things, warfare based on delusory ideas. The Neptune-Pluto conjunction moves human beings to a new awareness (opposition) of the uses of aggression (Mars) and its relation to self-centered thought or assumptions about regality as a source of rulership (Leo). Mars in Scorpio suggests aggression based on the emotional fixations just discussed (those that arise from fixed ideas about reality); Neptune suggests delusion. The transiting Neptune-Pluto conjunction suggests idealistic developments related to new ideas and earth-based values (Taurus), all in a process that challenges the natal square symbolizing humanity's tendency, since the onset of the Long Count, to engage in conflict based on delusions and arising from the worship of kings. The period in question brought a pervasive revolt against the militarism so characteristic of, and perhaps inseparable from, the megamachine. (We might recall, here, the earlier discussion of the square from Mars-Neptune to Mercury-Venus. Mumford tells us that in the "earlier stages of Neolithic culture," before the development of "the megamachine," we find "not even a hint of armed combat between villages; possibly . . . the massive walls around ancient towns like Jericho…performed a magico-religious function before they were found to furnish a decided military advantage," and that what is "conspicuous in Neolithic diggings is rather the complete absence of weapons, though tools and pots are not lacking."[1])

The t-square has its empty leg in Aquarius,[2] ruled by Uranus and Saturn, so we find ourselves back to the theme developed above: the development of new (Uranus) social forms (Saturn)—or, the need to develop them, evident at the Long Count's midpoint. We also find the development of written philosophy as a new discipline (Mercury-Neptune) as well as quan-

---

[1] Mumford, 216.

[2] Many astrologers compare t-squares to three-legged tables. They refer to the fourth "leg" as the "empty space." It contains the so-called "karmic degree," the degree opposite the focal planet. Of course, the Long Count has two such, for it has two focal planets in close conjunction; but Venus seems a better choice, for its aspects have lower orbs of aspect.

tum-leaps forward in the fine arts (Venus-Neptune) such as sculpture, music, drama, and poetry. But again, we find this impetus coming from the Neptune-Pluto conjunction, an aspect whose "effects" distributed themselves (so to speak) for the next five hundred years, until the next conjunction. Taurus emerges here through the emphasis on ordinary, fruitful living; a new impetus in relation to this constituted a demand for social change.

So as we would expect, the conjunction brings with it a host of new ideas. These ideas challenged prevailing notions that one should go to war for the king or ruler or that one can find meaning in ruthless aggression. The revolt against social constraint so characteristic of the period was also a revolt against the pride-driven, illusion-laced, power-mad aggression symbolized by the Mercury-Venus-Mars-Neptune square. That the conjunction takes place in Taurus suggests a pervasive desire to return to a more earthy, grounded way of life connected with the Taurean emphasis on fellow-feeling and deeply-rooted growth. The Sabian Symbol for the conjunction degree—A Red Cross Nurse, symbol of "the compassionate linking of all men"[1]—also tells us much about the period, reminding us of, among other developments, the teachings of Buddha and Lao Tse.

The t-square's empty leg, directly across from Mercury and Venus, falls on the positions of SP Saturn and SP Pluto at the Long Count's conclusion, suggesting that in the latter period people would experience the results of the earlier period's successes and failures and that developments in the earlier period could do much to mitigate problems in the later one. In Aquarius, that empty leg suggests the importance of humankind's ideas about social formations, how people deal with the Saturn-Uranus conundrum discussed above.[2]

Secondary Progressed Saturn

By 551 BC, secondary progressed Saturn has moved to 6 Scorpio 09, opposing the transiting Neptune-Pluto conjunction, conjoining natal Mars, moving toward a conjunction with natal Neptune. It also closely squares the Mercury-Venus conjunction in Leo. In doing all this, SP Saturn sets off the t-square just discussed (the one created by the Neptune-Pluto conjunction of 578 BC at 10 Taurus) and reiterates its importance. Saturn here suggests karma, form, and limitation; at the same time, it suggests the need for new forms (Saturn) of idealistic self-assertion (Mars-Neptune). As to the former, we see that people experienced the results of the Leo-Scorpio square: seeing the results of delusion-based warfare (Mars), many sought new ways to work with their spiritual yearnings and ideals (Neptune). If Mars-Neptune arises as aggression based on delusion, it can also indicate compassionate action; Saturn shows the results of the former

---

[1] Dane Rudhyar, *An Astrological Mandala: The Cycle of Transformations and Its 360 Symbolic Phases* (New York: Vintage, 1974), 77.
[2] We can see the Saturn-Uranus challenge in current attempts to deal with climate change. We seem to have the technical means (Uranus) available to deal with the crisis, but rigid and pervasive social forms (Saturn) frustrate efforts to act insightfully.

and the potential of the latter if a person would apply discipline. Thus we see in Buddhism the development of the *paramitas* and in Greece a widespread concern with ethics as a foundation for social ordering. Taken together, these aspects (SP Uranus opposing natal Saturn; transiting Neptune-Pluto opposing Mars; SP Saturn conjoining Mars and squaring Mercury-Venus) provide symbolic testimony to the "revolt" discussed above.

Yet though SP Uranus suggests innovation and rebellion, and though TR Neptune-Pluto suggests new ways of perceiving the world, and though we see clear challenges to the prevailing pattern of aggression based upon royal (Leo) dispensation, the Saturn influence (SP Saturn) suggests that many of the insights would get co-opted by the prevailing order, always a danger with Saturn and with Aquarius, the sign at the empty leg of the t-square. Thus Socrates, one of the more influential "axial" prophets, preached a doctrine that, though surely groundbreaking and revolutionary in its way (e.g. in the use of the Socratic method), has found a use ever since in the justification of the prevailing order.

Despite this, we can see that the Long Count's midpoint period truly brought a new dispensation to human beings and a new impetus to people living in organized societies. We find an emphasis on self-control, self-awareness, and self-cultivation not evident before. We find, too, powerful developments in what Mumford calls "technics," though these involved items related to domesticity more than (as in 3114 BC) things related to domination and war: though we find no great advances in approaches to either war or domination, we see all sorts of inventions that alleviated daily life in a positive way.

We find, above all, a challenge to the prevailing dynamics of the Long Count and to the development of the megamachine, particularly those dynamics associated with the Leo-Scorpio squares discussed above. Mumford reminds us:

> The revolt began in the mind, and it proceeded quietly to deny the materialistic assumptions that equated human welfare and the will of the gods with centralized political power, military dominance, and increasing economic exploitation—symbolized as these were in the walls, towers, palaces, temples of the great urban centers. All over Europe, the Middle East and Asia—and notably out of the villages rather than the cities—new voices arose. . . .[1]

Saturn suggests the new forms; the conjunction to Mars suggests, particularly when combined with SP Uranus' opposition to natal Saturn, that these new forms emerged out of an objection to the prevailing militaristic order; the square to Mercury and Venus suggests new ways of thinking and valuing, though with the danger, already noted, that these changes would end up incorporated into the status quo.

---

[1] Mumford, 258.

II. The Renaissance

1. SP Pluto squares Mars-Neptune and opposes Mercury-Venus.

    We see here another t-square, similar to the one we found via transit around 551 BC. In discussion of the earlier period, we looked at the TR Neptune-Pluto conjunction of 578 BC at 9+ Taurus, forming a t-square to Mercury-Venus by opposing natal Mars-Neptune. The empty leg of that t-square fell at 7-8 Aquarius, the area that SP Pluto reached by 1500 A.D.[1] At the later date, Mars and Neptune become the focal planets. (See the horoscope on page xxiii. The heavier lines indicate the t-square; the dotted line points to the empty leg of the 551 BC horoscope and to the part of the t-square (SP Saturn and SP Pluto) for the Long Count's concluding phase.) Furthermore, the empty leg falls right where the Neptune-Pluto conjunction of 578 BC took place (just as the empty leg of 578 BC falls on SP Pluto's Renaissance position), again suggesting a relationship between developments around 500 BC and developments around the time of the Renaissance. As we will see, these astrological factors reflect the fascination of Renaissance scholars with the "classical learning" that developed in the earlier period.

2. TR Neptune conjoins TR Pluto in Gemini.
3. SP Jupiter Return just a few years earlier.
4. Transiting Neptune-Pluto conjunction square natal Jupiter.
5. SP Uranus conjoining SP Jupiter a few years later.
6. SP Saturn conjoining natal Moon.

The most important progressed factor affects (again) the natal square from Mercury-Venus in Leo to Mars-Neptune in Scorpio, the aspect symbolizing, among other things, the military aspect of the megamachine—and again it involves Pluto, though this time by secondary progression instead of by transit. Recall that in 578 BC, *TR* Pluto conjoined *TR* Neptune at 9 Taurus, opposed to natal Mars and Neptune; in 1398, we find this longer-lasting indicator (SP Pluto) applying toward a precise square with Mars.

We can summarize these developments and their interconnections as follows:

- 578 BC (very close to the Long Count midpoint) had a t-square involving the natal square from Mercury-Venus to Mars-Neptune; this t-square resulted from movement

---

[1] Some dates for SP Pluto's aspects to natal planets: squares Mars 1466; opposes Mercury 1471; StRx 1541; opposes Mercury 1612; squares Mars 1618; StD 1705; squares Mars 1788; opposes Mercury 1793; opposes Venus 1848; StRx 1907; opposes Venus 1967; opposes Mercury 2038; squares Mars 2049. As SP Pluto remains retrograde in 2049, we know that it will go through the same series of aspects (squaring Mars, opposing Mercury and Venus) at least one more time, after it turns direct again. We can see, here, that the aspects-in-question have relevance not only to the Renaissance, but to the entire period between the Renaissance and 2012—and beyond.

of transiting Neptune and transiting Pluto at 9+ Taurus, opposing Mars-Neptune and squaring Mercury-Venus. The t-square's empty leg fell in Aquarius, right at the position occupied by SP Pluto and SP Saturn (as we will see) at the Long Count's end, and within orb of the position of SP Pluto during the Renaissance and for centuries thereafter.

- 1398 AD had a t-square involving the natal square from Mercury-Venus to Mars-Neptune, the t-square resulting from the position of SP Pluto at 5 Aquarius, opposing Mercury-Venus and squaring Mars-Neptune but closer to Mars. The empty leg fell at 7-11 Taurus (opposite Mars-Neptune), conjoining the positions of transiting Neptune and Pluto during the conjunction of 578 BC.
- Thus we see numerous connections between the 501 BC period and the Renaissance—connections reiterated, as we will see, at the Long Count's end, all involving the natal square (Mercury-Venus in Leo closely square Mars-Neptune in Scorpio), some movement of Pluto (by transit in 578 BC, by SP during the Renaissance and at the Long Count's conclusion). These connections suggest the importance of power and transformation (Pluto) in their various relations with aggression (Mars), and idealism-delusion (Neptune), all driven by unconscious factors (Pluto, Scorpio) and intellectual development for the individual (Mercury-Venus in Leo). Furthermore, we would expect to find important causal relations between events in the earlier period and events in the later period, particularly when we relate those events to the basic drives of the Long Count as a whole. The factors indicate the potential for enormous creativity, but, unless people could bring these energetic factors (particularly those involving aggression: Mars) under control, tremendous destruction as well, particularly considering Jupiter, which expands on whatever it touches.
- On the other hand, Jupiter's progressed return suggests new developments in both learning and travel, neither one of which, taken in isolation, seems problematic, but both of which led to enormous problems in connection with both the material just mentioned and the natal factors discussed in the previous chapter. These problems appear in the relationship between the time-analysis factors (SP Jupiter's conjunction with natal Jupiter) and natal ones (the natal yod and t-square, as we will see).

Secondary Progressed Pluto squares Mars-Neptune and opposes Mercury-Venus Transiting Neptune conjoins Transiting Pluto in Gemini

In the centuries after 551 BC, SP Pluto moved further into Aquarius, forming, by the Renaissance, a t-square involving Mars, Mercury, Venus, and Neptune. The square from SP Pluto to natal Mars perhaps accounts for the widespread cruelty that characterized the Renaissance and the entire period since. Though we generally consider the Renaissance as a time of enlightened learning—and not surprisingly, astrologically considered, with the progressed Jupiter suggesting expanded perspective *through* learning or travel, and with SP Pluto's opposition to Mercury, suggesting a transformation and empowerment of intellect and curiosity related, as discussed above, to developments around the Long Count's midpoint—it also brought the decimation of millions of people and the accelerated destruction of the biosphere. The intellectual developments and the aggression intertwined in numerous ways, as Mumford reminds us when he points out that between the fifteenth and seventeenth centuries, "the New World opened by terrestrial explorers, adventurers, soldiers, and administrators joined forces with the scientific and technical new world that the scientists, the inventors, and the engineers explored and cultivated":

> [One mode] was concerned with abstract symbols, rational systems, universal laws, and repeatable and predictable events, objective mathematical measurements: it sought to understand, utilize, and control the forces that derive ultimately from the cosmos and the solar system. The other mode dwelt on the concrete and the organic, the adventurous, the tangible: to sail uncharted oceans to conquer new lands, to subdue and overawe strange peoples. . . . In both modes of exploration, there was from the beginning a touch of defiant pride and demonic frenzy.[1]

If Pluto-Mercury suggests a powerful explosion of intellect, and if the Jupiter influence suggests philosophy, travel and long journeys,[2] Pluto-Mars suggests the fusion of all of that with a power-urge driven on by the demons of the unconscious. The combination produced the "demonic frenzy" that Mumford and other historians have noted. Mumford reminds us that "the hostility that the European displayed toward the native cultures he encountered he carried even further into his relations with the land." As to the cultures and their peoples, we need only point to the slaughter of millions of Native Americans and Africans and to the routine enslavement of the latter over many centuries. As to the land, we need only look around us to see the results.

The astrological connections seem clear. By 1400 AD, SP Pluto had reached 5+ Aquarius; the progression had come into effect in the time before the Renaissance and has lasted until the present day, getting progressively stronger until by the end of the Long Count, Pluto will have moved to 8+ Aquarius, still well within range of an opposition to Venus and a square to Mars, and still applying to a square to Neptune. Thus the Pluto-Mars square marks the entire last 600-plus years, what we might call *the modern era*. Further, during that period, we have been under the effect (so to speak) of the t-square involving SP Pluto and the aforementioned natal square: the t-square has Mars-Neptune focal in Scorpio and points to a major issue: aggression (Mars) based on delusion or idealism (Neptune), driven by a lust for power and a concern with

---

[1] Lewis Mumford, *The Myth of the Machine: The Pentagon of Power* (New York: Harcourt Brace Jovanovich, 1970), 4.
[2] The period brought two Jupiter influences: the SP Jupiter Return and the square from the (transiting) Neptune-Pluto conjunction to Jupiter. Another such would occur in the late 19th century. See the discussion of Wounded Knee below. (Jupiter symbolizes long journeys, philosophy, religion, and social expansion; more generally, he has to do with activities that provide perspective. Jupiter in Pisces suggests, of course, the religion of the fish/Jesus.)

regality, matters discussed above. The powerful destructive capacities emerge from SP Pluto's square to Mars along with its opposition to Mercury, the latter suggesting powerful intellectual growth (Mercury), often directed via aggression toward destructive ends (Mars).[1] The empty leg falls in Taurus, the sign ruling the aeon of the Long Count's birth, directly conjoined the position of the Neptune-Pluto conjunction of 578 BC, suggesting that the developments of earlier period would receive their greatest challenge late in the Long Count. It also suggests a need to consider the demands of the Earth itself (Taurus), particularly those deeply-rooted processes that develop over time, whether measured in centuries or aeons.

The developments of the Axis Period (c. 500 BC) would, if understood correctly and used wisely, serve as an effective and important balance to later developments. We might consider, for example, the aforementioned aversion to the megamachine and to the shell of civilization, an aversion that seems even more appropriate as we approach the Long Count's conclusion. However, though we often read of the Renaissance as a rebirth of culture, it also brought the rebirth of the military drives of the megamachine, drives now able to express themselves globally due to new developments in technical design brought about by new discoveries in the sciences (Pluto-Mercury; Jupiter-Jupiter).

Though SP Pluto in Aquarius certainly suggests the power of the social group to transform itself, and though in some sense this occurred during the Renaissance, it also suggests the obsession of the organized[2] social group with power—with what we might call negative obsessions *about* social power. Though SP Pluto in Aquarius demands a transformation of the social order, either through internal change or external destruction, the obsessions (Pluto) about that social order (Aquarius) stand in the way of any hopeful inner transformation. These obsessions have their root in the dominant illusions of the age, those suggested by the Neptune-Pluto conjunction(s) in Gemini, a series that started in 1398-1399 and that will go on for many centuries, symbolizing the conviction, widely held, that people should use their minds to conquer a world that seems to stand outside—a dualistic fixation aptly symbolized by Gemini. The natal quintile between Neptune and Pluto suggests not only the creative developments we see with every Neptune-Pluto conjunction, but also the problems with power suggested by the quintile through its connection with the pentagram.[3]

---

[1] Throughout history, we find an unmistakable connection between technical development and warfare. This doesn't mean that we find the two inseparable, but they often went hand-in-hand, reflecting the natal Mercury-Mars square; that we so often see self-deception regarding values at the same time (in the way those in power contextualized the aggression) suggests the Venus-Neptune part of the multiple square.

[2] I have added the modifier "organized" because Pluto's natal sign, Capricorn, symbolizing order, carries forward through Pluto's progressions.

[3] The quintile divides the circle by five; if we trace points along a circle at intervals of 72 degrees, we will draw a pentagram. Notably, I have drawn much of the historical material here from a book with the word *pentagon* in the title: Lewis Mumford's *The Pentagon of Power*, the second volume of his *Technics and Human Development*, the first volume of which, *The Myth of the Machine*, I have already quoted from extensively in discussing earlier periods.

In other words, the Neptune-Pluto conjunction in Gemini, the first in a long series in that sign, points to the what we see quite clearly in the development of that period: an emphasis on accurate measurement of the external world, on seeing that external world as a place with clear extension and into which one could move, notions reflecting the dualism of Gemini. During the Renaissance, we see a shift, in architecture, painting, and other arts, from an emphasis on the world as a kind of ante-room to the hereafter, to a place in which activities valued for their own sake took place, characterized by rules that humans could discern, discuss, and delineate. On the one side stood humans; on the other side appeared the world—the dualistic fixation of which many spiritual teachers have spoken, here appearing through the arts. We see another Gemini-element in the persistent projection by Europeans of the dark-twin qualities (for many mythic twins have a dark twin and a light one) onto "more primitive people" wherever Europeans, traveling and conquering, found them.[1]

That the t-square formed by SP Pluto has its empty leg in Taurus suggests that people will need to cultivate Taurus in order to navigate the period successfully. That this empty leg falls so close to the degree of the 578 BC Neptune-Pluto conjunction suggests that the changes in world-view ushered in by that earlier conjunction—discontent with the constricting demands of a mechanized and aggressive society—must play an integral role in social development for the Renaissance (and, as we will see, thereafter). Not surprisingly, therefore, we find scholars returning to classical knowledge during that period, seeking insights that might prove useful. However, those who returned to the classics did not always do so in order to cultivate a helpful skepticism. Too often, the increased knowledge furthered the movement toward financial and military dominance instead of serving as a helpful counter-balance.

Taurus has to do, not surprisingly, with the management of resources, with fruitfulness, with value, money, and accumulation, and with the relationship between money as an abstract symbol of value that might accumulate,[2] and the more tangible values of earth, values that, if cultivated, might accumulate. Taurus includes in his symbolism the Tyrant Holdfast,[3] an archetypal ruler who, like King Minos in Crete (he with a close relationship with a bull), tries to take as private gain that which the gods offer for the public good. So whereas the t-square suggests that we must cultivate Taurus—develop a way to work creatively with resources in order that they

---

[1] This tendency has reached a crescendo at the end of the Long Count with the United States. The United States horoscope has Mars in Gemini in a Gemini-ruled seventh house (open enemies): the United States constantly sees itself (so to speak) as acting upon principle (Sagittarius ascendant) and just as constantly finds aggressive and "primitive" enemies (Mars), the hooks upon which to hang the nation's projections before attempting to subdue them (though with SP Mars having recently turned retrograde in the United States horoscope, the United States military has had more and more trouble doing the subduing).
[2] An example: a bank yielding interest. At the Fifth Lateran Council in 1517, the Church ended its "age old prohibition against usury." (James Trager, *The People's Chronology* (New York: Henry Holt and Company, 1994), 170.)
[3] Joseph Campbell's term, if I recall correctly.

might augment naturally, as a good farmer works to progressively enrich his soil—it also suggests that human beings will too often manifest the darker side of Taurus.

In short, Taurus has to do with many of the problems that beset us today, even as it suggests within its symbolism some solutions to those problems. Surely most political problems have a financial root,[1] and just as surely our efforts to deal with global warming constantly run up against roadblocks at least partly financial in nature and having to do with resource-management. None of this should surprise us: the Long Count began in the Age of Taurus; we would expect Taurean themes to continue. Taurus, a sign associated with money, reminds us that our abstractions (e.g. money, finance, and all that arises from these) must retain their connection to what we might call real or tangible value (e.g. food, shelter, basic necessities including aesthetic ones and soil-related ones) or we will find ourselves well stuck in the civilized mud. The financial crisis of 2009 and thereafter, and its connection to pressing environmental concerns, surely demonstrates the thickness of this mud. Some of it might turn up along coasts due to rising ocean levels.

The ongoing square from SP Pluto has clearly brought on a type of social organization that has encouraged activities usurping resources, properly considered a commons, for private gain, a process robbing the earth of its richness (Taurus). This seems to have resulted from the competitive mindset indicated above. That SP Pluto forms the t-square suggests a need to transform the natal tendency to act aggressively (Mars) on delusions (Neptune), the tendency to think in terms of what one can get instead of in terms of the common good—tendencies we can trace back to the dawn of what we generally call "civilization," when the cooperation characteristic of the Neolithic village gave way to the harshness of the hierarchically organized societies of Egypt and Mesopotamia, a development brought about, at least in part, by the presence of a surplus (Taurus). However, the square suggests a problematic result: heightened aggression based on fixed ideas. Positively, SP Pluto in Aquarius suggests a transformation of collective social value; negatively, it suggests restrictive power arising from fixed ideas about social organization, from which agglomeration results environmental destruction. Social organizations (Aquarius) apparently resist transformation even more than humans do, so SP Pluto in Aquarius presents a challenge for all human beings, but one that we will find difficult to meet. For better or worse, the Long Count's SP Pluto will remain in Aquarius for many centuries.

The Neptune-Pluto Conjunction
Though *SP* Pluto appears to function, here, as the major table-setter, those who study the Renaissance without reference to the Long Count will generally see the TR Neptune-Pluto conjunction, the first in a series of conjunctions in Gemini, as the main symbolic marker of the pe-

---
[1] Like trees (closely connected to Taurus), finances (also closely connected to Taurus) in the modern, interest-driven system augment on their own, as long as the right conditions prevail. We could say the same for debts.

riod.¹ The first two Gemini conjunctions, in 1398-9 and the second in 1891-2, have gone a long way towards defining the period from the Renaissance to the present; SP Pluto does so only in connection to the Long Count horoscope.

As noted above, Gemini usually brings a pervasive dualism, primarily between self and world, perceived and perceiver, related to the "dualistic fixation" of Buddhist philosophy. Gemini tends to see the world as "other," as independent, even though self and world come from the same seed just as twins do, suggesting that Gemini has to do with overcoming the very dualism that invites Gemini's famous curiosity. The Neptune-Pluto conjunctions in Gemini suggest that during the period in which they occur (see chart on page 128) people will tend to see the external world as an objective something-or-other subject to examination with some purported objectivity. Not surprisingly, then, during what we call the Renaissance, the world came to seem (to Europeans, at any rate) something with extension and space that one could analyze through various mentally generated coordinate systems and into which one's curiosity could extend in a manner deemed reasonable. Furthermore, once one moved into that world, one found one's life increasingly mediated by various kinds of written communications, generally with a practical purpose. Thus the first of these conjunctions, marking the Renaissance, brought the development of perspective in painting, an increased emphasis on bills of trade, and the proliferation of devices that made long-distance travel more feasible. Through these and other means, people found themselves turning away from a world-view that had dominated the medieval period.

We can see the shift with particular clarity in the field of painting. Artists began to paint the world not merely as a prelude to Heaven or Hell, but as a place worthy of exploration in its own right. Thus this age brought exploration of the world as a whole, not only physically but intellectually. People saw the world not as an anteroom to the afterlife, but as a place inviting curiosity, a place about which to have ideas (Gemini) not merely a place in which one longed for a non-earthly existence—the longing suggesting Taurus, the sign in which the previous series of conjunctions took place.² In both art and technology, people perceived a world organized according to an arbitrary and specified set of coordinates (e.g. longitude and latitude). We see this strongly implied, and sometimes explicitly stated, in the painting of the period; and we find it in the work of scientists who saw the world as operating according to laws that humans could un-

---

¹SP (secondary progressed) Pluto doesn't exist, we might say, without the natal horoscope that one can progress to a specific date, the term "progressed" implying that we progress a particular horoscope to a particular date. Transit-to-transit conjunctions, on the other hand, have meaning in themselves, without reference to any natal horoscope. We can see transiting planets in the sky; we will never see a progressed planet there.
²Taurus, ruled by Venus, or Aphrodite, has a close symbolic connection with Hephaestus, whose father, Zeus, tossed him from Olympus; on earth, he fashioned all manner of things of what we might call heavenly beauty, likely reflecting his longing for his original home in the heavens. Astrologers know Venus as the goddess of beauty, and Taurus has a well-documented connection with music, song, and earthy aesthetics.

derstand and explain. This way of experiencing the world took myriad tangible forms, including but not limited to the coordinate systems that people used to measure space, and the mechanical clocks developed during that period, machines that produced minutes and seconds (a phrasing I've borrowed from Mumford).

Business dealings took place based on a system of objectively understood abstractions. Barter—dealing in tangible items—played a central role in the Taurean period;[1] bills of sale have dominated (and dominate) the Gemini period. Thus the Gemini period prompted world travel and exploration, suggesting Gemini and its polar opposite Sagittarius, with the former arising through curiosity and ideas, and the latter through what astrologers have traditionally referred to as "long journeys over water." Gemini's inventiveness clearly played a role here, as the travel would not have happened without a variety of developments that seem to reflect Gemini much more than Taurus. Mumford writes:

> If the 12th century witnessed the introduction of the mariner's compass, the thirteenth brought the installation of the permanent rudder, used instead of the oar for steering, and the 16th introduced the use of the clock to determine longitude and the use of the quadrant to determine latitude—while the paddle wheel, which was not to become important until the 19th century, was invented as early as the 6th century, and was designed definitely by 1410. . . .[2]

Mumford also notes that the three-mast ship, which could beat more effectively against the wind and thus made long ocean voyages possible, appeared by 1500, and that as shipping improved, people developed harbors and built lighthouses. The globe opened up to people's curiosity; Europeans encountered all sorts of non-Europeans. And the Europeans promptly projected onto these people all sorts of qualities: the "dark twin" of Gemini symbolism. To Europeans, those people, the so-called "primitives" of the world, seemed to embody everything dark, mysterious, and unregenerate that Europeans had rejected from their own self-conception.

We might see this distinction also through the terms offered by S.I. Hayakawa in *Language and Thought and Action*:[3] we see on the one hand the handlers of symbols (e.g. the Europeans) and on the other the handlers of things (e.g. the people the Europeans encountered). As handlers of symbols, the Europeans seem connected with Gemini; as handlers of things, the non-Europeans seem connected with Taurus. During that period, then, millions perceived the world not as a place in which to relate to the spiritual qualities of earth (Taurus), but as a place in which to exer-

---

[1] The term "Taurean period" refers the time in which the Neptune-Pluto conjunctions took place in Taurus. The chart above (page 128) gives the dates for this period, one not to be confused with the Age of Taurus, though we find in both cases the influence of Taurus. For the "Age of Taurus," see chapter one.
[2] Lewis Mumford, *Technics and Civilization* (New York: Harcourt, Brace, and World, 1962), 120-121.
[3] S.I. Hayakawa, *Language in Thought and Action* (New York: Harcourt, Brace and Company, 1940), 196-7.

cise curiosity and "objectivity" (Gemini), about which to have ideas and to communicate; a place for commerce and trade, a place for all sorts of negotiations (with people whom one suspected of dark motives). Throughout, we see rather questionable moral values as, in the spirit of Gemini, projection ran rampant.[1] This occurred, it seems, at least partly because instead of integrating the skills and wisdom of the handlers of things, the handlers of symbols often rejected those skills and the attendant wisdom. In doing so, they ensured that they would experience them as problematic projections.

The process hasn't finished yet: we will have, for many centuries (or, actually, millennia: between now and 5339-40 AD) five more conjunctions in Gemini—or, five and a half, as the conjunction of 5339-40 takes place partly in Cancer and partly in Gemini. So it seems that human beings have, and probably *need*, a lot more time to figure out these Gemini-related matters and the projections that arise from them: the proper use of curiosity and intellect; the results of our tendency to see the world as "other" and as inviting curiosity but not responsibility; the need to integrate, not reject, the potentials of the Taurean period; the need to deal more effectively with those mental processes as a result of which one person projects his "darker" qualities onto others; the need to communicate more effectively and develop a clearer understanding of the communication process altogether (seeing, for example, the effect that language structure has on any attempt to communicate[2]); the need to deal with problems related to expansion (Jupiter[3] and Sagittarius, Gemini's polar opposite) and long journeys; and the need to deal with those ideas that arise from communal life and that eventually produce and propel what we call civilization.[4] We can probably categorize ourselves as "in the infancy" of this development, as witnessed by the pervasive communication difficulties on the planet, the evidence for which arises in the number of wars humans fight, despite our allegedly advanced state of social development.

Jupiter

The Neptune-Pluto conjunction took place square the Long Count's natal and progressed Jupiter. That it squared both the natal position and the progressed one points to one of the other important astrological developments of the period: the SP Jupiter Return (which means that natal and progressed Jupiter occupy the same zodiac position, secondary progressed Jupiter having moved through the entire 360 degrees of the zodiac), an aspect that human beings never

---

[1] Readers should not take this to mean that those with planets in Gemini project more often or more virulently than the rest of us. They don't seem to do so, as far as I can tell.
[2] Recall that SP Saturn squared Mercury back around the middle of the Long Count. This suggests some limiting of the mental function even as it suggests the development of form, of what we might call "intellectual structures," such as the birth, at that time, of what we call "written philosophy." Thus we have the development of forms of reasoning anchored in specific language-forms, Aristotle's "Laws of Thought" major among them. These forms, both limiting and empowering at once, remain with us today, at least in the so-called Western world.
[3] The Neptune-Pluto conjunctions of 1398 and 1891-2 both took place square to the Long Count Jupiter. See below.
[4] The Age of Gemini lies between that of Cancer (village life) and Taurus (the rise of "civilization").

have[1] but that an abstraction like an aeon might well have, should it go on long enough. The SP Jupiter Return suggests, along with the square from transiting Neptune-Pluto to natal Jupiter, that the new perception of the world would result in social expansion and travel (Jupiter) instead of inner search; natal Jupiter's position in Pisces reiterates the *water* theme connected with the traditional connection of Jupiter with "long journeys over water."

Above all, we see Jupiter in the drive for imperialistic expansion and domination that increased parabolically during and after the Renaissance. Much of this domination took place because of the inventions mentioned above; armed with these inventions, Europeans went out to conquer people with darker skins, accumulating booty of all types, aided along the way by improvements in communication (Gemini):

> The commercial intercourse necessary to exploit [the industrial advantages that Europe had over the remnants of the Ottoman Empire to the East] was made possible by ships and letter-writing. The Mediterranean, the eastern Atlantic, and the North Sea were alive with trading vessels of Italy, Spain, and the Netherlands, and also with the numerous pirates who preyed on them. . . .
>
> The letter was essential because commerce required the frequent exchange of information and instructions between merchants operating in widely separate places. Commerce also required a system for the transfer of payments over long distances without the impossibly dangerous carrying of coin. This was provided by bills of exchange. . . . As the seas were alive with shipping, the roads were alive with the carriers of innumerable letters between commercial centers: from Florence to Lyon and London, from Venice to Bruges and Constantinople flowed an endless interchange of pieces of paper, like the telephone system in the modern world. . . . No merchant could survive without writing many letters.[2]

As noted, Jupiter symbolizes social expansion; the square suggests tension; the Neptune-Pluto conjunction in early Gemini suggests new means of communication and an entirely new perception of the world; the Jupiter Return suggests tremendous expansion, not only via imperialism, but also in knowledge. As to this last, Holmes writes of the word "Renaissance" in terms that remind us not only of Jupiterian expansion, but also of Gemini's tendency to see the world primarily in rational terms:[3]

---

[1] Humans have a Jupiter Return, but not a *Secondary Progressed* Jupiter Return. The former takes place every 11-12 years; the latter takes place about every 4200 years (because in secondary progressions, a day equals a year: if Jupiter moves through the zodiac in 11.5 years (an approximate figure), we multiply that by 365 days to get the approximate number of years in the Progressed Jupiter Return: about 4200 years (365x11.5 = 4195.5).

[2] George Holmes, *Renaissance* (New York: St. Martin's Press, 1996), 14.

[3] We see, here, the Gemini-Sagittarius polarity, for Jupiter rules Sagittarius. We see Mercury and Gemini in the information; we see Jupiter and Sagittarius in the long journeys connected to that information.

> In this book, [the term *Renaissance*] is taken . . . to mean the evolution of a new and distinctively modern European conception of man and the universe, involving individual identity, space rationally observed, society and history as the work of cooperating and conflicting individuals, and artistic excellence as a high value. Though these may seem to be a miscellaneous collection of items, they were all in fact connected with the revival of antique culture, which provided not only models of individual personalities and of social and historical analysis, but also, for instance with the recovery of Ptolemy's *Geography*, inspiration for the reinterpretation of space.[1]

As to this "reinterpretation of space," Holmes writes of Brunelleschi that he "made the experiments that constituted his invention of perspective drawing" in connection with his architectural plans:

> Earlier artists had been interested in space but had not given the picture of space mathematical exactitude. This was what was done in the early fifteenth century. As a result, it became possible, by using plans before drawing a picture, to give the space an absolutely clear accuracy, to make it a picture of what we actually think we see.[2]

"Space rationally observed" could become space rationally conceived and put to use: people extended out into it with the various "rational" plans that we call "commerce"; they saw the world as a place in which to rationalize, a place in which to apply curiosity and purportedly rational intellect. We see the results of this even today, and not surprisingly, as we find ourselves only at the beginning of the Gemini period. The Long Count horoscope reminds us of the imperialistic designs characterizing all of this: the new developments in intellect, perception, and world-conception resulted in an overstated Jupiter: an unstinting expansion in which principles and abstractions ruled over the specificity of individual people. Europeans therefore felt quite smug and justified as they subjected non-Europeans to European principles (Jupiter), principles purportedly benevolent but seeming, from a more objective point of view, extraordinarily ruthless (SA Pluto square Mars).

That SP Uranus conjoined Jupiter around this time points again to the inventiveness of the period and to the way that inventiveness spurred expansion and travel. SP Saturn's conjunction with the Capricorn Moon suggests, though, that such developments would augment the structural securities of individuals and states. Though with a potential to liberate people from limiting and possibly-harmful social forms, Uranus-Jupiter more often than not served the dictates of the power-model of civilization.

---

[1] Holmes, 18.
[2] Holmes, 33.

III. The Battle of Wounded Knee and the End of the Long Count

The ruthlessness mentioned above reached a culmination during and after the second Neptune-Pluto conjunction in Gemini. This conjunction coincided closely with the elimination of the last organized resistance of native peoples to the European onslaught and advance: the Battle/Massacre at Wounded Knee took place within weeks of the conjunction of 1891-2. After that, though Native People still resisted domination (as we can see still in South and Central America), they did so in what we might call fits and starts. The presence of the Gatlin Gun at Wounded Knee signaled the arrival of a kind of modern weaponry that made organized resistance futile in the "rational and organized space" that the soldiers represented and served. After that event, though we see many guerilla campaigns in Vietnam and elsewhere, we see no further attempts to directly confront capitalistic imperialism (derived from the factors mentioned above) in the way Native Americans had done for centuries.

Though the Battle of Wounded Knee took place just over a hundred years before the end of the Long Count, the progressed planets won't move very far during that final period: with only a few exceptions, the progressions for 1891 don't differ very much from those of 2012; in some cases, the progressions for the latter period have moved backwards through the zodiac since the earlier date.[1] The transits, on the other hand, will differ a good deal, manifesting as triggering factors for the ongoing situation symbolized by the progressed outer planets. A discussion of the events at Wounded Knee will therefore provide an appropriate segue into a discussion of the end of the Long Count.

The Battle of Wounded Knee, which many historians understandably categorize as a massacre instead of a battle, took place a few days after Christmas in 1890 in the area around what we now call Wounded Knee, South Dakota. Early that morning, soldiers in the 7th Cavalry of the United States Army opened fire with a Gatlin Gun and other weapons on a largely defenseless and semi-starving group of Dakota Indians, killing around two hundred. The army had categorized

---

[1] As noted above, this results from the retrograde movement of secondary progressed planets. This retrograde movement takes place when the Sun moves toward an opposition with the outer planets. Note that 1890 finds the SP Sun in early Taurus, moving toward a square with SP Saturn and SP Pluto. By 2012, the SP Sun (moving at about a degree/year) has reached Virgo, having gone through the opposition to SP Saturn and SP Pluto, both of which have progressed backwards a few degrees. Some years after the Long Count's conclusion, those (SP) planets will inch forward again. This tells us that the aspects we find at the Long Count's conclusion have not yet run their course, so the years after that conclusion will show the continued working-out of that energy. We see something similar in the horoscopes of nations. For example, even after the end of the Soviet Union, the national horoscope for that entity still showed the "effect" of transits, particularly in the areas formerly within the Soviet Union. Similarly, too, we sometimes see the charts of creative people continue to express after the person has died, as for example through the effect of the person's work. (Side-note: one of Lewis Mumford's early works, his biography of Herman Melville, had much to do with a revival of interest in Melville's work, a revival connected with specific transits to Melville's horoscope.)

these people as resisters, as thus as threats (much of this having resulted from the fact that Big Foot's band had left their designated reservation, an action that, from the army's point of view, meant that they qualified as "hostiles"). Perhaps some of them, wearing Ghost Shirts that they believed made them impervious to the white man's bullets, saw themselves in a similar light, though by any objective view, they certainly did not constitute a threat. However, they *did* form some sort of organized resistance, however weakened by that time, so we can say that the event brought organized resistance to an end.[1]

By 1890, SP Pluto had reached 9 Aquarius, opposing the natal Mercury-Venus conjunction and squaring the Mars-Neptune conjunction in the Long Count natal chart. As significantly, SP Saturn has joined Pluto in an exact conjunction and thus makes the same aspects.[2] In reaching 9 Aquarius, these two progressed planets not only formed a t-square (with Mars-Neptune and Mercury-Venus); they also reached the "reaction point" of the natal yod (Mercury-Venus, Jupiter, the Moon) discussed in chapter three; in other words, they opposed focal Mercury and Venus.

In the discussion of the natal horoscope, we associated the yod with collective illness brought about by expansion (Jupiter), bureaucracy (Moon in Capricorn), and the ongoing sense of bureaucratic regality (Leo), all driven by the highly organized aggression (Mars quintile Saturn and square Mercury-Venus) that has characterized the Long Count. We said that humankind would come to a "fork in the road" when important planets came to the yod's reaction point (directly opposed to focal Mercury-Venus). As Saturn and Pluto do that, we see breakdowns of all sorts indicating a need to chart a new course. These developments have resulted from 5000

---

[1] A bit more background may prove helpful to some readers.
a. We can trace these events back to the visions of Wovoka, a Paiute shaman from the Great Basin area. Wovoka's vision told him that the white men would all disappear and that native peoples should wear the Ghost Shirts. By the time the story made its way to the Dakota tribes, it said that the shirts would protect people from the white man's bullets.
b. That the events took place on the Pine Ridge Reservation may tell us a lot. On that reservation, we find the Lakota branch of the Dakota (though Big Foot's band came from a different branch of what some now refer to as the Dakota Nation—or even the "Sioux Nation," though the Dakota did not like that term, for various reasons; in any case, the U.S. Army did not make fine distinctions when dealing with Native Americans). The Lakota remain the only independent nation ever to win a declared war against the United States. The government's irrational fear of the Lakota apparently remains to this day, evidenced by the mile long jet-strip just outside of the town of Pine Ridge—the only place in South Dakota aside from military bases, I've been told, that military jets can land. It seems that though the Lakota live mostly in dire poverty, the government still wants to be able to fly in the troops if "necessary."
[2] One might argue that both had *passed* that opposition; however, if we look at SP position for 2012, the end of the Long Count, we find that Pluto has returned to 8 Aquarius and Saturn to 6 Aquarius, so their back-and-forth movements due to retrograde tell us that we should consider the progression as "in effect." In any case, as noted above, the secondary progressions of the outer planets define the basic situation; the triggering events arise with more quickly developing factors such as transits that we can consider as catalysts.

years of history, but they have accelerated in the past few centuries, punctuated by the Battle of Wounded Knee, and will climax, the Mayans tell us, in 2012 AD.

Mumford tells us that the megamachine had been reassembled by early in the twentieth century, Stalin having "rehabilitated and magnified all [its] most impulsive features,"[1] but that the re-assembly process had started much earlier, with the first stage occurring during the French Revolution. So during the last three centuries of the Long Count, we see the megamachine returning, with its desire for complete control, its paranoid need to crush all opposition, and its attempt to extend its power into all areas of life from education, to health, to behavior, to service. During this period, SP Saturn and Pluto went through the reaction-area to the natal yod.

An observant person could tell, with increasing ease as time went on, that something, and perhaps almost *every*thing, would have to change. Environmental degradation increased in a parabolic curve; war became endemic, increasingly destructive, and unending; propaganda spread everywhere, controlling minds to a degree unthinkable in the 4th millennium BC; the paranoia of those in power, never very rational, took increasingly psychotic forms. The megamachine, built on an acquisitive model and apparently unable to see beyond the clouds of pollution it creates, has shown no signs of abating.

All of this seems aptly symbolized by the conjunction between SP Saturn and SP Pluto at the reaction point of the yod and square the Mars-Neptune conjunction.[2] The activated yod suggests the above-mentioned need for a marked new departure (the "fork in the road") in modes of production (Capricorn, plus Jupiter: expansion), ways of thinking (Mercury), and approaches not only to food (Moon), but to all matters having to do with creature needs (Moon), particularly as these get subverted by the demands of the megamachine. Mumford speaks to some of these changes when he talks about a collective situation that "opens the way for a constellation of formative ideas, which themselves come into existence partly by reaction against the dominant culture, and yet are constantly conditioned, and even temporarily supported by the very customs and institutions they seek to replace."[3]

The yod symbolizes the gradual accretion of *a pressure to change*; the activation at the trigger point suggests that the pressure reaches a threshold: change must happen as the present system reaches a *point of no return*. Of the possible resulting breakdowns, Mumford writes:

---

[1] Mumford, *Pentagon of Power*, 248.
[2] In the 1890 progressed chart, the two planets square the Mars-Neptune midpoint quite precisely. They oppose Venus with just over half a degree of orb—and they turned retrograde during the 20th century, passing back through a precise opposition with Venus and Mercury. Also worth noting, here and in any discussion of this combination of factors: even if we were to limit our discussion to the t-square (thinking, perhaps, of the Moon's natal position as open to doubt), we would still have more-than-ample cause for concern.
[3] Mumford, *Pentagon of Power*, 427.

> What has brought on these breakdowns usually turns out to be due to a radical failure in feedback: an inability to acknowledge errors, an unwillingness to correct them, a resistance to introducing new ideas and methods that would provide the means for a constructively human transformation. If once recognized, many of the defects could be corrected, provided that prompt action were taken with the agents already at hand; but failing this, a more dire pathological situation, demanding surgery rather than diet, comes into existence.[1]

Mumford's words recall our remarks about the natal chart with its lack of oppositions and lack of air: difficulty making use of feedback from the world. Furthermore, yods, with their emphasis on ritualization, do not integrate feedback very well; the quincunxes suggest developments not seen straight on, developments that don't come into focus. The configuration lacks the opposition that could bring matters into focus—or, it lacks the opposition until a planet or planets arrives at the focal point. This development suggests events that set the yod into dramatic motion simply because the problems emerge clearly, objectively, and inescapably.

The quincunxes suggest, through their emphasis on ritualization, that the engrained patterns will prove highly resistant (resistant because ritualized: driven by unconscious factors and because of purported necessity). Because of the lack of oppositions, the resultant yod suggests a situation characterized by a lack of objective awareness about the nature of the problem. Paradoxically, the yod *does* often generate awareness, but this generally occurs through illness or imbalance resulting from the lack of awareness. This illness or imbalance appears clearly when important transits or progressions arrive at the reaction point, for then we *do* have oppositions (to the focal planet). Unfortunately, this objectivity, too, often results from unfortunate events instead of from an insight that might prevent them. The problem, inherent in the yod but hidden in the myriad details of the life-ritual, at last appears clearly in the external situation. The nature of Pluto (here appearing by secondary progression) suggests that the change will have to cut extremely deep, not merely to social rituals, but to the psychological patterns that gave them birth. Pluto-Saturn itself, apart from any connection to the natal horoscope, suggests profound changes in social structure.

The square to Mars-Neptune suggests a more flagrant problem, one arising from highly organized (Saturn) destructive forces (Pluto) working in a highly tense tandem with the aforementioned aggression driven by delusion (Mars-Neptune) and a deeply rooted death wish (Scorpio). Certainly we see in contemporary events numerous clear indications of the delusion and the death-wish: though wars have generally made problems worse rather than alleviating them, and though this has certainly occurred in the 20th century, nations still resort to organized violence when confronted with what they deem as problems. Furthermore, they have developed weapons

---

[1]Mumford, 428.

with such destructive capacity that one can only wonder why any creature would create even one, let alone thousands.

The aggression seems endemic (i.e. the natal horoscope has an afflicted Mars); the progressed square suggests that the endemic tendency has reached a level of intolerable destructiveness. So whereas the yod appears in all matters related to collective health including not only the health of the planet as a whole but also such developments as mass starvation and psychological dislocation, the square appears in more direct threats related to destructive weaponry of all sorts: destructive (SP Pluto) use of weaponry (Mars) occurring because of the delusions (Neptune) within the prevailing social order (SP Saturn). The square appears in the unending wars that characterize the modern period, with terror (Pluto) having reached a rigid form of organization (Saturn), not only among the dispossessed, but also in the armies of nation-states. And, of course, if humans continue to fight against each other, they will have difficulty marshalling their forces to make changes required by everyone (e.g. changes in social structure needed to address climate change).

Further, whereas Mars suggests weapons, Pluto conjoined with Saturn suggests viruses (Pluto) in the hands of the prevailing hierarchy (Saturn); the progressed factors therefore include in their symbolism the threat of disaster resulting from disease-causing agents released by organized hierarchies (not necessarily deliberately, but through delusion or misplaced idealism, or even simple carelessness, all marks of Neptune). They also suggest compressed heat (Pluto) bursting free of its containers (Saturn) as in volcanoes. (This last possibility doesn't seem the most likely, but it seems the one most in line with the predictions of the Mayans themselves: that this age would end in fire.[1]) Finally, we can see the compressed heat (natal Mars plus SP Saturn and Pluto) as the heat compressed in our atmosphere, a heat that may kill millions, perhaps sooner than we have expected.

The second major factor—the Neptune-Pluto conjunction of 1891-1892, the first since 1398 and the second in the Gemini-series (see page 128 above)—links Wounded Knee with the Renaissance. This second conjunction, at 8-9 Gemini, squared natal Jupiter just as the previous one did, though not quite so closely. (On the day of the Wounded Knee massacre, Mars at 9 Pisces conjoined Long Count Jupiter and squared the Neptune-Pluto conjunction, another configuration suggesting aggression in the immediate situation.) The conjunction forms yet another yod, this one to the sextile between the natal Moon and Mars-Neptune.[2] This astrological situation

---

[1] Recent volcanic indications in Yellowstone give one pause, particularly because the entire Yellowstone basin qualifies as a single volcano. If it erupts, the destruction will make the destruction of, say, Krakatau seem unimportant.

[2] Those who feel uncomfortable including the Moon, considering the arbitrary birth time, should remember that, Moon or no Moon, the TR Neptune-Pluto conjunction quincunxed natal Mars and natal Neptune. Isolated quincunxes may point to illness even more than yods do, for the latter has a more balanced dynamism than the unbalanced quincunx.

therefore suggests not only the highly organized, genocidal aggression suggested by SP Saturn-Pluto through its square to Mars, and not only unbridled expansion or imperialism suggested by the conjunction between TR Neptune and TR Pluto, but also a tendency to remain blind to the assumption, present since the Long Count's inception, that aggression (Mars) promotes security (Moon).[1] Consisting of quincunxes, the yod again suggests an increased illness of the planet and of the prevailing social order: an illness brought about by the shift in perception mentioned above in connection with the Renaissance: seeing the world as a realm in which to extend one's interest and aggression. We see in 1890 the results of that perception: curiosity and new technology prompted world-conquest; in 1890, organized resistance to that process in the New World effectively ended, later guerilla actions notwithstanding.

The progressed conjunction between Saturn and Pluto suggests that this assumption (that aggression promotes or ensures security: natal Mars sextile natal Moon) would emerge through increased violence, for the two planets forming the square to natal Mars-Neptune (SP Saturn and Pluto) disposit, respectively, the Moon and Mars, the planets that, through their sextile, suggest the assumption itself.[2] Neptune's discovery in the mid-19th century brought another factor to the table: that if one sought security through aggression, one would do well to deceive the persons involved on both sides of the conflict, often through reference to some purportedly higher truth (Neptune) such as we see in the deception of "Manifest Destiny" that left such huge piles of corpses.

The transiting Neptune-Pluto conjunction in Gemini tells us that the perception of the world as a space that invites human curiosity, a perception that had so much to do with the abominably cruel world conquest spurred into motion by developments of the Renaissance, had in a sense come full circle: because of curiosity, and because of the tendency to project negativity onto dark-skinned peoples, Europeans had conquered nearly the whole planet, some Pacific Islands excepted. (This exception didn't last long: a few years after the massacre, the United States sent troops and gunships into the Pacific, there to garner territory for the American empire.) The space had certainly invited curiosity (Gemini), but that curiosity manifested through military aggression (Mercury, ruler of Gemini, squares Mars in the Long Count natal horoscope).

A more hopeful vantage comes from SP Uranus, which by 1890 had reached a sextile with natal Uranus. The sextile here suggests increased inventiveness, Uranus having to do with the new, the revolutionary, and the insightful. The evidence for this inventiveness surrounds us, and certainly Uranus' discovery in 1781 stimulated the whole process. We cannot deny that the modern

---

[1] The sextile and trine often point to assumptions. The sextile, though, connects to the air element and thus to ideas consciously held. So, here we have the articulation of a specific idea arising from the assumption that native peoples had to "make way" for the "more advanced" European invaders.

[2] In other words, Saturn disposits the Moon in Saturn-ruled Capricorn and Pluto disposits Mars (and Neptune) in Pluto-ruled Scorpio.

age has brought astounding inventions in myriad technical fields ranging from the mapping of the human genome, to the developments in computers of all sorts, to the augmented power of highly technical weaponry. In considering these developments and their relationship to the crises that confront and threaten to engulf human beings and their various social orderings, we can again recall some passages from Mumford, passages emphasizing on the one hand the (to astrologers) well known connection between Uranus and individual liberty or initiative, and on the other the observation that the problems that face us now have to do not with a lack of knowledge but with a lack of will on the part of those with political power. In other words, we have difficulty solving these problems not because we don't know how, but because of the kinds of social orderings we have adopted and because of our assumptions about aggression and security.

In the face of social rigidity, though, individual inventiveness still gives us reason to hope. Mumford wrote (in 1970):

> Though no immediate and complete escape from the ongoing power system is possible, least of all through mass violence, the changes that will restore autonomy and initiative to the human person all lie within the province of each individual soul, once it is roused. Nothing could be more damaging to the myth of the machine, and to the dehumanized social order it has brought into existence, than a steady withdrawal of interest, a slowing down of tempo, a stoppage of senseless routines and mindless acts. And has not all of this in fact begun to happen?[1]

Of technical capacities and their connection to progressive social change, he wrote:

> But if mankind overcomes the myth of the machine, one thing may be safely predicted: the repressed components of our old culture will become the dominants of the new one; and similarly the present megatechnic institutions and structures will be reduced to human proportions and brought under direct human control. Should this prove true, the present canvass of the existing society, its technological miscarriages and its human misdemeanors, should by implication give valid positive directions for working out a life-economy.[2]

Having reached the sextile with his natal position (a progression that remains in effect through the Long Count's end), Uranus brings into effect yet another yod, this one with natal Saturn at the focal point and the two Uranus positions (natal and secondary progressed) as the base planets: inventiveness develops to such an extent that it effects—or should effect, and certainly *can* effect—a change in social structure (Saturn), a reconsideration of everything symbolized by Saturn in Leo (bureaucratic royalism; the bureaucracy seen as having royal prerogatives; the

---
[1] Mumford, 433.
[2] Mumford, 429.

king/president exerting himself through bureaucracy), matters we have discussed in an earlier chapter. Certainly we can see this occurring now through new technologies that often have a decentralizing effect.[1]

Certainly Uranus' sextile suggests that we have at hand the necessary technical knowledge and psychological insight. Whether we can effectively bring these to bear on the prevailing order (Saturn) remains in question. We know from myth that Saturn and Uranus don't generally work together very well, Saturn taking away Uranus' life-giving power (i.e. Saturn castrates Uranus). On the other hand, as Uranus' son, Saturn suggests a new social order born from insight, despite the resistance of the social order *to* insight, as suggested in the ancient myth. If we give birth to such a social order, we find the hidden harmony between mythic figures who have found themselves at odds for so long. The yod suggests that the ruling hierarchies of the planet need to get with the program if they hope to avoid the catastrophes of which the ancient Maya spoke so often.

We can summarize the many factors of 1890 and thereafter in a list:

- The "progressed" yod that characterizes the end of the Long Count (Uranus-Uranus-Saturn) had come into effect and indicates not only exponentially increased technical capacities, but also revolutionary changes in social structure resulting from a simple but cumulative development: the huge imbalances resulting from the prevailing social structures (the megamachine) had reached a level where the supporting organic matrix will no longer support it (Saturn disposits the Moon), thus necessitating a major change both in the structures themselves and in the ideas that underlie and support them (or, more precisely, that no longer do).
- The conjunction of SP Saturn and SP Pluto at the reaction point of the natal yod (Mercury-Venus; Jupiter and the Moon) and square Mars-Neptune, two developments that contain, in their various symbolic referents, many of the major problems of our age, problems ranging from ecological disaster to addictive (Neptune) militarism (Mars) to (possibly) plagues brought on by viruses (Pluto) to the danger of nuclear annihilation (Pluto-Mars plus Saturn) or eruptions from the underworld (Pluto-Saturn).
- The transiting Neptune-Pluto conjunction of 1891-2 suggests a further development of the trends already discussed: people perceived a world conquered by the twin (Gemini) developments (scientific and exploratory) mentioned above: the explorers had killed off most of the native populations in the countries to which they traveled either as conquerors or harbingers of conquerors, aided by weaponry that, with the

---

[1] Some will find it interesting that as we approach the end of the Long Count, the United States, still the dominant military and economic power in the world, has elected a president with his Sun in Leo, his Ascendant in Uranus-ruled (and Saturn-ruled) Aquarius, and his Moon conjoined the two Neptune-Pluto conjunctions in Gemini.

development of the Gatlin Gun (followed shortly by the warplane and other devices), had reached new levels of effective destructiveness. The explorers had opened the entire globe, save uninhabited regions, for commerce, exploitation, and "rational" distribution.

- The conjunction between secondary progressed Saturn and Pluto suggests the death (Pluto) of the old gods (Saturn), considering the "old gods" not only as the older Neolithic orderings of human society, but also as the gods of the technocratic order. At the same time, it suggests the kind of organized (Saturn) ruthlessness (Pluto) that has characterized the period leading up to and following 1890. (We should remember, here, that because the conjunction took many years to form, we can see it as indicating the entire conquest of what we now call The United States, particularly the events of the 19th century.) Organized (Saturn) barbarity (Pluto) made possible by the growth (progressions) of civilization (Long Count horoscope). Surely this term—*organized barbarity*—applies to much of 20th century history, when one Plutonian figure after another came to power, starting perhaps with Teddy Roosevelt, extending through Woodrow Wilson, Franklin Roosevelt, Adolph Hitler, Joseph Stalin, Winston Churchill, and on up to the Bush Dynasty in the United States.
- Triggering factors on the day of Wounded Knee suggest its importance: Mars has just passed its conjunction with the Long Count's natal Jupiter and closely squares the (Neptune-Pluto) conjunction degree; the transiting Sun at 7 Capricorn sets off both yods: first the one formed by transiting Neptune and Pluto (the Sun quincunxes those planets, conjoins the natal Moon, and sextiles Mars-Neptune); then the natal yod (in conjoining the natal Moon, TR Sun quincunxes Mercury-Venus and sextiles Jupiter). Thus the Sun triggers aggression related to the health of the ecosystem altogether.

IV. The Conclusion of the Long Count

Triggering factors at the end of the Long Count give, as we will see, a distinctively troubling emphasis, though not without some causes for hope.

As noted, the main table setters remain in effect: SP Uranus remains in the sextile to its own position, effecting the yod to natal Saturn (from natal and SP Uranus), though here the orb of aspect has narrowed to almost zero; SP Saturn and SP Pluto remain near the positions described above. As we have seen, SP Pluto had begun to affect this position as far back as the Renaissance, Saturn having arrived more recently.[1] Transiting factors unique to December 21, 2012 provide dramatic corroboration and triggering:

---

[1] The Renaissance found Saturn in the second decanate of Capricorn. During that period, he conjoined the natal Moon and quincunxed natal Mercury and Venus, thus affecting the natal yod involving those planets plus Jupiter). By 1890, Saturn had joined Pluto in the tenth degree of Aquarius, at the focal point of the yod. (See previous section.)

- TR Pluto approaches the Long Count's Capricorn Moon, suggesting a death and rebirth of those security patterns provided by the forms of social ordering (Capricorn) that marked the Long Count's birth. The transit could also indicate the death (Pluto) of some elements of the sub-lunar realm itself (i.e. the biosphere, associated with the Moon), that death resulting from the mentioned forms of social organization (Capricorn). Because of developments in human social orderings indicated by natal Moon and other factors in the Long Count horoscope, the ecosystem has, by the Long Count's conclusion, deteriorated into illness, no longer providing any sort of security for the prevailing kind of social ordering. In short, death (Pluto) of a wide-variety of life-supporting ecological processes (Moon), with the possibility but not the guarantee of rebirth. After the death, humans will need to give birth to new forms of social organization, forms that provide security for the coming age. The Capricorn Moon symbolizes security through social forms, not the most reliable type of security, for social forms change even when nature's patterns remain unaltered; the Moon in Capricorn suggests ecological patterns pervasively affected by forms of social organization, particularly hierarchical forms (e.g. the megamachine). The position also suggests insufficient attention to natural processes altogether, Capricorn preferring the organizational to the organic.[2] The natal position suggests that humans had traded the security found in nature's patterns for the security found in social forms. At the Long Count's end, we experience the results of this trade: the stifling of the sub-lunar realm by the results of hierarchical ordering. That SP Saturn conjoined this position at the time of the Renaissance suggests organizational process initiated then, affecting the eco-system and reaching a crisis point at the Long Count's conclusion as TR Pluto goes over the same position. In any case, Pluto's conjunction suggests death of these forms, which have apparently run their course.
- TR Mars precisely conjoins natal Uranus, setting off the mentioned yod (composed of natal Saturn, natal Uranus, and SP Uranus) and suggesting either sudden (Uranus) anger or aggression (Mars) or highly innovative action emerging through a change in social form.
- TR Saturn, at the Mars-Neptune midpoint, precisely squares both natal Venus and SP Pluto, thus triggering the t-square already mentioned (the one formed by natal Mars-Neptune, natal Mercury-Venus, and SP Pluto and SP Saturn). Karma comes home to roost, with Saturn symbolizing karma: the inescapable, formal results of action. (Transiting Saturn of 2012 conjoins SP Saturn of 551 BC, suggesting a close connection between the demand for some limiting of delusion-driven aggression announced during the earlier period and the results, experienced during the later

---

[2] Astrologers refer to Capricorn as the Moon's detriment position, suggesting that the Moon must function in ways not in harmony with its nature. For an individual, this can produce great awareness; for an aeon, it suggests the detriment of the lunar function (e.g. the ecology) as a result of the environment provided by social forms (Capricorn).

period, of any failure to limit. More hopefully, the two positions suggest the possibility of finally establishing some limits as part of recognized structural elements of the status quo.
- SP nodal axis has just passed the natal Moon. SP Moon (which moves a degree each month) conjoins Sun-Venus midpoint.

Before discussing the triggering factors, let's review the influences of the secondary progressed factors: SP Uranus, on the one hand, and SP Saturn and Pluto on the other. In sextiling its own position, SP Uranus creates a yod to natal Saturn. In discussing the natal horoscope, we spent a lot of time investigating the precise Saturn-Uranus quincunx in the natal horoscope, suggesting that it had to do with a deeply-rooted imbalance between the human need for free expression (Uranus) and the kinds of social structure (Saturn) that developed around 3114 BC, with the latter getting the upper hand (because Saturn disposits natal Uranus in Capricorn), so that human beings, so free during the Neolithic period, found that they had to find their freedom within increasingly rigid social forms. The aspect also suggests the ongoing co-option of human inventiveness by the centralized bureaucracy, so that inventions served the centralized bureaucracy more often than not.

SP Uranus' sextile to his natal position suggests an awareness of this but also an increased tension in the prevailing order as human beings throughout the world demand, either by direct statement or collective necessity, pervasive change based on insight, demanding that human insight, inventiveness, and technical brilliance serve a more useful purpose than heretofore. SP Uranus' position may suggest that humans do not lack the technical means to solve their problems. But recalcitrant Saturn in Leo must adjust: the ruling (Leo) order (Saturn) must use the available technical means to make those changes demanded by the situation, working to help the larger situation (Aquarius) instead of merely the ruling class (Saturn in Leo).

Thus the inner tension hidden within the prevailing order, the ongoing cooption of invention by the social order, resulting in what we can now see so clearly: the technical power exercised by the prevailing order over anyone who would seek freedom *from* that order. This destructive process comes to a point at which no further progress will result without a major change of course (the yod: a fork in the road), a change that includes disruption of all that had degenerated into blind ritual for collectivities (the natal quincunx). Activated yods suggest the need to make decisions, so heretofore hidden and ritualized imbalance metamorphoses into a demand for change of structure (Saturn) resulting from developed insight and technical advance (SP Uranus at the sextile point). Circumstances demand that expertise now serve different ends.

As we have seen in earlier chapters, a second natal quincunx runs parallel to the one from Saturn to Uranus, this one from Mercury and Venus up to the Moon, the signs again being Leo and Capricorn. This second quincunx (Mercury-Venus to the Moon) forms one half of a natal yod made up of Mercury-Venus, the Moon, and Jupiter. The second major progressed factor of 2012 involves SP Saturn and SP Pluto, both of which have arrived at this yod's reaction point (the point directly opposite Mercury-Venus).[1] In coming to that reaction point, these two progressed planets square the Mars-Neptune conjunction in Scorpio. The natal sign placements again suggest the tension between royalist tendencies (Leo) and bureaucratic ones (Capricorn) within the prevailing order. The aspects suggest not only challenges to the prevailing patterns of living developed over the past 5000 years, but also the danger of destructive (Pluto) and organized (Saturn) aggression (Mars) driven by illusions (Neptune).

The astrological point: in opposing Mercury and Venus, SP Saturn and SP Pluto not only activate the yod, but also turn the natal square (Mercury-Venus to Mars-Neptune) into a t-square. Thus the interweaving of ecological factors (yod) with factors based in overt aggression (the squares). The natal yod symbolizes entrenched patterns involving a search for security (Moon) through expansion (Jupiter) driven by royalist tendencies (Leo); a drive that consumes (Jupiter) resources (Moon) in a search for security (Moon) driven by the unfortunate relationship between hierarchy (Capricorn) and central power (Leo). These patterns have become so entrenched that people take them for normalcy and often don't question them until a crisis arises in the form of illness, this one involving the planet as a whole. We can see this as typical for the yod formation, symbolizing as it does patterns that have developed into blind rituals; the squares arise in the more clearly delineated forms of war and empire.

We have seen that SP Pluto in Aquarius can suggest a transformation of all fixed ideas about social ordering. Its position at the Long Count's end suggests that some kind of social transformation must and will happen, either one directed by human beings in their attempt to reorder their societies, or as a result of transformations of present conditions, as in some kind of environmental catastrophe. We can expect powerful and organized forces to oppose any vestiges of royalty or elite rule. As Dane Rudhyar wrote some decades back, Pluto not only brings transformation, he also sets up the conditions that require changing. So Pluto symbolizes (and fuses) the destructive conditions that surround us and the power to transform those conditions; the symbolism suggests that we may find the power within the destructive conditions.

We have also seen that the conjunction between SP Saturn and SP Pluto, an aspect that will remain in effect for many years after the end of the Long Count, can suggest a resistance (Saturn) to that transformation (Pluto)—a resistance emanating from the old order itself. Natal Saturn in Leo suggests crystallized bureaucratic structures around an autocratic center. At the Long Count's end, many humans surely see the need to change a kind of ordering that has outgrown whatever usefulness it might once have possessed.

---

[1] Saturn has reached it and then retreated. In the years after the Long Count's conclusion, it will move over the reaction-point point again.

To effect the transformation demanded by a yod, one must cultivate a precise understanding of the factors involved in the presenting situation and develop a willingness to let go of anything preventing change. The change comes from the nature of the materials themselves, from what we can call "the contemporary situation." Those materials develop to a point where they ignite the needed change even though they had remained invisible, felt as an inner but unacknowledged tension, for quite some time.

At the end of the Long Count, both yods (the natal one and the one formed by SP Uranus) suggest extreme tension and crisis: the need for pervasive change in our mode of social ordering. The problems that beset us here at the end of the Long Count reveal long-standing tensions within all processes born around 3114 BC, inherent to what we call *civilization*. In particular, we should note those tensions mentioned earlier in connection with the sun god-king (Leo) and the organization (Capricorn; Saturn), both of people and of land, that surrounded him: the basics of the *megamachine*. The tensions also come, as noted, from three major assumptions that humans have for thousands of years taken as a matter of course, as the way things purportedly are: that addictive militarism or aggression (Mars-Neptune) somehow provides security (Moon); that to govern well, one must combine royal and bureaucratic modes (e.g. Saturn in Leo); that expansion leads to well-being (Jupiter-Moon).

But as we always find with challenging aspects, we can see more hopeful possibilities as well: a transformation (Pluto) of thinking (Mercury), particularly about order (Saturn); a change in the approach to aggression (Mars); a recognition of the limits of the present social ordering; a pervasive challenging of problematic assumptions. We should recognize all this as possible, and in the horoscope for a person, we might have reasonable hope that some or all of this would occur. Though when dealing with an aeon or any collectivity we will feel less hopeful, the doubt itself may rest on an assumption we should question: that in order to effect change, we need to find a "central point around which the impetus to change might organize." This assumption may arise from factors already mentioned: the Sun in Leo conjoined Saturn; the various quincunxes between Leo planets and Capricorn planets. Perhaps the energy of change will take quite a different form as we enter a new era.[1]

The Triggering Factors at the Long Count's End

We call them "triggering factors" because they "trigger" the longer-lasting secondary progressed factors into manifestation. In non-astrological terms, we would say that specific events catalyze reactions arising from long-standing patterns of behavior. In doing this catalyzing, these triggering factors tell us something of the significance of the Long Count's concluding point, not only because we consider these factors as triggers for more long-lasting developments, but also because their positions at the end of the Long Count give us information about

---

[1] Events in the Middle East, particularly in Egypt, in early 2011 may give us hints about this new form.

the "cataclysm" that will purportedly bring the Long Count to an end—about the specific events doing the triggering. The longer-lasting factors (SP Pluto, Uranus, and Saturn) set up the reaction; the factors of shorter duration (various transits, plus secondary progressed positions of inner planets) catalyze that reaction into manifestation.

We can look at these factors in at least two ways: as triggers, in which case we take into consideration their relationship to natal and progressed positions; or as the factors in play at the Long Count's end-point and thus as having significance in themselves as regards both isolated events and the next Long Count, for the transits of December 21, 2012, taken by themselves, give us an entirely new horoscope. We will deal with the first of these here and the second in the next chapter.

Because the Maya gave us a very precise end-date for the Long Count, as we look at that end-date we can look at the astrological factors in a way that we haven't up to this point. For the earlier dates, even as we took a precise date to set the progressions, we spoke of a larger period and gave interpretations relevant to that longer period, not to the precise date alone. For example, when we looked at the Long Count's midpoint, we didn't interpret events associated with a specific date that the Mayans had set; we looked instead at astrological developments for that general period. (In any case, we can consider the date as somewhat arbitrary: we set the progressions for the precise midpoint of the Long Count.) Here, because we work with a precise date, we can look at the Long Count's conclusion not only as the culmination of developments taking place over many centuries, but also as indications of a very specific date and thus to specific events instead of just general developments. Nevertheless, we should remember that just as the Long Count's birth-date doesn't seem to point to particular events that happened on that day, but rather seems to encapsulate changes of longer duration, so with the Long Count's end-date.

We can start with TR Saturn's conjunction to the Mars-Neptune conjunction and square to the Mercury-Venus conjunction, setting off the natal square between those two conjunctions (Mercury-Venus; Mars-Neptune). Saturn gives form to whatever the square indicates: aggression (Mars) based on delusions (Neptune) put in service to the dictates (Mercury) and values (Venus) emanating from the centralized ruling-complex (Leo), the aforementioned cult of kingship that arose five thousand years ago in connection with solar cults resulting from the observations of astronomer-priests who tracked the regular movements in the heavens, seeing there a pattern from which developed social centralization. Thus we see in the square the activity of the centralized power-system (Sun in Leo) with immense creative and destructive power (Scorpio) at its beck and call. At the Long Count's end, TR Saturn crystallizes this conflict into definite form.

However, this transit of Saturn had occurred every twenty-eight years since the beginning of the Long Count cycle, so we should ask what about this final one seems unique. To answer this question, we look to the factors already mentioned, starting with the conjunction of SP Saturn and SP Pluto in Aquarius and square to transiting Saturn and the natal conjunction. Transiting Saturn, suggesting restrictions coming from the ruling hierarchy, sets off (the square suggesting structural change) the tension, already discussed, arising because of the bureaucratic restrictions (Saturn) put on the drive for necessary change and transformation (Pluto) of those aggressive impulses (Mars-Neptune) so exacerbated by what we call civilization (Long Count).[1] The square doesn't necessarily suggest destructive warfare, but certainly includes such warfare in its symbolism, Mars as the god of war, Pluto the god of destruction, and Saturn having to do with tension.

We also need to look at factors more specific than TR Saturn. Though the progressed Saturn-Pluto conjunction had been in effect for centuries, and though Saturn had crossed through the Mars-Neptune conjunction many times during that span, it had not done so very often with *transiting* Pluto closely conjoining the natal Moon and transiting Mars precisely conjoining natal Uranus and quincunxing natal Saturn. This significant series of triggers seems too much to attribute to coincidence, and its interpretation doesn't seem very encouraging: transiting Saturn sets off aggressive drives (Mars) already under extreme tension from secondary progressed Saturn and Pluto just as Pluto hits the Moon and demands a death and rebirth of all security patterns found embedded in social structures *and* as transiting Mars hits Uranus, suggesting sudden aggression related to, or arising from, the long-standing imbalance suggested by the natal Saturn-Uranus quincunx—or, more hopefully, innovative action.[2]

So SP Saturn and SP Pluto not only contact the reaction point of the natal yod, a matter discussed above, but they also form a t-square to the Mars-Neptune conjunction (a t-square that includes, as noted, Mercury and Venus) that we find under additional pressure from *transiting* Saturn at the focal point (conjoining Mars-Neptune). Since transiting Saturn symbolizes (among other things) the pressure of events, the reaping of karma from decisions made about structure, particularly by those in authority, Saturn as trigger suggests pressure from bureaucratic intransigence, not only in 2012 (suggested by TR and SP Saturn) but also as part of the Long Count as a whole (suggested by natal Saturn conjoining the Sun and quincunxing Uranus). Because we read natal factors as part of all transiting and progressed developments, TR and SP Saturn suggest the result, at the end of the Long Count, of authority-regimes' restrictive

---
[1]This sentence interprets the following astrological factors: SP Saturn conjoins SP Pluto, and both square the Mars-Neptune conjunction—which TR Saturn conjoins. Remember, too, that SP Saturn and SP Pluto also oppose natal Mercury and Venus, forming a t-square.
[2]The positions are all extremely close, particularly taken in aggregate. Though Pluto remains just under two degrees from the Moon, we would still consider it an effective conjunction; and the triggering factors have very small orbs of aspect: Saturn to Venus 0A13; Saturn to Mars 1S08; Pluto to Moon 1A52; Mars to Uranus 1S03; Mars to Saturn 0S46; Venus to Jupiter 0A38; and TR Saturn separating from a squarewith SP Pluto 0S38. We also find a transiting yod (formed by TR Jupiter), though of wide orb, a matter discussed below and in the next chapter.

activity over a 5125 year period. As a triggering factor, *transiting* Saturn suggests an intransigence visible in developments specific to December 2012 or thereabouts, developments that the people of 2012 will see as having a wide range of contemporary relevancies but that astrologers can see as typifying patterns with their roots long in the past. The contemporary events will surely involve intransigent authority structures hindering necessary transformation and thus exacerbating military drives (Mars) still under the sway of "realistic thinking" (Mercury).

Still, by itself, transiting Saturn doesn't give us a definitive or unique triggering factor. As noted, Saturn had moved through this area of the zodiac over thirty times since the Renaissance, and only one of that passages—lasting from December 1776 through December 1778—took place with Pluto also in Capricorn, thus creating a mutual reception between these two bodies,[1] and during the earlier period, Saturn didn't conjoin Mars and Neptune anywhere near the time that Pluto conjoined the Moon. (In other words, we don't find in the earlier period any time with the mutual reception *and* the coinciding conjunctions.). So the situation at the end of the Long Count seems unique as long as we take into consideration all the factors: unlike during the other periods with Saturn and Pluto in mutual reception, December 21, 2012 finds them in more-or-less simultaneous conjunctions (Saturn with Mars and Neptune, Pluto with the Moon).[2]

TR Pluto's conjunction with the Capricorn Moon sets off the natal yod (Mercury-Venus focal, plus Jupiter and the Moon), so the death-and-rebirth process connected to bureaucratically structured security (Moon in Capricorn[3]) affects and arises from the long-standing imbalances already discussed. So we find the yod under pressure not only from SP Pluto and SP Saturn at the reaction point (opposite Mercury-Venus) but also from *transiting* Pluto (conjoining the Moon) and *transiting* Saturn (squaring focal Venus and Mercury).

---

[1] Pluto in Saturn's sign (Capricorn) and Saturn in Pluto's sign (Scorpio).
[2] As noted, since the Renaissance, Saturn and Pluto have only had one other period of mutual reception. Pluto spent 1762-1778 in Capricorn—for the most part, the precise dates being: 1/7/1762-7/7/1762; 11/9/1762-4/4/1777; 5/26/1777-1/26/1778; 8/20/1778-12/1/1778. Saturn spent the following periods in Scorpio: 12/7/1776-4/20/1777; 9//3/1777-11/25/1779. If we put those dates together, we see that 12/7/1776-4/20/1777, 9/13/1777-1/26/1778 and 8/20/1778-12/1/1778 found Saturn in Scorpio with Pluto still in Capricorn. However, this took place with Pluto in *late* Capricorn, well past conjunction with the Long count Moon and thus not forming the conjunction to the Long Count Moon when Saturn went through 7-11 Scorpio to conjoin Mars and Neptune. Thus the uniqueness of the positions on 12/21/2012. We might note two things about the earlier period. First, Saturn had entered Scorpio at a time when Pluto remained within orb (though loosely) of conjoining the Long Count Uranus and quincunxing the Long Count Saturn, thus setting off that aspect. Second, the same period found Pluto in conjunction with the United States' natal Pluto. The United States' birth took place very close to the mutual reception dates. (The United States has Pluto in late Capricorn and Saturn in the second decanate of Libra.) Notably, the United States has probably done more than any other nation to further the destructive processes and imbalances under discussion here.
[3] To be distinguished from security resulting from harmony with natural patterns, for example.

When we add transiting Mars to this mix, we see a trigger specific to the period right around December 21, 2012. At midnight on that day, we find Mars at 26 Capricorn 22, separated by less than a degree from his quincunx with Saturn and by 1°03' from his conjunction with Uranus. Mars-Uranus has a well-established connection with sudden aggression, sudden anger, and sudden self-assertion, and an equally well-established connection with progressive, revolutionary action. Here, we would expect aggression or assertion through technical means (Uranus), though we might also see the more hopeful manifestation. Mars's quincunx to Saturn suggests that the aggression comes as a result of or for reasons connected to the kinds of social structuring we discussed earlier in connection with the Saturn-Uranus quincunx (co-option of genius by the status quo). One thinks, at the time of this writing, of recent upheavals in Egypt and other Middle Eastern countries, and of the turmoil in Greece as a result of financial difficulties in the European Union. Such uprisings—the people taking issue with the kinds of social structuring in which they find themselves enmeshed—seem likely to characterize the Long Count's final period.

We have seen that the Long Count horoscope suggests not only a tension between two approaches to governance (the regal, symbolized by Leo, and the bureaucratic, symbolized by Capricorn), a tension that has resulted in a kind of illness (quincunx) in the social order and the planetary ecosystem. We have also seen aptly symbolized in the Long Count horoscope the rise of highly organized aggression and sadism, with the natal tendency suggested by the Mars-Neptune/Mercury-Venus square and the periodic manifestations suggested by various transits, progressions, and directions. Though we can see this aggression and sadism as based on illusions (Neptune) regarding regality, predominately illusions regarding the king or centralized power or energy source (Leo), its results (hecatombs of corpses) certainly don't qualify as illusory. Transiting Pluto's conjunction to the natal Moon and quincunx to natal Venus at the Long Count's end reiterates the need for a transformation of the social order altogether (the quincunx suggesting social ritual), a transformation of anything that brings security through hierarchical order and centralized authority—one of the basic tensions indicated by the Long Count horoscope[1]—and the possibility of ecological (Moon) death and rebirth (Pluto). Under many variations, the form of social ordering under discussion has existed for thousands of years; the triggering factors strongly suggest that it has reached a breaking point—or, a point at which it will break unless those with the power to make adjustments (for example those with important posi-

---

[1] Another note on timing: One might argue, correctly, that Pluto would have transited that point before—every 240 years or so—without making a similar demand. True enough, but at this point we consider Pluto as triggering the more long-lasting developments indicated by the secondary progressions (Uranus' sextile to its own position; Saturn-Pluto squaring Mars-Neptune and opposing Mercury-Venus, thus at the same time forming a t-square and triggering the yod (from its "reaction point")). All of this plus the mutual reception discussed above. Because these factors suggest challenges to the basic structural factors of the Long Count horoscope, we can conclude that we will see challenges to all developments symbolized *by* that horoscope. Pluto's transit to the Moon, though significant in itself, acquires much more power as it triggers these more long-lasting developments.

tions in the hierarchy or enough financial, social, or military power to effect changes) decide to stop resisting the necessary transformation. At present, much evidence suggests that we should expect the more problematic manifestations, but the more creative ones remain possible.

That transiting Saturn has reached the midpoint between Mars and Neptune suggests that the possible cruelty or misguided aggression indicated by the natal aspect finds a particular form, possibly directed by a specific hierarchy with deeply entrenched power (Scorpio). We have seen Mars-Neptune's connection with aggression throughout the Long Count; the transit could easily trigger a military confrontation of some sort, possibly one involving nuclear or germ weapons as Scorpio acts through its ruler, Pluto (plutonium; viruses), which conjoins the Moon (security). It could also suggest aggression based on the delusions of underground or hidden forces, perhaps people who feel powerless in terms of organized government (e.g. so-called terrorists[1]) or those who hold power behind or beneath organized governments (governments that we could categorize as *terrorist* as well). So an honest appraisal of the evidence tells us that the dire warnings of disaster at Long Count's end don't seem at all far-fetched. They seem, rather, aptly symbolized by the astrological configurations.[2]

This "doomsday scenario" arises from a combination of the factors discussed: sudden aggression (Mars-Uranus) prompted by illusions (natal Mars-Neptune); a challenge to all forms of socially-constructed security (Pluto-Moon); events crystallizing because long-standing tensions within the pervasive social hierarchies (Saturn-Uranus) reach a breaking point. All of this could obviously spell "massive war" as the tensions inherent in what we call "civilization" come to a breaking point; or it could mean environmental disaster (suggested by the various quincunxes): disaster resulting when long-standing imbalances come to a point at which further progress cannot happen without a change of direction, all having its roots deep in the past, with the kinds of social structuring that arose around the beginning of the Long Count. If quincunxes and yods often suggest illness, then we would expect illness on a planetary scale—an illness that comes to a crisis that could bring civilization to an end or could trigger a healing crisis that would set in motion another cycle of human development.

We have here interpreted these factors in terms of social structures, but we should note that astrological symbols can arise in various forms. We might consider Saturn not as a symbol of social restriction and structure, but of geological restriction and structure; we might consider Pluto

---

[1] So-called. I don't much like the term unless we apply it to organized governments as well as groups not aligned with any government. I accept the following understanding of this term (though I didn't invent it): we should consider someone or some group as *terrorist* if they kill innocent civilians in order to achieve economic or military ends.

[2] One might argue that, because of the imprecise birth-time, we should not rest all that much weight on Pluto's transit to the Moon. Even if we eliminate the Moon from the picture, though, we have TR Pluto forming a yod from the natal Mercury-Venus-Jupiter quincunx. The resulting yod would indicate a gathering illness brought into focus by TR Pluto.

not as a symbol of power and transformation, but of highly pressurized magma held deep within the earth (what we might call the geologic unconscious). Viewed in this way, the symbolism suggests volcanism, the eruption of massive volcanoes, particularly like the one under Yellowstone. This doesn't strike me as the most likely manifestation, but merely as one suggested by the symbolism—and one that has a curious connection to predictions that some say come from the Maya themselves.

Should we see these as the only possibilities? Would we say that the astrological symbols predict only disaster, appearing as a kind of suddenly-manifesting fate? Or can we see other scenarios as at least possible? The Long Count's conclusion finds TR Jupiter at 8 Gemini, which might seem an apparently innocuous position at first. However, at 8 Gemini, Jupiter forms and participates in two additional yods, both involving the energies already discussed: through his sextile with the 3114 BC Mercury-Venus, he forms a yod up to the 3114 BC Moon, and therefore to TR Pluto, an aspect just discussed; then through his quincunxes to both the 3114 BC Moon and 3114 BC Mars-Neptune, and therefore to TR Pluto and TR Saturn, he becomes the focal planet of a yod formed by the natal sextile between those planets. So we have back-to-back yods locked together, both involving Jupiter.

Compared to the other factors we have looked at, TR Jupiter moves quite quickly, making a circuit of the zodiac every eleven to twelve years. Thus, considered in the time-analysis, it arises as a triggering factor. (The quincunxes to both TR Saturn and TR Pluto form one of the yods in the horoscope for the *next* Long Count, a matter discussed in the next chapter.) On the one hand, TR Jupiter's position further corroborates the intense triggering we see at the end of the Long Count; the triggers set into manifestation the two most problematic and important configurations in the natal horoscope. First, Jupiter triggers the natal yod by a) squaring one of the base planets (Jupiter), b) quincunxing the other (Moon), and c) sextiling the focal planets (Mercury and Neptune). Second, Jupiter triggers the natal square involving Mercury, Venus, Mars, and Neptune; he does this by a) sextiling one end (Mercury-Venus) and b) quincunxing the other (Mars-Neptune). Further, the yod to 3114 BC Moon-Mars-Neptune brings the two configurations together. We have seen another aspect—the long-lasting conjunction between SP Saturn and SP Pluto—that also brings the aspects together: making a t-square of the natal square and simultaneously arriving at the reaction point of the yod, matters discussed above.

The reader can see, then, that the transiting and progressed factors for December 21 2012 do seem rather extraordinary, bringing together all of the major configurations of the natal horoscope. I have no idea if the Maya had any of this in mind in choosing their dates.

Transiting Jupiter doesn't have the power of the secondary progressions. As a triggering factor, it suggests some degree of perspective and foresight. While on the problematic side it suggests triggers resulting from over-expansion, hardly a surprise considering the ecological factors we've discussed, on the other hand it suggests good fortune arising through the capacity to coordinate all factors involved, for Jupiter brings perspective, and thus (as the "greater benefic" of astrological tradition) hope; it encourages people to join together for a common purpose and a sense of fellow-feeling. The trine from TR Jupiter to SP Saturn and Pluto corroborates.

This is not to deny that the various yods suggest, as already discussed, the accumulation, since the beginning of the Long Count, of the troubles that beset us on all sides. Considering the current state of the world, we would probably categorize these factors as undeniable! The various yods (whether natal, formed by transit, or as a parts of the next Long Count's horoscope) point to choices; they suggest that the curious entity we can call civilization has come to forks in all available roads, a situation suggesting confusion and perhaps destructive stasis. At the same time, yods suggest the focalization of potentials not yet brought to bear, potentials that have heretofore remained in a state of incubation but that now get called forth by circumstance. Though human civilization has clearly come to point at which it must change direction, that change could involve bringing the human potential more fully to bear through new social forms and rituals that serve as more harmonious vehicles for it.

This assertion sounds quite abstract, but evidence related to it appears right before our eyes and has come up in our discussion already: human beings have the ability to solve their problems, but entrenched social forms—the mentioned power structure and much of what we have discussed in connection to the mega-machine—often *seem* to make it well-nigh impossible to bring that ability to bear on those solvable problems. The Long Count's conclusion seems to mark a point of no return, a period when those abilities, whether intellectual, spiritual, imaginative, or artistic, will no longer make the necessary impact. Jupiter symbolizes the process of drawing different energies into a larger whole, and thus symbolizes a necessary cooperation: conflicting nations and groups must solve problems by working together if for no other reason than that *everyone* will suffer (though the poor will surely suffer first—and more) unless *everyone* commits to solving the problems together, putting aside selfish, parochial, or national interests to do so. The Long Count's conclusion marks a time when this had better happen—when, we might say, that curious institution we call "the state" must dissolve, making way for something more suitable to current circumstances.[1]

Decision-makers both with and without power will find their hands forced, at least by ecological factors, with the danger of destructive warfare looming in the background, the threat probably deriving from factors related to resources (Taurus as the empty leg of the t-square discussed above), and thus to the same set of imbalances that have led to environmental catastrophe. The benefic Jupiterian energies suggest that people may succeed in setting into motion such pro-

---

[1]Something else that probably must dissolve: industrial farming conglomerates. These institutions must bear much of the responsibility for the decrease in the available seed-varieties for crops upon which the human population depends.

grams or individual initiatives as will promote either collective well-being or individual harmony. But the fact that one finds one's hand forced (so to speak) suggests that one has limited options: cooperation or disaster. This limitation reflects the yod configuration, which astrologers have long referred to as "the finger of god." The phrase suggests a focus of attention or demand: all human beings will have to concentrate energy on a specific set of concerns, surely including environmental ones, that limit the available choices and force people to do what they *must* instead of merely what they *would*.

As we approach the end of the Long Count, though, we should remember that just as the Long Count's birth-date did not, as far as we know, coincide with specific events of profound importance, so the end-date of the Long Count may pass just like any other. Perhaps the symbolism of the end-date, like the symbolism of the birth-date, encapsulates trends more than it indicates specific events. In other words, we shouldn't necessarily expect catastrophe on December 21, 2012. Perhaps the catastrophe encapsulated in the astrological symbolism has been taking place for some time now and will continue. People living during the Renaissance didn't notice change taking place suddenly, on a particular day; nor, I would wager, did the people of the 4th millennium BC. With the perspective that comes with time, we see those changes as unprecedented and swift, but to the people of the time, those events perhaps appeared simply as daily life.

One factor among all of these *does* seem to threaten extreme destruction set in motion through warfare: the position of the SP Saturn-Pluto conjunction. It opposes the important Mercury-Venus conjunction, and oppositions suggest projection, particularly when we see them as marks of collective developments. In general, the outermost planet or grouping of any opposed pair will receive the projection that will appear in the world as an event. Saturn-Pluto as a projection could well arise as highly organized (Saturn) destruction (Pluto), with destructive forces (Pluto) breaking free of social restriction (Saturn), or as long-buried fires (Pluto) breaking free of geological restrictions (Saturn). And because these progressed planets square natal Mars, the organized aggression would probably involve the military, or perhaps fire, released from the underworld (Scorpio).

Square aspects formed by transit or progression demand the conscious and deliberate development of new forms in order to house the energy-demands of the moment. The militaries of the world will either need to disband or (more likely) find new ways to operate. We have seen that in the past the military served as a major impetus in the maintenance of the mega-machine. In the present, no form of social organization has more power-in-action than the military, so probably that power needs to work in more creative ways, probably under the direction of non-military people who seem to start from a different set of assumptions than military people generally do. The military training, too, needs transforming so that personnel can more readily act, with their usual organization, in creative ways instead of destructive ones. To those who say that we should disband the military entirely because military units so seldom act in any but destructive ways, I can only reply that we would do better to engage an afflicted Mars constructively than to pretend it doesn't exist. The military organizations do not seem likely to disband, so we must find ways to use them to help the collective situation. (This discussion of the military has a close connection to a matter important to the next chapter: the December 21, 2012 Mars gives and receives no major aspects and thus qualifies as "unaspected." It can operate as a loose cannon; it can also operate as a unique set of potentials.)

Some will say that Saturn-Pluto could also indicate a beneficent death of old forms as a prelude to the rebirth of new ones, all as a result of ecological crisis, with Mars entering the picture as highly focused energy, and Neptune as idealism or selflessness. We should see as one of the possibilities the use of military units to help, for example, outfit homes with more appropriate technology in all parts of the world. The military organizations of First World countries have vast resources; leaders must redirect them toward enlightened and compassionate (Neptune) action (Mars).[1] I fully admit that though we should see this as one of the possibilities, we shouldn't delude ourselves into seeing it as likely—and without an enormous amount of pressure from the governed millions, it will surely not happen at all.[2]

If we had to do, here, with the horoscope of an individual, we could see how that individual could marshal his or her psychological energies to effect such a transformation, but we may have more difficulty seeing how a collectivity (humankind altogether?) would do so. Still, the symbolism suggests the potential and the need for such change, and it could occur if people (either people in authority or, taking into consideration the Age of Aquarius, *groups* of people acting on their intelligence and insight) with the power to enforce their will on events find themselves willing to use that will to empower change. (As noted, recent rebellions and mini-rebellions surely give us some reason to hope.)

We might remember, here, the significance of the septile and quintile measures to the Long Count. If we emphasize the septile-energy, we will think that change must occur through hierarchies; if we emphasize the quintile-energies, we see that change occurs when we fully understand the nature of the world in which we live—or, that each person does. The former, the more evident of the two, emphasizes the inertia of the collective karma, the collective order, and the collective mindset; the latter, less evident but just as important, emphasizes the creative power not only of consciousness but of people who can bring to bear the natural transformative powers of the phenomenal world altogether.

---

[1] Chogyam Trungpa, Rinpoche, one of the most important Tibetan teachers to come to the West in the 20th century, organized, as part of his mandala of teachings, a military unit he called the Dorje Kasung, a group devoted to compassionate but organized activity undertaken to support enlightened activity and always connected with meditation. Interested readers can contact Varjadhatu via internet connections.
[2] Recently in Egypt, however, the military restrained from immediately acting against demonstrators, an impressive departure from the norm.

That we see a development as unlikely doesn't mean that it couldn't take place, and because we can't really afford despair, we should probably try to work constructively with the quintile-related potentials. One of the messages of the Long Count, both at beginning and end, has to do with powerful changes in forms of social organization, a description suggested by the quintile-septile relationship *and* various factors in the Long Count natal horoscope. Just as the people in the years leading up to the Long Count's beginning saw the advent of heretofore unimagined forms of social organization, so we might see the birth of social forms that we can't intuit clearly at this point. We must admit this as a possibility, and as we do, we should note, as Mumford does, that though the new forms of the 4th millennium BC were prefigured in earlier forms (in the rise of the powerful hunter in opposition to the Neolithic village farmer), so any new forms will arise from factors *in* our current situation, factors that would pervade our situation to such an extent that we might not see them as individualized forms at all, or factors that act in one way now but which could act much differently later.

At the beginning of the Long Count, the hunters emerged as the military class that has dominated civilization increasingly ever since. The hunters had played a vital role in pre-civilization economies, but they had split further and further off from the Neolithic village farmers and eventually took over as rulers. The further metamorphosis of the current period needs more conscious direction than what occurred over 5000 years ago. We have the organizational structure in place; we have not infused it with the necessary values, for we have imbued it with values inimical to human survival. The transformation thus must take place at the level of value (Venus, a focal planet of the yod) before it affects the social forms (Saturn) imbued with that value. Perhaps we needn't tear down all the structures of civilization—at least not all at once!—but we certainly must step beyond the paranoid parochialism that has characterized human civilization since its inception. Unlike the people of 5000 years ago, we *must* change if we wish to avoid catastrophe.

The transits and progressions suggest that at the Long Count's conclusion, imbalances truly "come to a head" and demand resolution; something in the nature of the forces themselves brings the imbalances to such a point that change *must* occur. We can expect these changes not only in the entrenched and ritualistic approaches to seeking security through hierarchies (Moon in Capricorn), but also in the tendency to think in terms of central, quasi-deified leaders (Mercury-Venus in Leo) and the tendency to seek security through expansion (Moon-Jupiter). Thoughts about self-development and personal value, about the value of a centralized self, develop largely through social settings, through an ongoing search for security obtained, here, through expansion.[1] We may see this as "part of the nature of the beast," but we should perhaps see it as an expression of a certain bestiality that has arisen within and received encouragement from the kinds of social development under discussion.

---

[1] This sentence refers to all of the planets in the yod: *security through expansion* suggests Moon-Jupiter; *thoughts of self-development and personal value* suggests Mercury-Venus; *the value of a centralized self* suggests Venus in Leo.

In all this, though, we should note that the "clearer focus" may refer not only to the events themselves as problematic forms crystallize before our eyes, but also to what happens within individuals. Individuals with "clearer focus" may find resolutions to the daunting problems that, as I write, arise on all sides. It may even happen that though we see events as shaping consciousness and awareness, really consciousness and awareness as readily shape events. If people have a clearer or more focused awareness, they can apply power at the right point. But the discussion of this "clearer focus" and what might result from it belongs more properly to the next chapter.

Chapter Five

The Next Long Count

THE FOREGOING MATERIAL AT TIMES seems to portray civilization as a kind of collective psychosis resulting in frenzied bouts of warfare and ongoing ecological destruction, driven by a lust for power and conquest. Certainly we could find abundant evidence in support of such a view, however much it may ignore the way the new form of social organization that arose in the 4th millennium BC opened the way for types of human thought and expression probably impossible in Neolithic societies. Still, whatever we say of the benefits of civilization, we could still say that if we consider our planet as a being, then the rapid development of that social form we call civilization, and particularly industrial-technological civilization, certainly looks like a kind of cancer: even if we acknowledge that cancer may coincide with great leaps in awareness, if ignored it usually expands until it threatens the body as a whole.

But even if we see civilization as a kind of psychosis or cancer, we can still acknowledge the brilliance it has brought; and when we look closely, we may find it difficult to separate the brilliance from the psychosis, for the two seem joined at some deep level and may express the same underlying tendency. And, of course, psychoses and cancers don't always lead inexorably to death. A physician may find ways to intervene that preserve the brilliance while saving the life. Sometimes human intervention produces remarkable results, though if one doesn't intervene until late in the process, one may have to do surgery instead of simply suggesting changes in lifestyle.

Some imbalances simply disappear with time, as if outgrown, or perhaps having run their course. Perhaps, too, the person's innate intelligence and wisdom begin to assert themselves;

perhaps the diet or social conditions change; perhaps even psychosis, as a process, may run its course, or change, or appear in a new light. Certainly the condition of the so-called psychotic doesn't seem cut in stone; not so certainly (but often, it seems, quite probably), the condition itself arises as a sane response to an insane situation,[1] an acute response to imbalance. If individuals can recover from the condition we label as psychosis, perhaps human society can recover from collective psychosis. To do so, people must recognize the sanity, brilliance, and intelligence that arise in the current situation, even while recognizing that the psychosis *does* indicate a deep imbalance of some sort. People will also have to realize that even if the psychosis ends, they will still have to deal with the results. I may recover from a psychosis during which I burn down my neighbor's house, but the ashes remain even after my recovery. Of course, psychosis differs from cancer at least in that it doesn't necessarily or always threaten the physical body; if we see current developments as cancerous, we may conclude that the living physical body—the planet itself, it seems—will not survive without some kind of surgery.

The conclusion of the Mayan Long Count may well bring the current experiment in social organization—the one called "civilization" and associated with all the problems mentioned in this text—to an end. But though this could occur simply because the process has run its course, we should expect that cessation will bring a crisis of some sort, for we should not expect more of civilization than we expect of the humans who make it up, and those humans generally wake up fully only when they experience some sort of crisis or difficulty. And, of course, the environmental problems won't go away just because humans wake up.

Writers have proffered various theories as to what will precipitate the changes associated with 2012. Some have suggested that various astronomical events (e.g. the galactic alignment, sunspot cycles) or geological changes (e.g. huge volcanoes, shifts in the magnetic field of the planet) will bring about changes of an unprecedented nature. Some have claimed that we will experience a major shift in human consciousness. I can't speak with authority on any of these matters and certainly don't wish to denigrate any of the ideas offered by those who have studied and pondered the matter deeply. However, we should keep two points in mind:

- First, just as the Long Count's birth horoscope doesn't seem to tell us of events that took place on that particular date, so we shouldn't expect major changes precisely on December 21, 2012. Perhaps such changes will occur, but perhaps the end-date, like the birth-date, encapsulates in its astrological symbolism changes that took place over a considerable period of time.
- Second, though the notions presented in this book suggest that the Long Count measures major changes in social structuring that do not happen suddenly or on a certain day, this does not mean that other investigators have misevaluated or that the

---

[1] I have borrowed this phrasing, I think, from R.D. Laing.

reader should accept my ideas instead of theirs; it does not suggest that we must opt either for physical changes (e.g. magnetic shifts) or sociological ones (e.g. changes in social structure), for presumably both could occur together, with one perhaps causing the other.

- Third, if we see external agents (e.g. astronomical events or magnetic shifts) as primary, we have perhaps taken on what we might call a septile orientation, putting more weight on changes in external scaffolding than on the awareness of individuals—what we can call a quintile orientation. In the Long Count, these approaches interweave, suggesting that we will find solutions only by uniting them. I cannot say for certain whether external forces like magnetic shifts have, will, or can change social structures in any way other than the destructive. When we look at the historical processes discussed in this book, we find ourselves looking at actions that humans have taken, decisions humans have made and continued to make. In other words, we can think what we wish about external energies impinging on us, but we should realize that changes take place on the spot, right here, where external and internal meet.

The Mayans tell us that the Long Count, which seems to measure the development of "civilization," will end on a specific date. As it does so, something else presumably begins. We should note, though, that not all Mayan scholars agree that the end of the present Long Count brings the beginning of another such. Nor do they agree that we should see the present Long Count as the culmination of four previous ones, the total number of years adding up to 25,625 years, quite close to the time it takes the equinoctial point to move backwards through the 360 degrees of the zodiac. If we see the present Long Count as the last of five, we would see December 21, 2012 as the end of an approximately 26,000 year period; if we see it as a period with no relation to other, similar periods, we would see that date as the end of a 5125 year period. But whether we see the 2012 date as the end of a 26,000-year period or a 5125-year period, we should ask whether December 21, 2012 ushers in a new period of the same length.

The Maya apparently attached great importance to the current period, predicting great destruction. Some climatologists have predicted dire changes in the coming decades, changes that will perhaps make it difficult for humans to live in the same way they have for the past five millennia—and perhaps to *live* at all, as we should not see our ecological niche as any more secure than that of many extinct species. Most certainly, our social structures will have to change, and drastically. Perhaps such changes will not avail us, coming along "a day late and a dollar short"; perhaps *homo* (purportedly) *sapiens* will not survive. Many who know more than I about ecological niches, species survival, and paleontology have made dire predictions.

Let us put those arguments to side, however, and assume, for the sake of argument, that human beings will survive in some form and for some considerable time. This leaves us with questions about the social forms they will develop, whether out of whim, wisdom, or necessity. If the previous Long Count told us about the social forms of the past 5125 years, perhaps the horoscope for December 21, 2112 will tell us about the social forms that will develop over the next 5125 years, or about our approach to social form altogether. Just as the new forms of the 4th millennium BC developed out of antecedent conditions, so the new social forms will arise from what we see around us right now, if we know where to look, within or beside (or in hiding from) present forms.

Let us (again for the sake of argument) also put aside questions about whether the ancient Maya predicted a new Long Count. Let us do so simply because in most of our experience, endings bring beginnings. Then let us assume that the horoscope for the new period gives us symbolism about a very long period of time, a period lasting at least as long as the last one and therefore having to do with a discernible stage in human development, though perhaps development of a sort as alien to us as the first civilizations in Sumer and Egypt probably seemed to the Neolithic farmers in whose locale they rose. Whether the period lasts 5125 years or five times as long, it will surely witness the development of technologies, social forms, and psychological alterations that we would find difficult to imagine. The horoscope for the new period won't tell us what specific developments will occur, but it will tell us about the general patterns that any growth will follow.

In discussing this new horoscope, we find ourselves in murkier waters than we did in discussing August 11, 3114 BC. Though we have before us a horoscope for a similar kind of entity, for the new horoscope we cannot consult historical records to check our theories. We cannot find out what happened when and from that information make deductions about the kind of entity we have under examination. Whereas for the 3114 BC horoscope we had abundant information about both the pre-natal and post-natal periods, for the 2012 horoscope we have only the former.

We must therefore extrapolate, and though this may at first seem a daunting obstacle, the situation seems, in at least a few ways, similar to that of an astrologer looking at an infant's horoscope. That astrologer has some idea of the circumstances in which the child emerged—the family environment, significant economic factors, parental psychology, and various elements in the collective that could prove important—and from this he or she can to some extent ground the astrological interpretation, not in empirical reality, but in conjectures with some tie <u>to</u> that empirical reality. Just as an astrologer would make one kind of prognosis about a Mars-Saturn square in the horoscope of the daughter of 18th century French nobility and quite another about the same square in the horoscope of the child of a Pittsburgh steel-worker, so here we can look at the environment marking the final phases of the present Long Count to get some idea of the circumstances in which the new period will emerge. To that we can add an assumption: that the new horoscope tells us a lot about social structuring, just as the previous one did, that we have before us a horoscope for the same "kind of thing."

The astrological symbolism from the previous Long Count, along with the available evidence gathered from observation, suggests that the birth-circumstances will involve chaos, breakdown, environmental difficulties, perhaps even environmental or socio-political catastrophe, and quite possibly widespread violence, some of which we have seen already and none of which seem about to abate. All of those developments have grown from the predominant ideas and assumptions of the previous Long Count, including ideals and assumptions about regality surrounded by a rigid bureaucracy, coupled with an often-sadistic drive for power. The 3114 BC symbolism also suggests tension between the prevailing order and the inventive mind, a tendency toward aggression based on delusion, an emphasis on bigness, on power, and on a kind of devouring aggression. Further, as we have seen in the previous chapter, some of the progressions to the horoscope of the previous Long Count will continue for some years into the future, quite likely telling us quite a bit about what will occur early in the new period.[1] Further still, we know that the Neptune-Pluto conjunctions will continue to occur in Gemini for many centuries.

But the same 3114 BC symbols (in which we can include time-analysis symbols) that seem to point so clearly to threat also point to a set of demands that, if met, can emerge as potentials. Most important, here, seems the SP Saturn-Pluto conjunction in Aquarius as it opposes natal Mercury-Venus.[2] Pluto suggests fusion not only in the external world in relation to the plutonium bomb and nuclear energy, but also in the inner world of each person as a living expression of the Long Count energy. This inner fusion has to do with a development within each person's awareness: a recognition of the pervasive and powerful fusion of apparently-external world and apparently-internal awareness. This awareness takes one beyond the scientific paradigm that has so dominated the last centuries of the Long Count, a paradigm in which the external world arises as wholly other, as something separate from the observer and therefore observable in the purportedly objective way that made possible what we call "science."

Pluto suggests a new mode of perception altogether, one in which humans recognize their own participation in the things they see, in phenomena altogether. As a symbol of rebirth and archaic energy, Pluto suggests a rebirth of something that has died, a something that Owen Barfield calls *original participation*: "an awareness which we no longer have, of an extra-sensory link

---

[1] As any astrologer will attest after studying the horoscopes of people long since passed away, or even nations purportedly no longer existent (such as the U.S.S.R.), horoscopes often continue to operate even after death.

[2] A note to non-astrologers: This aspect will not appear in the natal horoscope for the new period. It arises through progressions to the 3114 BC horoscope, so it doesn't appear in the sky. We put the SP (secondary progressed) planets where we do because of mathematical calculations, not physical observations. Progressions for a certain date refer to that date only in reference to the horoscope that we have progressed, not to the more general situation. However, in this case, the horoscope that we have progressed seems to have to do with the sort of social structure in which we find ourselves enmeshed.

between the percipient and the representation,"[1] the participation of observer with observed rediscovered in the laboratories of quantum physicists and the explorations of analytical psychologists (and never absent from ideas of many Buddhists and others involved in spiritual work). From the scientific point of view that prevailed until around 1930,[2] and that still prevails in the popular mind, such participation qualifies as a delusion, a lack of that purported objectivity upon which science has purportedly rested; from the point of view of many scientists since that time, a view supported by experimental data, this "delusion" seems a verifiable element of the world we see represented before us.

This brings us again to the conjunction between SP Pluto and SP Saturn that marks the conclusion of the Long Count. Pluto suggests a transformation of the way we think and perceive; the transformation involves the above-mentioned fusion. Saturn represents our view of consensus reality: the way we think that the world "is," the physical and social structures built from that consensus, and the way we express our convictions in the crystallized structures that we call "language." The conjunction suggests, therefore, a transformation of the way we program our world,[3] with the gamut of transformation running from habitual tendencies of perception, to habitual ways of learning and using language, to habitual ways of structuring society. We might remember, here, that the rise of the kind of civilization that the Long Count seems to measure took place around the same time that humans developed written language, crystallizing a previously changing form into a more rigid one. This crystallizing may well have led to the freezing of idea-structures, thus making possible the kind of civilization that developed—and, most importantly for our purposes here, for the kind of creativity and destruction that ensued.

The conjunction suggests a potential: the development of a new mode of perception in which the perceiver recognizes, as part of the way he structures his world, the dynamic role of the individual and collective consciousness in creating the representations that everyone takes for "reality."[4] Thus we access power (Pluto) if or insofar as we recognize and work actively with the way we create and recreate our world constantly, using language (and the concepts one derives from the language one uses) as a major tool to effect that process. Pluto suggests the de-crystallization of what has crystallized; but because Saturn, the faster-moving planet of the pair, will move

---

[1] Owen Barfield, *Saving the Appearances: A Study in Idolatry* (Middletown: Wesleyan University Press, 1988), 34.
[2] When astronomers discovered Pluto.
[3] Robert Hand, *Planets in Transit* (Atglen PA: Whitford Press, 1976), 317.
[4] I have borrowed the term "representation" from Barfield, though I take responsibility for the use to which I put it, particularly if it conflicts with Barfield's notions. Barfield uses the term "idolatry" to refer to the process in which humans take representations (whether as physical idols or ideas such as scientific theories) as the reality itself—as "the effective tendency to abstract the sense-content from the whole representation and seek that for its own sake, transmuting the desired image into a desired object" (110-11). He also sees idolatry as (135) turning the models (what I would call the habitual collective representations, connected to Saturn) into idols. When we worship an idol, we take the representation as really, whereas really it only *represents* something.

steadily away from Pluto in the early decades and centuries of the new era, the aspect suggests the development of new versions of "reality" emerging as a new set of structures or representations (whether verbal, situational, or physical) in the world.

Pluto generally brings a breakdown phase first and then a rebirth; the rebirth in this case will emerge through the new structures just mentioned. That the conjunction takes place in Aquarius suggests that the new representations will arise fused with the modern scientific view, and that the new representations must find application in the social realities and social structures we confront: structures combining the best of the past and the possibilities for the future (for Aquarius, as we have seen, has two rulers: Saturn and Uranus, representing the crystallized structures of the past and the ideas that arise to shape the future.[1]). All of this connects to the transit-to-transit Neptune-Pluto conjunctions in Gemini, a series that began with the arising of the modern form of idolatry mentioned above: taking the representation as the reality and failing to distinguish the representation from what it represents. This idolatry, integral to the "scientific view" naively understood, made possible the world we see around us, and got its first major impetus back in the Age of Gemini when humans began their long experiment in written language, an experiment that led to the crystallized forms that underlay the initial civilizations of the Middle East. But as centuries pass and one Gemini-conjunction follows another, we can expect a dissolving and a transformation of the dualistic version of "reality" that we so much take for granted. People will eventually recognize (literally: they will begin to *know again*, to know in a new way) that both parts of the duality—on the one hand the world that seems to arise as appearances, on the other the perceiver—come from the same seed, just as twins do. This new recognition will arise as a new power. Though this recognition probably won't stabilize for quite some time, we can see it already, though perhaps just in chrysalis stage.

The astrological symbolism of the new Long Count suggests not the monolithic, royalistic-bureaucratic-militaristic structures of the previous Long Count, but something less organized, less obsessive, and containing different formative ideas,[2] ideas that as yet have probably not even achieved sufficient form to deserve the name "ideas," but which, as time go on will emerge through new forms of social organization and new institutions, guiding myriad choices made by people ranging from leaders to apparently inconsequential citizens.

Transiting Pluto in Capricorn on December 21, 2012 becomes natal Pluto in Capricorn for the new aeon, for the transits for that end-date equal the natal positions for the new horoscope. In many ways, Pluto's position in Capricorn (ruled by Saturn) in the new horoscope reiterates SP

---

[1] Pluto, here, does not represent the new ideas themselves. It represents the process by which we fuse, say, verbal structure with molecular structure, *and* the process by which we transform that original fusion (Barfield's *idolatry*, I would say). Pluto symbolizes the power to transform the world through a development in awareness, not the specific ideas that further that process.
[2] The term comes from Lewis Mumford.

Pluto's conjunction with SP Saturn (ruler of Capricorn) at the conclusion of the previous Long Count, just as does transiting Saturn's placement in Scorpio (ruled by Pluto), the two planets forming a mutual reception.[1] Pluto in Capricorn suggests a pervasive death-and-rebirth of structure and hierarchy. That it conjoins the Long Count Moon suggests a pervasive death and rebirth process related to all social structures (Capricorn) that had provided security and nourishment (Moon), two elements vital to all people on earth. This suggests, among other possibilities, mass starvation as social structures that previously had played a major role in food transport now fall apart. It could also suggest death of many of the taken-for-granted powers of the "sub-lunar realm," the realm of vegetation and natural or organic growth.

However, the same aspect can suggest the birth of social forms possibly more friendly to humans. The close sextile to Saturn in Scorpio suggests a helpful flow of practical ideas related to this rebuilding (with the closeness of the sextile reminding us of the closeness of the SP conjunction discussed above) following the death-phase sketched above. Again we see the death and rebirth of structure, but Pluto in Capricorn points more directly to the breakdown of government structures,[2] while Saturn in Scorpio points more directly to the death (Scorpio) of psychological approaches to world-structuring (Saturn), to the prevailing mode of seeing the world in one way and not in another. The mutual reception suggests the power of the breakdown phase; when we add the symbolism of the sextile, we see human ingenuity leading to new social forms, even group endeavors.

These two planets both quincunx Jupiter, forming an extremely close yod that can suggest healing and adjustment, the adjustment having to do with cooperation and the need to learn more about the social implications of the dualistic mode of thinking mentioned above (Jupiter in Gemini). Pluto in Capricorn suggests that power comes through organization and pragmatism, even though it also suggests that an old form of organization must die before the new can arise. This conundrum may suggest that the new Long Count begins in chaos and destruction: human beings, having reached the terminus of one mode of social development, must now let go of that mode and give birth to something new. The symbolism of Jupiter, the greater benefic, suggests some optimism and hope, though that optimism and hope will come to fruition only if people can coordinate (Jupiter) the multifarious results of human curiosity (Gemini).

That Pluto squares the natal (2012) Moon in Aries reiterates the (transit-to-natal) Pluto-Moon conjunction at the end of the Long Count. The Moon in Aries has little importance as a transit to

---

[1] In other words, we find Pluto in Saturn's sign (Capricorn) and Saturn in Pluto's sign (Scorpio). This suggests mutual influence. In addition, the two transiting planets are in a close sextile. So the Saturn-Pluto theme seems dramatic and important—reiterating, as noted, the symbolism of the Saturn-Pluto conjunction at the conclusion of the previous Long Count, though without the dire implications associated with that aspect.

[2] It also suggests Plutonic powers controlling the prevailing hierarchies: the powerful moneyed interests that we unfortunately know so well (or, perhaps, so little).

the 3114 BC horoscope, but it has great importance in the new horoscope, symbolizing the primary security-orientation characterizing the new period: a formative idea, we might say, related to security. It suggests a search for security through a pioneering mentality, not through connection *to* social structures (as with the Moon in Capricorn) but through moving away *from* them. It suggests the paradox of finding security (Moon) through pioneering (Aries), though *pioneering* suggests moving away from places where people generally *find* security. Because Pluto has much to do with space travel, the new structures that enable pioneering may involve space travel. The idea of colonizing other worlds seems suggested as one possibility connected with the aspect—but perhaps not the most hopeful, at least in the short run for most people on the planet, or the most likely. Quite likely the pioneering will involve new modes more than new places. In moving away from civilization as he knows it, the pioneer shows not only dissatisfaction with the prevailing mode of living, in this case the prevailing way of finding security, but also a need for a new approach to the matter of security altogether, other approaches having proven unacceptable, overly confining, or simply destructive.

The square suggests, as do all squares, a need for structure. Here, the Moon-Pluto square suggests a need for structures to unite the pioneering drives of the Aries Moon with the bureaucratic and organizational power of Pluto in Capricorn, though that position suggests a complete overhaul of existing organizational modes. Conflicts arise because the individualistic drives of Aries do not settle easily with the bureaucratic demands of Capricorn: Aries' desire for immediacy of expression challenges and must adjust to Capricorn's concern for structures that last through time. On the other hand, the combination suggests that the transformation of social structure (Pluto in Capricorn) must unite with new approaches to security (Moon in Aries). The square surely suggests that the new modes will appear incompatible with the old ones, though, as Mumford tells us, as a

> . . . once fully-formed culture becomes dematerialized . . . the way opens for a new constellation of formative ideas, which themselves come into existence partly by reaction against the dominant culture, and yet are constantly conditioned, and even temporarily supported by the very customs and institutions they seek to replace.[1]

Pluto in Capricorn surely suggests transformative new ideas with roots in the past; the square to the Aries Moon suggests that new approaches to security, despite their pioneering quality (and despite the fact that pioneering seems *necessary*), will never arise completely separate from the results of the past. New approaches reflect dissatisfaction with a past it apparently must to some extent carry forward. To overcome obstacles, people will need to draw on the organizational structures that sometimes seem to qualify *as* the obstacles.

---

[1] Mumford, 427.

If the end of the previous Long Count brings any sort of widespread destruction, new security will not arise at all without pioneering. New structures will have to arise if the old ones have disintegrated or proven materially or morally bankrupt. Pluto in Capricorn suggests that the pioneering must incorporate hierarchy, structure, and organized effort, but the transformation of structure will bring new approaches to security and the sub-lunar realm altogether (the sub-lunar elements including environmental factors). We can see a danger here, for Pluto in Capricorn also suggests the controlling power of monolithic government set against the search for simple home security. This power clearly could arise in the wake of any destruction, driven by ecological or military factors resulting from the previous aeon. But the new will arise through connection to the aforementioned curiosity (Jupiter), for in squaring Pluto, the Aries Moon sextiles Jupiter—and thus the two bodies become the base of a yod to Saturn:[1] structures arising from the detritus of the old (Saturn in Scorpio) arise because of the beneficent combination of pioneering mentality (Moon in Aries) and curiosity (Jupiter in Gemini), of risk-taking and social cooperation. The yod suggests the development of structures infused with approaches to security arising from knowledge and information newly minted.

Despite its emphasis on the transformation of structure, Pluto in Capricorn also suggests the power and influence of the old or traditional. Pluto always brings paradox: the old gods may have died, but they still exert influence. Humankind, having habituated itself to the social forms we associate with civilization, will have difficulty finding viable new approaches unless there arises a determination to transform (Pluto) the most basic approaches to daily living (Moon), a process of transforming (Pluto) the old structures through relation to the new impetus, a process we might call rebirth (Pluto, particularly in connection to the Moon). The new structures (square) must enable people to express humankind's new power, a power paradoxically rooted in tradition, *through* a pioneering mentality that can manifest as either adventure or irresponsibility.

With the presence of destructive weapons in so many hands, people clearly must devise new, more adventurous ways to find security, ways different from those indicated by the previous Long Count's Moon in Capricorn (security through, or derived from, bureaucratic structure and hierarchy). If we see Pluto in Capricorn as a reflection of the nation states that house the bureaucracies, we might welcome a movement away from such states; those states have, after all, created the weapons and maintained the destructive systems that have and will threaten all security (for, we might say, it's a funny kind of security that builds weapons of destruction and destroys the environment). Thus the old dispensation has run its course; however, the square suggests that people will find no security by simply trying to reject the old.

---

[1] The second of the two interlocked yods in this horoscope. The first has Jupiter as focal planet and Saturn-Pluto, in close sextile, as base planets; the second has Saturn as focal planet and the Jupiter-Moon sextile as base-planets. And, as noted, Jupiter quincunxes Saturn, the Moon squares Pluto, and Venus, opposite Jupiter and thus at the reaction-point of the first yod, trines the Moon. So we see an interlocked and complex pattern of planetary energies. See the horoscope on page xxii.

Pluto also squares Uranus, which conjoins the Moon in Aries and adds a note of rebellion to the mix. Uranus-Moon reiterates the need for new modes of security, but whereas Aries points to highly individual initiative, Uranus suggests new ideas and technologies. The pioneering will probably arise through ideas and technical expertise; the challenge will involve finding the correct application for these. We can already see the seeds of such approaches, whether in new techniques for winter harvesting, new methods of generating energy, or new ways of organizing social groups. As we have already seen, the Uranus-Uranus sextile (SP Uranus sextiles natal Uranus) at the end of the previous Long Count suggests the availability of technical means, so we should feel no surprise to find Uranus emphasized again. Moon-Uranus suggests an intellectual rebellion linked to one related to survival, with Aries adding the pioneering element: pioneering linked to new ideas or technics related to feeding and bodily health. Uranus generally refuses to accept old ways if they do not accord with new insights, understandings, or technical capacities. On the other hand, this symbolism – not only Moon-Uranus, but Aries and Pluto – could suggest a marked lack of security altogether, for what kind of security do we find in constant pioneering (Aries), constant transformation (Pluto), and constant rebellion (Uranus)? If people wish to find security, they will have to cultivate and welcome new approaches to gaining it—a daunting task (suggested by the afflictions to the Moon), as most people alive have no experience or knowledge of any viable alternatives.[1]

Because Uranus rules Aquarius, the Moon-Uranus conjunction could also suggest that in the Aquarian Age, people will find security not in isolated homes, bur rather in groups based in shared ideas or social principles, a kind of new-age Neolithic village in which new technologies further group-survival. We have seen already that the Age of Aquarius may well bring environmental barrenness resulting from long-standing modes of social organization; Uranus as ruler suggests a need to break away from those modes of organization, to find something new and less socially and environmentally destructive. Moon-Uranus suggests that people will find security only through adventurous associations that provide security. We can expect, then, to see marked increase in such movements as community gardening within cities, shared living quarters that make more effective use of resources, and group living that enhances security through shared resources and the application of new technical means.

The previous horoscope had Uranus and Pluto in conjunction in Capricorn, an aspect suggesting (along with the close Saturn-Uranus quincunx) the co-option of human inventiveness (Uranus) by the powers (Pluto) of the status quo (Capricorn), a particularly strong tendency in that horoscope because Saturn disposits both planets and conjoins the Sun in Leo (the royal imperative). The symbolism of the new horoscope suggests adventurous, renegade inventiveness (Uranus in Aries) challenging (square) the entrenched powers (Pluto in Capricorn), but with Pluto again in Capricorn, it seems that evolution will occur largely through structural or organizational chan-

---

[1] People still living in Neolithic villages seem like exceptions, here.

nels, and that individual human beings will find their most ready means of creative self-expression by working *through* such channels. Because of the emphasis on pioneering (Aries Moon) rather than security through structure (Capricorn Moon), we can expect these channels to exist apart from the major agglomerations of power. The renegade inventiveness reminds one of the isolated, independent centers that occupy center stage in Marge Percy's *He, She, and It*; the evolution through bureaucracy reminds one of *The Lord of the Rings*, where the magical and transformative powers always retain their connection to social hierarchy.[1]

The 3114 BC horoscope had Mars in a close conjunction with Neptune, a close square to focal Mercury and Venus, a close trine to Jupiter, a close sextile with the Moon, and a precise quintile to Saturn. In other words, Mars, symbolizing the military (among other things), insinuated itself into diverse areas of life, so much so that people had a hard time conceiving of social living without a military presence. The new horoscope has an unaspected Mars in Capricorn, suggesting highly organized military groups (Mars in Capricorn) operating largely outside the larger organizational matrix of society, perhaps outside the purview of the nation states or their remnants (as the aspects already discussed suggest a diminished emphasis on nation states altogether). We know that many different groups now have access to highly effective weaponry, suggesting the proliferation of organized military groups (Mars in Capricorn); we could see, in the coming centuries, more and more renegade armed groups in all sorts of places, as organized martial energy operates without clear connection (unaspected) to established social trends or legal restriction. Unfettered but disciplined, the energies of Mars can work either tremendous good or tremendous harm, for though we might see great danger in the situation just described, we might also see such a situation as an improvement upon what has developed in the past centuries.[2]

Unaspected planets often do not integrate constructively with the rest of the horoscope early in life, which in this case may mean for several centuries, or until important transits or progressions bring that planetary energy into coordination with other horoscope factors. But such planets often symbolize a special talent or interest. If we accept the assumption offered above that on a collective level planets often operate in their most problematic way, we would see in unaspected Mars good reason for concern, particularly seeing the harm, in our era, coming from renegade military groups (e.g. Blackwater, Al Qaida) just as we see it in organized governments (e.g. The United States and Israel) who use their militaries without regard for international law. Though we might fear organized and unaffiliated militias roaming the planet, we should not assume that they will wreak more havoc than have nation-states.

---

[1] Of course, Tolkien seemed at pains to reiterate the value of the Christian religion, whereas Percy, despite her use of Jewish lore throughout *He, She, and It*, does not seem driven to reiterate the value of Judaism.

[2] We might think, as so many pundits continually declare, that the military must remain under the direction of the political arm of government, but that approach (assuming of course, that it actually happens in the world outside the rhetoric of politicians) has apparently done little to prevent endemic and ongoing warfare, hecatombs of dead bodies, and an ever present threat from armed military groups.

Mars symbolizes the energy of survival, the energy with which a person says to the world, "I am this person and none other, and here is my territory, and I will defend it if necessary, particularly if I see that as necessary for my survival." It represents the energy with which a person pushes back at the outside world or at atmospheric pressures, symbolic and literal, that press inward with crushing force. In the chart of a larger social body, an integrated Mars suggests that the military, or the assertive forces generally, operate in union with other social factors to protect organized groups (e.g. nations) from purported external threats.[1]

However, when Mars operates independently, without aspects, we cannot assume any connection between military and any self-protective functions. Rather, we can expect the military to operate without particular social goals (real or imagined) in mind, a tendency we see more and more late in the Long Count, particularly in the military adventures of the United States, but also in the aggression of various other renegade groups. We can expect this tendency to increase as we pass 2012, for the symbolism strongly suggests that instead of seeing military organizations as integral elements of the megamachine, we will see military elements operating on their own. The term "loose cannons" comes to mind. As the new era progresses, transits and progressions to natal Mars will tend to bring about increased integration (starting with the conjunctions of Saturn (2020) and Pluto (2021) to that Mars), but even then we will probably not see the central military machine that has done such damage in the era coming to an end.

We can expect benefit if these highly organized groups, equipped with modern tools of all sorts, can direct their efforts toward ends that serve the greater good. For example, one can envisage (though one should probably not expect) military groups organizing to retrofit various buildings for more energy-efficiency. Because we have seen, for many centuries but particularly recently, that nation states have generally retarded necessary developments rather than furthered them, we can easily see how organized groups not controlled or limited by national governments could do much good if they directed their energies wisely.

The two important and interlocked yods suggest (as did the yod in the 3114 BC horoscope) ritualistic behavior, but because this horoscope has different yods than the earlier horoscope, the rituals operate in different life areas and move toward different ends. The earlier horoscope had yods (one in the natal horoscope, one formed by progression) to planets in fixed Leo, symboliz-

---

[1] However, when Mars has a challenging aspect to Neptune in the chart of a nation or an era, as in the horoscopes for the United States and the Long Count, we can expect some delusion about what constitutes self-protection. We can see this clearly in the United States' horoscope with its close Mars-Neptune square: the United States constantly imagines enemies where none exist, constantly creates threats through self-assertion (instead of using assertion to defend itself from already-existing threats), and constantly uses deception that results, intentionally or not, in increased threat-levels. With Neptune in the ninth, the United States deceives itself either about foreign nations or about ideology (e.g. "Manifest Destiny"). The Long Count natal horoscope has, the reader may recall, a Mars-Neptune conjunction in Scorpio, suggesting a set of delusions that we can trace in the historical record.

ing the fixed role that kingship played throughout the Long Count. This horoscope has one yod to Jupiter in Gemini, suggesting not kingship but heterogeneous learning and wide-spread curiosity, and a looser yod to Saturn in Scorpio, suggesting authority regimes connected to hidden factors (perhaps underworld operators of various sorts). Whereas the earlier horoscope had Mercury and Venus focal, the 2012 horoscope has first Jupiter, suggesting a search for social integration less centrally organized, and then Saturn, suggesting bureaucracy. Whereas Saturn can anchor the horoscope via his emphasis on form, Jupiter in Gemini, particularly when sextile the Moon and (more loosely) Uranus, suggests a possibly helpful intellectual restlessness. Gemini certainly seems more vicarious and exploratory than does Leo, though without such a clear sense of direction. Where Leo emphasizes centrality and rulership, Gemini suggests mental vivacity as its own reward.

Negatively, the yod could suggest problematic accumulation (Jupiter). The base planets, Saturn and Pluto, suggest the power of the bureaucratic order operating intelligently and efficiently (sextile) in ways leading to expansion (Jupiter), though the Gemini influence suggests expansion of ideas more than territory. The yod altogether can suggest social (Jupiter) power (Pluto) expressing itself effectively (Saturn) through intelligence and adaptability (sextile) but sometimes with too much exuberance (Jupiter), though it could also suggest an ongoing emphasis on the "dark twin" element of Gemini. If this occurs, Jupiter's expansion will lead to conflict based on projections of the darker element. The symbolism also suggests the danger of ritualized and disconnected profligacy driven by ritualistic behavior connected to hierarchy and restrictive social organization (Saturn).

Altogether, though, the 2012 yod to Jupiter, with the focal planet in a mutable sign, seems more flexible and adaptable than the earlier one (3114 BC) with the focal planet in a fixed sign. Though the new one can suggest a problematic accumulation (Jupiter), it can also suggest expansive good will that helps to alleviate the environmental imbalances and social malfunctions that seem destined to occur. This interpretation doesn't seem far-fetched, particularly with Venus-Jupiter opposition anchoring the yod: though the two benefics in close aspect can, again, suggest profligacy, they can also suggest the mentioned expansive good will (Jupiter) connected with either artistry or optimistic and open human connections spreading throughout the world (Venus in Sagittarius).

Connected with the yod to Jupiter, we find the much looser one to Saturn from the Moon-Jupiter sextile.[1] The 3114 BC horoscope also had a Moon-Jupiter sextile at the base of a yod. Also, as in the previous horoscope, we find a quincunx from Saturn to Uranus. However, in the previous

---

[1] Both yods have the quincunx from Saturn to Jupiter as a structural element. The yod to Jupiter has a sextile between Saturn and Pluto, quincunxes from Jupiter to both planets, and an opposition from Venus to Jupiter. The yod to Saturn has that planet quincunx Jupiter and the Moon, a sextile between those latter two bodies, plus Uranus in a peripheral role.

horoscope, because that quincunx had less than a degree orb of aspect, making it one of the closest aspect in the horoscope, it had a defining character that dominated life throughout the past five thousand years, and particularly during the last few centuries as secondary progressed Uranus moved to form a yod to natal Saturn. The 2012 quincunx has an orb of four degrees, wide enough that many would not even see it as a quincunx,[1] though many would agree that the horoscope has the aforementioned yod to Saturn.[2] The 2012 yod to Saturn demands an adjustment of status-quo structures and bureaucracy according to revolutionary demands (Uranus) coming from the people (Moon) and to a pervasive human ingenuity (Jupiter in Gemini) directed toward the provision of basic needs (Moon).

Further, the Moon in Aries, unlike the Moon in Capricorn (3114 BC), does not gravitate toward bureaucracy, structure, or hierarchy; instead, it wants individual assertion. Coupled with Uranus, it can indicate vociferous, strong-willed demands for quasi-revolutionary alterations in the status quo (Saturn). Jupiter in Gemini wants communication; its sextile to Moon-Uranus suggests a strong demand to open communications-channels as a means to make changes in the existing social structure (Saturn) with its entrenched power bureaucracy (Saturn in Scorpio sextile Pluto in Capricorn). So though we see some problems, here, with hierarchy (Saturn), we find stronger counter-balancing forces emerging as demands and volatility not amenable to the kinds of social structures and control evident in the earlier horoscope. The close sextile from Saturn to Pluto may reflect the strong conjunction between SP Saturn and SP Pluto at the end of the Long Count.

Altogether, the interlocked yods can indicate illness—and not surprisingly, considering what we know of the earlier horoscope. The cure lies in a consciously undertaken alteration of social ritual. No doubt many will find this evident and necessary as the present Long Count concludes, quite possibly due to a world-wide awareness of illness on a planetary scale and widespread famine (Moon square Pluto), as the ecological situation seems to worsen each day. All of this suggests that during the next Long Count, people will have to put their attention toward activities that help to reduce or reverse trends in this area.

The 2012 t-square (Chiron, Jupiter, Venus) reiterates these demands. Chiron, the focal planet, suggests illness and the need for healing by taking a more holistic approach. As the ruler of Virgo, Chiron has a close relationship to all quincunx aspects[3] and thus to illness. However, the mythic Chiron also has a close relationship to healing. We can see him as the archetypal

---

[1] Many astrologers use a 2-3 degree orb of aspect for the quincunx.

[2] Not all, however; and much depends on the birth time. The midnight horoscope has the Moon at 11Aries35 and Saturn at 8Scorpio38, an orb of just under three degrees. However, in the hours after midnight, the orb widens at the rate of a degree every two hours, so by 10 AM it will have widened to just under 8 degrees, far too wide for a quincunx. On the other hand, the orb-of-aspect to Uranus remains at 4 degrees. Some, though, would prefer to see this as a slightly more precise bi-quintile (144 degrees).

[3] Virgo lies 150 degrees from the beginning of the zodiac.

Wounded Healer, for he had a wound that he could not heal yet served as a healer and stands at the fountainhead of the Greek medical tradition. During the late 1970s, when Chiron was discovered, myriad groups made public statements or initiated activities emphasizing more holistic approaches to healing of all sorts. Some will see Chiron as indicating a planetary wound that humans cannot heal.

Chiron conjoins Neptune, in its dignity in Pisces. The symbolism suggests illness and healing connected to the power of the oceans (Neptune), and we know not only that the oceans have begun to rise as a symptom of the planetary illness,[1] but also that many scientists have warned that much ocean life may not survive the twin assaults from heat and humans. Jupiter, square Chiron and Neptune, again suggests over-expansion, while Venus in Sagittarius, also square Chiron-Neptune, suggests expanded value and, particularly in connection to Jupiter, abundance in many forms, though with an emphasis on the intellectual (Sagittarius-Gemini) rather than the organic. The Venus-Jupiter opposition, though an afflictive aspect, involves the two traditional benefics and so suggests richness and good will. Of course, abundance and richness, though perhaps beneficial to an individual, in the chart of a collective may prove problematic, particularly when suggested by a hard aspect that in this case suggests over-extension, and particularly given what we know of world climate. So we see here, among other possibilities, an illness and a rising of the oceans caused by over-abundance: the oceans rise because of various economic choices, particularly those related to capitalism and the creation of abundance. Venus-Jupiter can suggest a problematic and unexamined luxury, or a current of fellow-feeling that can alleviate any number of difficulties.

The t-square certainly suggests sociability (Venus-Jupiter) as a response to illness (Chiron). The opposition points to restless human relationships based on principle as avenues to heal planetary wounds. Here we see an emphasis on the personal instead of the bureaucratic, the affable instead of the official, the interpersonal rather than the international. As the wounded healer, Chiron suggests that by relating directly to wounds and illness and their causes, people can find a way to heal them, but only through simple human openness. Chironic healing deals not so much with symptoms as with causes, so the t-square suggests that if, in the new era, humans relate more openly to each other, they can discover the cause of planetary woes. Because Chiron also makes helpful aspects to Saturn (trine) and Pluto (sextile), mitigating the problems from the yods, we can see assistance coming from the entrenched and still powerful bureaucracy even as we see that no healing can take place, planetary or otherwise, without a full acknowledgment of the illness that needs healing (Chiron as wounded healer archetype).

The horoscope offers no guarantees, however. Venus-Jupiter can also manifest as irresponsible and possibly dilettantish approaches to problems, for neither planet wants to emphasize work,

---

[1] The reader might recall the material in chapter one: half a Great Year ago, during the Age of Virgo, ocean-levels rose as the ice-caps melted. Today, we face similar results though from different causes.

and together they can easily gravitate toward irresponsibility. The t-square can bring increased woundedness as a result of irresponsible behavior, a not unlikely consequence when we consider the involvement of Neptune, a planet prone to delusion and self-deception, particularly when connected to Venus and Jupiter. The combination suggests confusion and disorganization related to opportunity and goodwill, a tendency to live the apparently-good life and to ignore not-so-apparent problems instead of engaging them. T-squares in mutable signs often lack organizing power; though this one has a helpful trine to Saturn, it suggests, through its otherwise healthy restlessness, difficulties organizing needed healing regimens.

The Venus-Jupiter opposition not only forms the opposition of the t-square, but also the central axis of the horoscope's closest yod, and Venus occupies the reaction point. This horoscope therefore has a configuration similar to the one formed by progression at the end of the previous Long Count: a t-square linked inextricably with a yod via an opposition that functions as the opposition in the former and the central axis of the latter. Here, however, we have Venus, the lesser benefic, at the reaction point (instead of SP Pluto and SP Saturn), Chiron-Neptune focal in the t-square instead of Mars-Neptune, and Jupiter in Gemini as the apex planet of the yod (instead of Mercury-Venus in Leo). Thus the 2012 yod/t-square combination doesn't appear as afflictive, intractable, or aggressive as the earlier one; it doesn't have within it the indications of military aggression driven by delusion and set off by the potentially sadistic energies of the underworld under the direction of the prevailing hierarchy (SP Saturn conjoining SP Pluto at the reaction point of the 3114 BC yod, plus a fixed sign at the apex). Instead, it has indications of overabundance that needs curbing, healing that needs clear direction, and social cohesion that needs to remain dynamic instead of escapist. Because the 2012 yod to Jupiter has very narrow orbs of aspect (less than a degree for every aspect), it will have a great effect and will need attention, and given the circumstances, ignoring it will lead to dire problems related to continual and unregulated growth. However, the aspects themselves don't seem as daunting; they only come to seem so because of the daunting problems in place as the period begins.

Saturn and Pluto, in mutual reception and in a precise sextile, suggest the possibility of intelligently mobilizing government forces in response to prevailing planetary illness; Jupiter in Gemini can suggest social application combining vision and necessary detail. The other sextiles—five in all: Moon-Jupiter; Jupiter-Uranus; Saturn-Pluto; Sun-Neptune; Sun-Chiron—the practical use of intelligence. The trines—four in all: Chiron-Saturn; Venus-Moon; Venus-Uranus; Mercury-Moon—suggest potential harmonies that, though they need direction, don't point to the calamitous conflicts suggested in the 3114 BC horoscope.[1] (In general, trine aspects point to a possibly benign, though often not very dynamic, flow of energy.) Further, whereas the earlier horoscope had no oppositions, suggesting that people had difficulty seeing through their projections and so mistook their delusions for reality, the 2012 horoscope has the important op-

---

[1] By contrast, the 3114 BC horoscope had only two trines (Mars-Jupiter, Neptune-Jupiter) and two sextiles (Mars and Neptune to the Moon).

position from Venus to Jupiter, the aforementioned benefics, to provide some measure of objective thinking as regards individual and social values. It could show that people will feel more prone to emphasize human relationship, and not bureaucratic structure, as they confront collective difficulties. It may also suggest that people will not find themselves besieged by their own inner demons.

Admittedly, many astrologers see t-squares as producing problems, particularly in the horoscopes of collectivities. This one *does* suggest difficulties, particularly environmental ones, but the involvement of Venus and Jupiter at least suggests a way forward. The focal planets (Chiron and Neptune) suggest illness and a need to heal (Chiron), the illness having to do with idealism, poisons, and possibly with the oceans (Neptune matters). Though the squares from Venus and Jupiter to Neptune certainly suggest problems related to over-idealism and disorganization, they have at least an undertone of good-will and benefit ("benefics"). The squares indicate a need to organize good will and magnanimity with a view toward healing, and to do this while limiting the excesses suggested by gregarious Venus-Jupiter. The problems, here, arise as a possible refusal to confront difficulties with their roots in the past, rather than newly intransigent difficulty and destruction. This statement also reflects the benefics' placements in mutable signs, for mutable signs have more to do with adjustment to circumstances than with initiating new projects (cardinal signs) or establishing intransigent patterns (fixed signs).[1]

The empty leg of the t-square, symbolizing that which needs cultivating in order to find balance, falls in Virgo. This suggests, again, healing, but in a particular way.[2] Virgo heals through adjusting life-rituals and ritualistic modes of behavior directed toward the ends we wish them to serve. We have seen the importance of ritual in the 3114 BC horoscope. There, problematic collective rituals of social organization led to destruction; here, Virgo suggests a need for a ritualistic reconnection to practical acumen, uniting (as so many rituals do) heaven with earth, aspiration with clear-sighted attention to the particulars of life. Virgo can arise as illness if the person or society in question adopts rituals that do not engage all of the available vital energies and energetic demands; it can arise as health if those vital energies and energetic demands find appropriate venues. With Virgo as the empty leg, people will need to pay more attention than they have in the past to the ongoing social ritual and to find ways to purify the environment. To do this, they will have to focus on particulars, and they will have to do so out of a sense of individual value (Venus-Jupiter).

---

[1] The 2012 horoscope has six planets in mutable signs, four in cardinal signs (unless we cast the horoscope for about six hours later, when the Sun entered Capricorn, a cardinal sign), and one in a fixed sign (Saturn in Scorpio). The 3114 BC horoscope has one planet in a mutable sign (Jupiter in Pisces), three in a cardinal sign (Capricorn), and six planets in fixed signs. As the new aeon develops, we will probably see fewer fixed, large structures and organizations and more flexibility. By itself, this seems to augur well, though to deal with widespread problems like climate change, large and stable organizations can play an important role, at least in theory.

[2] I feel that Chiron, along with Mercury, rules Virgo. Thus the similarities between what I say here of Virgo and what I said above about Chiron.

We see in this horoscope, then, a pervasive but not always obvious Virgo-symbolism: Chiron, ruler of Virgo, lies at the focal position of the t-square; the empty leg of that t-square falls in Virgo; the yods further suggest Virgo, particularly because they contain the "lower quincunxes"[1] from Jupiter to Pluto and both the Moon and Uranus to Saturn. This symbolism can suggest disorganized energy possibly leading to illness, but it can also suggest the mentioned ritualistic organization that marshals healing capacities. It also suggests practical intelligence enabling people to reconnect "the above" with "the below"—activity with vision, vision with unconscious drives, heaven with earth. All of this has the imprint of Virgo.

Virgo symbolizes attention paid to the essential particulars that make up a ritual: only by paying attention to those particulars can one gain benefit from one's participation *in* the ritual; only by paying attention to specific elements of a problem can one see how to solve it. Only by paying attention to those particulars can people set the ritual into a healthier pattern—particularly important, as "ritual" refers here to the patterns through which people live their lives, as for example the one, common in the United States, in which people drive to work, heat their homes with fossil fuels, send their money to large corporations, buy most of their food through stores that purchase from large agribusinesses, and so forth. Fortunately, though the mutable t-square suggests disorganization, it also suggests a potential harmony based in compassion, openness (Neptune), and applied service (Chiron)—a movement from imbalance to new balance, with that term suggesting the constant adjustments needed to maintain balance.

This last suggests the movement from Virgo (imbalance) to Libra (balance). Virgo lies between Leo and Libra, between self-concerned radiance (Leo) and formal relationships between equals. This movement can occur through ritual, work, and the demands of necessity, Virgo matters all. Unless people find ways, probably through the aforementioned good will, to coordinate their efforts, to put service ahead of personal gain, the lack of coordination will continue. However, a t-square's empty leg energy often manifests on its own—manifests, we might say, as a result of the tension of the t-square itself, as if called forth from some recess, hidden but already present. In this case, I would guess that circumstances related to purity and impurity will compel people to coordinate their efforts.

Fixed sign squares (3114 BC) suggest intransigent energy: in the 3114 BC horoscope, this intransigence arose through fixation on central authority (Leo, Sun conjoining Saturn in Leo). Mutable sign squares (2012 AD) suggest difficulties related to disorganization and adjustment-to-circumstance, as all the mutable signs have to do with moving from one level of awareness or activity to another. Quite possibly the problems arising after 2012 AD will have to do with reactions to social structures falling apart, perhaps the replacement of nation states by smaller groupings, a process that can have obvious benefits but which can also create difficul-

---

[1] In the lower quincunx aspect, the faster moving planet has moved 150 degrees ahead of the slower-moving planet; Virgo begins 150 degrees from 0 Aries.

ties in tackling projects (e.g. related to global warming) that seem to require concerted, coordinated efforts from millions of people. Thus, problems may go unaddressed. The horoscope suggests this as a major difficulty arising in the coming age. Though this writer finds it hard to see how such smaller groupings could present greater obstacles than nation states have done over the past several hundred years, it often seems that to deal with problems like climate change, some sort of large-scale organization must occur.

Though mutable signs bring more flexibility, this flexibility doesn't always lead to benefit. The 2012 horoscope doesn't lend itself as easily to huge agglomerations of power; rather, it suggests a dispersion (Gemini) of learning (Jupiter) and a proliferation of relationship (Venus-Jupiter). It has no planets in Leo, so the emphasis on regality seems to have dissipated. Whereas in the previous Long Count we saw the danger from too much fixity, here we see problems arising from frivolity and diversity, perhaps a reaction to the disastrous consequences of the previous period, perhaps simply a difficulty finding the resources necessary to make necessary changes. Nero's fiddling had little effect on the spreading flames.

In considering all this, we should recall the Aquarian symbolism. As we move into the new Mayan aeon, we also move into the Age of Aquarius. As stated earlier, astrologers see Aquarius as a barren sign connected with group enterprises, ideas, and (as an air sign) communication of ideas within those group enterprises. It often has little connection to organic processes, yet these are what will probably need renewing in the coming era. On the positive side, the Aquarius symbolism suggests the galvanizing of group energies around a fixed idea; on the problematic side, Aquarius too often ignores organic necessity.

This symbolism, combined with what we have seen in the 2012 horoscope, points to the domination of social factors over organic ones, a tendency to live in a world of conceptual elaboration (Jupiter in Gemini) and entrenched or fixed ideas (Aquarius). Though the symbolism suggests beneficial social interactions arising from curiosity, it also suggests difficulties in applying ideas in ways that will ensure the continued health of the planet and of the body social. More particularly, Jupiter in Gemini can suggest a tendency to accept conclusions not based on an accurate assessment of the data, but based rather on some joy at dealing with the ideas themselves. Yet the t-square points to the need for practical application of intelligence. We see here the problematic (square and opposition) relationship among some of the mutable signs: Gemini takes an interest in ideas for their own sake; Sagittarius prefers the sweeping abstraction to the precise observation; Virgo, while eschewing the notion that ideas have value in themselves, seeks the application of those ideas to practical circumstances; Pisces may eschew ideas altogether, seeing the universal as having practical value.

Gemini plays a further role here, as for the next few thousand years, the Neptune-Pluto conjunctions will continue to take place in Gemini. The first two conjunctions of the series have produced a mode of perception (Pluto) in which the perceiving mind (one twin) sees the phenomenal world (the other, purportedly darker, twin) as a place inviting curiosity, as a place into which to extend one's activity and mental investigations, initially confident in the objectiveness (so to speak) of that world into which one extends. In other words, this series of conjunctions began with a collective delusion (Barfield's *idolatry*) in which individuals ignored the twin-element of experience. In mythic stories of twins, we generally find one light twin and one dark twin, one allegedly good and one allegedly bad or unregenerate. Here, the twin in the light represents the individual's awareness; the twin in the dark represents either the unregenerate earth or the material world altogether (that of which one purportedly *has* awareness). Once these conjunctions began in Gemini, conquerors looked out into the "objective" space of the world and saw two kinds of darkness "in need of improvement": the dark minds of "primitives" and the unimproved earth—the field, from the conquerors point of view, in which to bring about regeneration (Pluto) and a specific version of delusion masquerading as spirituality (Neptune) through the bringing of the word (Gemini), all terms receiving their definitions from the conquerors and not the conquered.[1]

But Mercury, traditional ruler of Gemini, functions as messenger for the gods and has a reputation as the lord of liminality. He rules borderlands, doorways, and portals of all kinds, whether in the world of the gods, the world of humans, or in the mind. Thus Gemini, with its ongoing and effervescent curiosity about the world, can prompt a movement taking place as a result of curiosity and interest even if that curiosity and interest doesn't at first have a practical orientation or goal. The series of Neptune-Pluto conjunctions in Gemini, then, may provide a kind of doorway: though we can see the dark side of the Gemini potential in the projection-driven fury visited by dominant societies upon all others, we may well find out as we enter the new Mayan era that the viciousness we have seen results not from the Gemini-series alone, but from its combination with the squares (involving Mars, Neptune, Venus, Mercury, Scorpio, and Leo) in the 3114 BC horoscope. Absent the cruelty suggested so strongly by those afflictive aspects, the new era may eventually bring a more positive development of Neptune-Pluto in Gemini, one not marked by intellectually-justified sadism but by curiosity, one in which natural human interest in the mind-world duality, and in the effervescent variety of human beings, prompts new developments in consciousness. And, indeed, it seems that we see hints of this already.

Recall that during the Age of Gemini, humans also found themselves dealing with dualism: the hunters separated further and further from the farmers and villages, until those hunters metamorphosed into the rulers and the farmers into the ruled. This split eventually led to the kind of civilization that has remained with us ever since. This split appeared in the behavior of the people in the two predominant groups (hunters and agriculturists)—or, we might say, in people with two approaches to survival—and one group dominated the other.

---

[1] Many of the Europeans invading North America felt that the native peoples did not have legitimate title to the land because they did not "improve" it via farming or industry.

When the Gemini series of Neptune-Pluto conjunctions began, the split began on a perceptual level—mind-world; civilized-uncivilized; intelligence-matter; "improved"—"unimproved"—and the shift in perception led to changes in action. I have already explained how these various splits had much to do with technical and social developments since the Renaissance. We should realize, though, that unless humans deal with these problematic perception-patterns, they won't solve the problems that will continue into the coming era, for the influence of the previous eon will not end all at once. Some of the difficulty has to do with Pluto itself, for though Pluto appears in the collective as the predominant collective idea (with the specifics indicated by the sign in which we find transiting Pluto), it tends to fuse. The fusion can lead to blindness as the idea gets fused with the external phenomena, seeming to abide there and describe the phenomena, the dark twin, quite nicely. On the other hand, the period after Pluto's discovery has brought remarkable developments in humans' ability to see more objectively the myriad ways in which mind and world constantly intertwine and thus to make a more compassionate use of this process. For if we can see the ways in which this fusion arises, whether in the mind or in the world that seems to lie outside the mind, we might work with it more effectively and creatively, realizing that to work on one means to work on the other.

During the coming age, people in all walks of life and in all nations must continue to cut through the problematic dualism described above. This can occur because of Gemini's curiosity, for if one wishes to see through the illusion, one must first take an interest in it. In this way, people can gain more and more objectivity; they can see that both of the twins, mind and world, come from the same seed, the same source. Once people begin to see this, they can move to solve the problems; they can deal more effectively with the barrenness of the Aquarian Age; they can more effectively galvanize the great social potential of the new aeon, a period in which new ideas can have great effect on social problems as long as the power-brokers don't co-opt the value for the benefit of plutocrats. But one thing seems clear: during the new era, people will need to work on their problems by moving beyond the aforementioned split, by seeing the way mind affects world and vice-versa. That way lies the journey.

Once people do this—once they see the way the collective idea fuses with the world—they can begin to use that idea more creatively, as a way to solve problems instead of as a way to get stuck in old ruts. It's a question, here, of seeing the power of mind to influence the world—the basic lesson of Pluto, a planetary energy that reminds us of how mind arises fused with the world, and that to see this is to access the full human creative power, not merely to take part in "the evolution of consciousness" as something separate from the ongoing karma of the world, but to take part in what we can call "co-evolution," a term we can understand as referring to the evolution of consciousness fused with developments in the world outside. I suspect that this won't occur right away, but we can each help to bring it about by working in the world as a way to affect mind and working on mind as a way to affect the world.[1] The Neptune-Pluto conjunctions tell us

---

[1] The discovery of Pluto in 1930 served to announce to us all that if we didn't work with the Plutonic en-

of the delusions and illusions that arise from the unconscious idea collectively held. Though individuals can work to get at the source of their projections in what Jungians would probably call psychological complexes and what Buddhists would call the dualistic fixation, the collective, having no individual will, has more difficulty seeing the collective idea objectively. Though individuals can see that collective idea working itself out, and though some historians (e.g. Mumford, Toynbee) do a remarkable job articulating the pattern through which this takes place, the problems persist because "the collective" has no localized consciousness and remains diffuse.

Furthermore, because the collective delusion has worked itself into a wide variety of durable social forms with their own momentum and their tendency to reinforce the delusions from which they arise, the problems seem intransigent. Astrology can help us, here, to deconstruct (to use a term from literary criticism) the maze, to untie the knot. The 3114 BC Long Count horoscope tells us, particularly when combined with the information from our own astrological tradition (e.g. the Ages, the transits and progressions), about the predominant perceptual and conceptual patterns of the period. Knowing these, we can begin to work more consciously with them. We can say something similar about our work in the coming era: by understanding the symbolism, we can work more consciously. We can see the tendency to split the dark twin from the light twin; we can question that tendency, seeing it as merely that: a tendency in human beings, not an accurate description of the vast set of operations we refer to as "the world." Further, we can harness the intellectual capacities and tools of the Aquarian era, for Aquarius, through its two rulers, Uranus and Saturn, has much to do with the social (air) application (Saturn) of new ideas (Uranus). Finally, the socializing emphases of the 2012 horoscope tell us what we must emphasize if we want to heal the illness suggested by the yods found in the horoscopes of both Mayan eras.

The era of bigness has apparently run its course, but we shouldn't expect all large institutions to vanish. Nor should we see this as desirable in all areas. While we should work to dismantle those large institutions that clearly do more harm than good—e.g. nation states that wish to dominate others, corporations too big to either fail or bring benefit, large agribusinesses that seem bent on ruining the soil and getting rid of one seed-strain after another, banks and other financial institutions that aid and abet whatever bigness they can find—we should also acknowledge that some elements of the "world problematique" require solutions that coordinate the actions of millions of people.

In discussing culture and its transformation, Lewis Mumford speaks of four main components: dominants, persistents, emergents, and remnants:

---

ergy more clearly and directly, we would find ourselves at its mercy. The rise of National Socialism and the atomic bomb suggested that human beings didn't quite understand the lesson plan.

> The dominants are what give each historical phase its style and color: but without the substratum of active persistents, and without the vast underlayer of remnants, whose existence remains as unnoticed as the foundations of a house until it sags or crumbles, no fresh invention in culture could achieve dominance. If one bears this in mind, it is legitimate to characterize a cultural phase by its largest visible new feature: but in the total body of a culture the persistents and the remnants, however hidden, necessarily occupy a far larger area and play a more essential part.[1]

The astrological factors in the two natal horoscopes we have examined, and particularly the strong and challenging configurations within those horoscopes, seem to represent the dominants of the age in question. However, the persistents for the new aeon have not yet appeared as such; certainly they have not yet taken root. To the extent that they depart radically from the dominants of the old aeon, they will surely appear as emergents. To the extent that the old forms extend into the new aeon, we can consider them as remnants, but we may not know for a while whether to consider them as persistents.

In general, it seems to me that we can find the persistents in those qualities of a culture or civilization that speak to or encourage the expression of persistent qualities in the human beings alive during those times. Hopefully the dominants will do that as well, but one never knows. As we saw earlier, the kinds of social organization that developed over five thousand years ago made possible some types of artistic, organizational, and technical expression that reflect something important, perhaps essential, in human beings; at the same time, those forms discouraged other potentials, and in our own age we see an overemphasis on the technical at the expense of other possibilities. We may have difficulty saying just what "something important in human beings" consists of—though I strongly suspect it has much to do with enabling and empowering the energies symbolized in our horoscopes—but the social forms that encourage its expression will surely persist in the new aeon. Hopefully, the ones that do not will go by the boards.

As we consider the horoscope for December 21, 2012, we should not forget the earlier horoscope, for the energies of that period persist, at least as remnants, possibly as persistents. Even as old forms deteriorate, new ideas arise, at first inchoate at best, that will develop into the dominants for the new period. The new horoscope can give guidance about how to work not only with the remnants, but also with the persistents and dominants—and surely it gives information about the emergents. At first, people may have difficulty distinguishing dominants from emergents, though the latter make possible the former. For example, about five thousand years ago, the development of new agricultural techniques made possible the social forms that came to dominate the aeon right up to the present. Surely we will see analogous processes in the coming years.

---

[1] Mumford, *Technics and Human Development*, 131.

Much difficulty, though, arises through the karma of the previous aeon. We could have said the same thing in 3114 BC as well, as no doubt people experienced all sorts of difficulties as a result of the hunter-farmer split, as from the Neolithic social forms that no longer served as sufficient carriers for creative endeavor (having developed, it seems, into mere routine). However, people in that era did not have to reverse current trends in the way that we apparently do; they did not face climate changes that, along with soil-depletion and other factors, threaten the food supply, and they did not have to deal with the kinds of weaponry that now threaten millions of people and even the ecosystem itself. (In fact, the changes that took place back then depended on new techniques that *increased* the food supply.)

Though we have obviously received much benefit from the past, we find that we must change course, and radically. We seem to have less latitude in our choices now than our ancestors did. Fortunately, some important factors in the horoscope for the new aeon strongly suggest a love of change, a willingness to adapt, and an effervescent curiosity that will make adaptation possible. Whether the changes will effect a sufficient cure remains in question.

Epilogue

I.

SOME OF THE MAGIC OF THE MAYAN time measurement that we call the Long Count lies in the way the astrological symbolism for its birth date seems to give us such a precise description of the cataclysmic social and cultural changes that took place during the several centuries to either side of that date. Despite the cataclysmic nature of the changes, though, I would wager that August 11, 3114 BC passed pretty much like any other day for the people of that period—even for the people of Mesopotamia and Egypt, the areas in which the cataclysmic developments took place, reminding us that what looks cataclysmic from the vantage of 5125 years may have looked completely ordinary for people at the time. Because people did not keep historical records and so did not have a recorded past available for comparison, and with writing still in a very primitive stage, I would wager that few if any people noticed what seems so evident to us.

We differ from the people of that era in many ways, of course, and we probably have more perspective on developments in our era than they or their forebears had on theirs. In saying this, though, we should remind ourselves not to overestimate the differences or ignore the similarities. Though we think we have an advanced perspective, born from our historical knowledge and our purportedly sophisticated state of intellectual development, both resulting from what we may see as our more sophisticated use of symbol-systems, a more objective observer might find us equally in the dark, just as immersed in events and our limited ideas about them, just as lacking in perspective or insight. During what some have called paradigm shifts (and assuming that the current era qualifies as one), the prevailing modes of analysis, or even description, may limit one's understanding more than enhance it. We may not have mental or symbolic models (insofar as we can distinguish those two) suitable to describe or analyze the future paradigm. Limited by a way of seeing that has developed through the sets of symbols connected to one culture or one period, people may have similarly limited notions of the future.[1] Surely the Neolithic villagers of long ago had no word for the kind of social development—"civilization"—that took place, we might say, right before their eyes. To alter slightly a phrase allegedly coming from Jesus (whom we associate with another paradigm shift), we could say that like our ancestors, we have eyes but do not see as clearly as we think we do.

Of course, we have at least one advantage over our ancestors: some people during the past 5125 years have called our attention to the ways that our symbolic patterning can get in the way of accurate seeing.[2] Though such awareness apparently does not enter the momentary consciousness of most people, at least we know that in different places and times, some people have attempted to see the problem clearly—having at least noticed that it exists—and to find ways to solve it. Nevertheless, we should take care every time we think we really understand the present or know what will happen in the future—and we should take particular care when discussing periods of what we call millennial change or paradigm shift, for if things change quickly or pervasively enough, current symbolic paradigms may not describe them as well as we think they do.

To a lesser degree, we deal with similar problems every time we apply a set of symbols to events that do not consist of symbols—in other words, continually. The world apparently does not consist of language or any set of symbols, so every time we attempt to describe or analyze that world with our symbols, we run the risk of creating a map that does not have the same structure as the territory[3]—and such maps can lead us badly astray. Nevertheless, because people often find some maps at least somewhat helpful, we can at least suggest two possibilities for the Long Count's conclusion: on the one hand December 21, 2012 may bring cataclysmic events (though, as suggested above, I doubt that), or its astrological symbolism may point to cataclysmic-but-not-immediately-obvious developments taking place all around us, developments of longer duration about which we perhaps have less understanding than we think we do.

---

[1] These "sets of symbols" include our astrological set of symbols, of course. As for interpreting new paradigms, we might remember the words of Louis Armstrong when someone asked him to explain jazz. He said something to the effect of, 'If you have to have someone explain it to you, no explanation will suffice.'

[2] The valid cognition teachings developed over a thousand years ago in India come to mind, as do the investigations of Alfred Korzybski, Edward Sapir and Benjamin Lee Worff, not to mention various Jungians with their discussions of projection, and a gamut of people who have investigated the matter experimentally (as, of course, did Jung and the valid cognition folk, though in their experiments they examined different material—often the inner contemplations, perceptions, and imaginings of people).

[3] The phrase comes from Alfred Korzybski. See his *Science and Sanity: An Introduction to Non-Aristotelian Systems and General Semantics* (Englewood, NJ: Institute for General Semantics). As for maps, territories, and structures, if you try to get from Philadelphia to Buffalo using a map that has the latter east of the former, you will likely get well and nicely lost in the swamps of eastern Pennsylvania instead of striding with assurance through the great north woods.

Though we know that at certain points in a process, form changes drastically (ice turning to water, for example, or water to steam; Prince Hal metamorphosing into King Henry), and that the new form will not accommodate old forms of activity (you can't ice-skate on water or swim in steam; Falstaff can't interact with the King the way he had with his former drinking buddy), we also know that acorns grow into oak trees, not into skyscrapers: though we may have difficulty identifying the acorn in the oak, we will at least see the changes as consistent with other processes we've observed. So though some will say that the magnetic poles will shift, and though that might happen, it also might not happen; I suspect that it won't occur on the 2012 winter solstice (though given the dramatic nature of the horoscope for that date, such a development would seem as much a confirmation as a surprise). Perhaps extra-terrestrial beings or Jacque Vallee's beings from other dimensions[1] will intervene in human history. However, even without such events, it seems likely that 2100 AD will differ from 2012 AD as drastically as 2000 BC differed from the period leading up to 3114 BC.

II.

We have seen that the 4th millennium BC brought unprecedented changes in human social organization, as humans developed institutions—and physical structures—larger and more tightly ordered than any developed before, institutions in which the god-king ruled through a strong bureaucratic hierarchy implementing policies emanating from the center. We have seen, further, that the horoscope for August 11, 3114 BC symbolizes these developments quite precisely and that we get startling results when we subject that horoscope to time analysis. We have seen, too, that the symbolism strongly suggests that here at the end of the Long Count, things have gone about as far as they can in the given direction. Some will want to add that the end of the Long Count will usher in a marked and comparatively rapid period of spiritual development, apparently some sort of spiritual breakthrough. Whether or not we see hints of such a development, we will probably wonder what the discussions of social development have to do with the discussions about spiritual development.

In earlier chapters, we noted that the social changes of the 4th millennium BC made possible the development of certain human potentials that had apparently lain mostly dormant in Neolithic village life, the form of social organization preceding what we call "civilization." If we think that human life has a purpose, we will probably agree that one such purpose has to do with the development of the full human potential; we will, therefore, applaud at least some of what occurred so long ago within or as a result of the new forms of social organization. With differentiation of function, what we now call "division of labor," came various kinds of specialization; from specialization came unprecedented advances in what we now call science, technology, and the arts.

---

[1] See Jacques Vallee's, *Dimensions: A Casebook of Alien Contact*. (New York: Ballantine Books, 1988).

However, if "civilization" brought hierarchy and division of labor, with people at or near the bottom of the hierarchy doing most of the heavy lifting and those at the top doing most of the purportedly heavy thinking, we might recall the words of Adam Smith:

> . . . the understandings of men are necessarily formed by their ordinary employments. The man whose whole life is spent in performing a few simple operations, of which the effects too are, perhaps, always the same, or very nearly the same, has no occasion to exert his understanding, or to exercise his invention in finding out expedients for removing difficulties which never occur. He naturally loses, therefore, the habit of such exertion, and generally becomes as stupid and ignorant as it is possible for a human being to become. The torpor of his mind renders him, not only incapable of relishing or being a part of any rational conversation, but of conceiving any generous, noble, or tender sentiment, and consequently of forming any just judgment concerning many even of the most ordinary duties of private life. Of the great and extensive interests of his country he is altogether incapable of judging. . . .[1]

Even if we find some of Smith's judgments a bit extreme (and perhaps evincing a class-bias), we will probably agree that the prevailing form of social organization in any period or place has a profound effect on what elements of the human capacity people develop or fail to develop.

Let's leave the term "human capacity" undefined for now, and similarly for "spiritual development." If, as seems reasonable, we take spiritual development as part of the human capacity, then by engaging in the former, we develop more of the latter. Thus we can see the relationship between our modes of social organization and "spiritual development" however understood, for each mode will encourage some capacities and discourage others. To borrow terminology from economics, we might say that each form of social organization presents not only opportunities, but also its own opportunity *costs*.

We can admit, surely, that hierarchical modes of social organization promote a kind of efficiency that non-hierarchical modes do not promote and may even retard. Hierarchical organization in purely mechanical operations seems essential in the inner workings of myriad mechanical devices, for example, where the function of one part must remain subordinate to the function of another part, and where the function of the various parts must have the proper inter-relationships for a device to function properly. In theory, hierarchy will enable more efficient function by ensuring or bringing about the optimal relationship among the various parts of a system. Such a mode promotes the kind of efficiency that enabled humans to build the pyramids, not to

---

[1] Adam Smith, *An Inquiry into the Nature and Causes of the Wealth of Nations* (New York: Modern Library, 1994), 840.

mention the complex, interwoven society that now surrounds us and in which each of us, however unwittingly or unwillingly, plays a role.

Military leaders have long recognized the relationship between hierarchy and efficiency. If you fight your wars with a strong hierarchically organized military force, you will usually defeat a foe lacking or deficient in the same.[1] Certainly most Native American tribes found this out. We may take the Dakota as an example, for when the Dakota fought battles, whether against other Native Americans or against the European invaders, they initially and for many decades emphasized individual gallantry and bravery over hierarchical efficiency; they held "counting coup," not efficient killing, as the most laudable and honorable action.[2] When the Dakota used such a method against the American army, however, the Americans mowed them down, the effectiveness of the onslaught being attributable not only to superior weaponry but also to the hierarchical mode of organization that found its most effective expression in armies developed according to mechanical principles.[3]

But even if we admit that hierarchy breeds efficiency and that sometimes humans benefit when or because they act efficiently, we will also recognize *efficiency* as a highly abstract noun without clear referent, and *efficiently* as an adverb that can modify any verb (e.g. *heal* or *kill*). Certainly we can do something *efficiently* and still not ensure long term benefit: corporate farming practices may sometimes yield more per dollar (though not, some would argue, per *acre*), thus qualifying as *efficient* in some sense, yet they may also deplete the soil. You can probably produce more Chevy trucks if you have a clear division of labor, yet you may do much damage not only to the larger environment, but also to the people who occupy (so to speak) the divisions. *Efficiency* clearly has no necessary connection to *value*.

As we come to the end of one arc of social development and seek an alternative, we at the same time seek ways to release different human potentialities. We see in the differences between the 3114 BC horoscope and the 2012 AD horoscope the differences in emphasis between the two periods. We should hesitate before concluding that one "is better" than the other, but we should certainly expect that from the change in social mode will come a change in some area of human

---

[1] Some will see the Vietnam War as an exception. However, though the Vietnamese lacked the technology of the American invaders, they did not lack clear, hierarchical relations, as even a cursory examination of events leading up to Dien Bien Phu will reveal. Interestingly, though, as we approach the end of the Long Count with its emphasis on hierarchy, organized military actions generally prove counter-productive for everyone involved, as if the time for such activity has passed. We might say that at one point, military activity at least accomplished *some*thing for *some*body (though usually at terrible cost), but that now such activity does *no-one* any good.
[2] To "count coup," a warrior would ride (or, in pre-invasion times, run) into the fray, hitting a foe on the head with a coup stick before making his escape.
[3] Of course, the Europeans could make effective weapons largely because the hierarchical mode dominated their society. In other words, we can't really separate the making of effective weapons from the hierarchical mode of social organization in which weapon-making technology developed to such a degree.

expression or development. Some will see this as a kind of "spiritual development," though it may not immediately appear in that light.

III.

Many predictions about December 21, 2012 seem to reflect a dualistic bias: they suggest that something outside of our everyday experience—alien life forms, polar shifts, some sort of galactic energy—will somehow affect human behavior in a dramatic way. We can even spin the facts about climate change to make them appear as outside agents, even though human beings seem responsible. Humans apparently have a tendency to look outside of themselves for both causes and solutions. We see this tendency in the spread of the theistic religions, whether monotheistic or polytheistic, patriarchal or matriarchal, and we see it in much Newtonian science, where the forces that purportedly make the universe tick seem to exist independently of the person watching it do so. The tendency to see externalities as the major causal factors behind our difficulties—and as the operant factors in our potential extrication—seems to reflect the symbolic *sevenness* discussed above. In the Long Count measurements, when we see sevenness (52 year cycles, 5125 year cycles, 5200 tun cycles), we see ideas about collective powers and external developments. Once we move to the individual emphasis symbolized by *fiveness* (7200 tzolkin), we find the counter-balance to these apparently external powers.

We find in many traditions the notion that power somehow descends upon human beings. Christian healers call on God; Muslims call on Allah; many Polynesians speak of *mana*; some Native Americans speak of the Great Spirit; even in Buddhism, a non-theistic set of practices, we see a pantheon of symbolic figures.[1] If we ask whether such external gods exist or not, we perhaps fall prey to the structures provided by our language, for the question seems to allow only one of two answers and thus to present a false dilemma. We might ask, instead, how we *feel* about or when we encounter the apparently external figures or icons. Do we feel that we can access helpful energies by visualizing an external source? Do we find that such an approach has a peculiar effectiveness? If we do, what occurs when we attempt that visualization or entertain that idea? We find iconography in almost every religious or spiritual tradition, and it seems that some people can access some sort of power by in some way visualizing or contemplating such. And the power seems to manifest whether the visualized figures "really exist" or not. The question as phrased above seems to suggest that *sevenness*, here taken as our versions of the world, and *fiveness*, individual creative power, go their ways separately, but the Maya seemed to think that they intertwined. We see this intertwining in the *tzolkin* and in *ollin*.[2]

---

[1] We might say, in connection to Buddhist notions, that though we may doubt that a visualized deity exists in a reliable way, the person doing the visualizing doesn't exist in a reliable way, either. Certainly the visualizer doesn't exist in the way he or she has come to rely upon or to imagine—and yet that person can develop in helpful ways by considering him or herself as existing in a certain way.

[2] See chapter two.

We can see something similar in many events in which people gather together in large, structured situations (rock concerts come to mind) and in various meditation-gatherings. In the latter, the space in which meditation occurs seems connected to sevenness; within that setting, people must work on themselves. When people do that work, they often find something peculiar happening, something that no-doubt lies behind the emphasis of many spiritual teachers on group meditation or group prayer: a development that seems to combine what we have called sevenness and what we have called fiveness. The effect looks something like the arising of harmonics in music: a new tone or awareness emerges that no-one creates individually.

Something similar can occur, at least in theory, in connection with social development. All social action takes place within some social context, but though the work takes place within the context, the context itself doesn't do the work. At the time in which I write, mid-2011, we have seen this principle—the interweaving of *fiveness* and *sevenness*—at work in various Middle Eastern countries, in Wisconsin, and in Greece. We can expect to see more. It seems that many of the current uprisings, and particularly the one in Egypt, have occurred not because large hierarchical organizations have gotten involved, but because when enough people act with sincerity and determination within a larger social context ripe for change, something can occur that no-one does individually. Though these uprisings have not yet established a clear new order, having merely threatened the old, it seems important that they have issued their challenge without resorting to the kind of organizational structures to which they objected. It seems that many of these people have issued their challenge not to the way things are done within a certain mode of organization, but to the mode of organization itself. I suspect that the new aeon will bring not only more of the same, but perhaps more importantly, people simply opting out of the larger hierarchical order, seeking to live on their own terms to the extent that they can do so. We see signs of this process, though only in a fledgling stage, in various parts of the world.

Millions of people have begun to realize that, given the nature of large institutions whether state-run or private, individuals cannot get what they want or deserve by propitiating the powers-that-be. No matter how many people call or write their congress-people or vote for the person "of their choice,"[1] they see little positive change. It seems to make little difference whether the large institutions are public or private, for something apparently "in their nature" resists any challenge. In our era such institutions generally seem to do more harm than good, whether they operate in agriculture, finance, manufacturing, industry, or government. We may take these as signs of the end of the aeon of bigness. We don't see very many positive results, these days, until individuals take power unto themselves (the potential of fiveness) as a counterbalance to institutional inertia and blindness (the dark side of sevenness).

---

[1] In *The Devil's Dictionary*, Ambrose Bierce put the matter a bit more precisely: in an election, one gets to vote for the man of another man's choice.

Though the jury remains out on whether developments in Egypt, Tunisia, Syria, Greece, and other places will yield the results envisioned by those seeking change, we can at least see that something important has occurred. In the terms we have used here, change has occurred on the level of sevenness once people have taken upon themselves the power of fivensss. We will not effect the necessary changes on a worldwide scale until millions more people take a similar approach, for though we need external changes—changes, for example, in social structure or organization—such change will certainly not occur if sevenness and fiveness continue to operate in their separate realms. As seen through the lens provided in this book, some of the magic of Mayan measurements, and particularly the Long Count and tzolkin, lies in the way they direct us to this conclusion.

IV.

If we get lost in the symbolism, though, we may pay insufficient attention to the developments to which the symbolism purportedly has a connection: the world around us at the end of the Long Count. The quincunxes in the natal horoscope have apparently manifested as a planetary illness brought about by the rituals connected with the kind of social organization that emerged around the Long Count's birth-date: a kind of social organization characterized by a dramatic increase in the size of structures, organized groups, initiatives, and institutions. As we have seen, this mode of social organization brought both harm and benefit. Now, though, it seems that we must deal with the problems if we wish to continue to develop. The horoscope for December 2012, with its emphasis on diversification, flexibility, and pioneering, suggests some solutions—important, because though many people can talk at length about the illness, they may not see how to cure it. We may say that we must stop using fossil fuels, but we will recognize that fossil fuels have integrated themselves (so to speak) so pervasively into our social structures that the system has apparently come to depend on them. This despite the fact that more and more scientists have come around to the view that if we don't make drastic changes extremely quickly—and, some will say, completely eliminating our use of fossil fuels—we will have to contend with a series of climatic feedback loops that will threaten human civilization. Some scientists have said that present practices threaten the human race itself. All of this should probably give us pause, particularly given the statements by some scholars that the Long Count's end will bring the end of the world.

I tend to think, though, that the changes to come, however pervasive, will have to do with modes of social organization, not the race itself, at least in the short run. We should note, though, that an increasing amount of evidence suggests that the survival of the race, or at least of the race as we know it now, may depend on the willingness of the people of that race to make pervasive changes in social structure. We may wish to take the signs of the times – more frequent and severe flooding, bigger and more dangerous tornadoes and hurricanes, famine that now seems endemic, heat waves taking on a more and more threatening cast—as merely temporary fluctuations, but perhaps we do so at our own risk.

The time-analysis of the August 11, 3114 BC horoscope and the symbolism of the horoscope for December 21, 2012 strongly suggest that humans must drastically alter the rituals that, taken together, we call "civilization." All of these rituals woven together present us with a knot that may take decades to untie, and by then irreparable damage may have occurred. Just as the horoscope for August 11, 3114 BC suggests rituals connected to royalty, bureaucracy, and environmental degradation, all driven by a delusional militarism, so the horoscope for December 21, 2012 suggests rituals required as ongoing adjustments to a given situation. We might say that the changes must begin and end with changes in "consciousness," for all human action seems to begin as ideas, though sometimes only vaguely conscious ones. True enough, but the quincunx seems closely related to the multifarious details of life on the most ordinary level; the aspect asks for a close analysis of all details and resultant rituals, for an understanding not only of others' values but also of the financial roots of current problems. We can say what we will about consciousness, but unless we also deal with the problems indicated by the quincunxes, increase in consciousness alone will probably not suffice. Nero fiddled while Rome burned, perhaps thinking he could simply go elsewhere; we do not have that option.

What must change? I have characterized the passing era as one of bigness; the coming era must, with its strong mutability and lack of fixity, emphasize smaller organizations of various types. Though this short epilogue doesn't seem the place for a long discussion about the details of this shift and how it might take place, we can say at least, following the arguments of people like Helena Norberg-Hodge and Bill McKibben,[1] that the shift will and must involve an emphasis on more local and diverse approaches, that we should not see the necessary changes as impossible to effect, and that, far from demanding a loss in the quality of life, those changes seem likely to *in*crease the quality of life for the vast majority of human beings (as long as, I think, we make the changes soon enough).

We can see quite clearly that large systems often generate great harm to the environment: many (most?) large farms use pesticides that poison both the ground and the food that grows in it; many large fish farms have analogous effects on fish and the oceans; many large lumber companies, fulfilling demands by other large corporations, damage forests; and the list goes on. If you have a large farm, you will make a profit by engaging in monoculture; you will ship your produce over long distances, increasing the cost of the product even as you harm the environment by using oil; you will encourage and support large supermarket chains. If, on the other hand, we encourage a system in which small farms produce for local consumption, we encourage diversity in crop-production, thereby promoting the health of the soil, and we reduce transport costs and support local markets. If this occurs in enough places, it will serve as a trend to counter the massive urbanization that depends on the system of bigness and that has done so much to harm

---

[1] I have borrowed, here, from these two people: Ms. Hodges' 2009 interview with David Barsamian for Alternative Radio, available at alternativeradio.org; Mr. McKibben's *Deep Economy*. See the bibliography.

the ecosystem. By emphasizing the small, the diverse, the personal, and the local, we can bring about a reduction in prices and an increase in useful productivity, on farms and elsewhere; we can also reduce the harm presently done not only to the ecosystem, but also to human communities all over the world. Instead of the ruling triumvirate composed of monoculture, long transport, and large agglomerations (whether of people, money, or power), we would have a triumvirate of diversity (not only in the plants on a given farm, but in the activities of the people and communities involved), immediacy (as in farmer's markets or solar collectors), and personalization.

If the earth experiences vast climate changes, humans will have to undergo vast changes as well, and because it seems unlikely that humans will undergo genetic mutation in the near future (though, of course, one never knows), we will have to make changes where we can, beginning with changes in our modes of social organization. The horoscope for December 21, 2012 suggests that human beings must and will make changes along the lines sketched above, but it doesn't tell us whether we will do so soon enough. Further, it doesn't tell us whether we will do so out of desperation, conviction, or some combination of the two. We have seen that the astrological symbolism for the new era suggests not the morbid and obsessional emphasis on military aggression and social agglomeration of the passing era, not the creation of more large institutions, but an ongoing adjustment to institutions already in place. The horoscope's greater emphasis on mutability and its reduced emphasis on fixity strongly suggests dispersion instead of concentration, adjustment instead of augmentation, the human more than the hierarchical, the immediate rather than the institutional. I suspect that if humans hope to thrive, and perhaps even to survive, they will have to break free of institutional blindness. Such a change would obviously qualify as a growth in awareness; one might even label it "spiritual."

Appendix

The Traditional System

Sign	Ruler	Detriment	Exalted Ruler	Fall[1]
Aries	Mars	Venus	Sun	Saturn
Taurus	Venus	Mars	Moon	-
Gemini	Mercury	Jupiter	North Node	South Node
Cancer	Moon	Saturn	Jupiter	Mars
Leo	Sun	Saturn	-	Mercury
Virgo	Mercury	Jupiter	Mercury	Venus
Libra	Venus	Mars	Saturn	Sun
Scorpio	Mars	Venus	-	Moon
Sagittarius	Jupiter	Mercury	South Node	North Node
Capricorn	Saturn	Moon	Mars	Jupiter
Aquarius	Saturn	Sun	Mercury	-
Pisces	Jupiter	Mercury	Venus	Mercury[2]

---

[1] A planet's detriment position lies directly across from it's the sign it rules. A planet's "fall" position lies directly across the zodiac from its "exalted position."

[2] Some will find what we might call cultural biases in these lists. For example, no planet has its exaltation in Scorpio, perhaps suggesting that no planet can feel "exalted" (so to speak) when working in the underworld. Similarly, the system seems to suggest that the Sun has such power over Leo that no planet qualifies as "exalted" in that sign. Another point worth noting: though some writers (Nicholas Divore, in his *Encyclopedia of Astrology*) have noted that trines and sextiles join the signs of rulership and exaltation (e.g. the Moon rules Cancer and has her exaltation in Taurus, signs in sextile; Jupiter rules Pisces and has his exaltation in Cancer, signs in a trine relationship), many writers do not mention the stressful relationships lurking in the traditional system (e.g. Venus' two rulerships lie in a quincunx relationship; so do Mars' two rulerships; Mercury's two rulerships square each, as do Jupiter's. Saturn's rulerships lie adjacent to others, in a semi-sextile relationship that belongs to the same 12-series of aspects as does the quincunx).

Not all sources give Mercury all of the above designations. For example, though some sources list Mercury as the *ruler* of Virgo, they do not list Mercury as the *exalted* ruler as well; those same sources list Mercury's *detriment* as Pisces, but they do not list Pisces as Mercury's *fall* position. Similarly, some sources do not have Mercury as *exalted* in Aquarius or *falling* in Leo. Not all sources include the north and south nodes, the list-makers perhaps feeling that as the nodes do not qualify as planets, or bodies of any sort, they not rule over signs.

Within this traditional setup, we can find the following orderly arrangement, in which each planet rules two signs, while the two "Lights" (the Sun and Moon) rule one sign each, and in which the order of rulerships moving either direction from the Lights follows the order of planets in the solar system, starting from the sun. In this system, Saturn's rulerships always oppose (lie 180 degrees away from) those of the Sun and Moon.

Saturn rules Aquarius	Saturn rules Capricorn
Jupiter rules Pisces	Jupiter rules Sagittarius
Mars rules Aries	Mars rules Scorpio
Venus rules Taurus	Venus rules Libra
Mercury rules Gemini	Mercury rules Virgo
The Moon rules Cancer	The Sun rules Leo

With the discovery of new planets and planetoids, astrologers have added to the traditional list (though most astrologers feel that the traditional rulers still have weight).

The Current System

Sign	Ruler	Detriment	Exalted Ruler	Fall
Aries	Mars	Venus	Sun; Pluto	Saturn
Taurus	Venus	Mars	Moon	-; Uranus
Gemini	Mercury	Jupiter	North Node	South Node
Cancer	Moon	Saturn	Jupiter; Neptune	Mars
Leo	Sun	Saturn	-	Mercury
Virgo	Mercury, Chiron	Jupiter, Neptune	Mercury	Venus
Libra	Venus	Mars	Saturn	Sun
Scorpio	Mars; Pluto	Venus	-; Uranus	Moon
Sagittarius	Jupiter	Mercury	Chiron; South Node	North Node
Capricorn	Saturn	Moon	Mars	Jupiter; Neptune
Aquarius	Saturn; Uranus	Sun	Mercury	-
Pisces	Jupiter; Neptune	Mercury	Venus	Mercury

Not all astrologers agree about the new designations. For example, not all astrologers see Pluto as exalted in Aries, though the designation makes sense if we consider Pluto as having to do with death and rebirth processes, for in the northern temperate zones, many plants go dormant during the Scorpio time of year and appear reborn during the Aries time of year, the period following the spring equinox. Further, not all astrologers see Chiron as the ruler of Virgo, preferring to see that body as the ruler of Sagittarius and the *exalted* ruler of Virgo; others (including me) flip those assignments around. Curiously, though many astrologers speak of the dignities of Chiron, not as many seem to speak out on the matter of Chiron's purported debilities. If we follow the traditional pattern, in which the debilities lie across the zodiac from the dignities, we would see Chiron as in detriment (or fall) in Pisces and in fall (or detriment) in Gemini. These designations also seem to make sense, as illness (Chiron) can result from absorbing poisons (Pisces) or from the habitual tendency to separate body and mind (a split that we might connect to Gemini).

To these systems, we can add Alice Bailey's system of rulerships.[1]

Constellation	Orthodox	Disciple	Hierarchies
Aries	Mars	Mercury	Uranus
Taurus	Venus	Vulcan	Vulcan
Gemini	Mercury	Venus	The Earth
Cancer	Moon	Neptune	Neptune
Leo	Sun	Sun	Sun
Virgo	Mercury	Moon	Jupiter
Libra	Venus	Uranus	Saturn
Scorpio	Mars	Mars	Mercury
Sagittarius	Jupiter	Earth	Mars
Capricorn	Saturn	Saturn	Venus
Aquarius	Uranus	Jupiter	Moon
Pisces	Jupiter	Pluto	Pluto

The "Orthodox" list duplicates the traditional listing given above, except that this one includes Uranus as ruler of Aquarius. The second and third lists come from sources that Alice Bailey discusses in *Esoteric Astrology*. I have often found that those two lists illuminate facets of the signs that we may have overlooked; they seem to me quite useful in the interpretation of the horoscopes of collectivities (e.g. countries, corporations), but I do not often use them in interpreting horoscopes for people. For example, if I see Sagittarius on the tenth house cusp of a person's horoscope, and I want to locate the house ruler in order as part of the vocation pattern, I will generally emphasize Jupiter, not Mars or the Earth. Along with many other astrologers, I would say that we need more investigation of these matters—and that Ms Bailey's lists do not provide the obvious connections that the traditional lists do. But, of course, we can often find great value in that which does not seem obvious.

I should also mention the multi-level system of rulerships used some centuries back by many European astrologers. In our era, Robert Hand and others have argued for the importance of these assignments. For further information on these, contact www.arhatmedia.com and consult the works of Robert Zoller.

---

[1] Alice Bailey, *Esoteric Astrology* (New York: Lucis Publishing Company, 1951), 68.

Mayan Bibliography

Arguelles, Jose. *The Mayan Factor*. Rochester: Bear & Company, 1987.

Bailey, Alice. *Esoteric Astrology*. New York: Lucis Publishing Company, 1951.

Barfield, Owen. *Saving the Appearances: A Study in Idolatry*. Middletown: Wesleyan University Press, 1988.

Barnes, Harry Elmer. *An Intellectual and Cultural History of the Western World. Volume I*. New York: Dover Publications, 1965.

——— (ed.) *Perpetual War for Perpetual Peace*. Caldwell, Idaho: The Caxton Printers, Ltd., 1953.

Barzun, Jacques. *From Dawn to Decadence: 1500 to the Present*. New York: Harper Collins, 2001.

Bierce, Ambrose. *The Complete and Original Devil's Dictionary*. Lexington, KY: Seven Treasures Publication, 2009.

Calleman, Carl Johan. *The Mayan Calendar and the Transformation of Consciousness*. Rochester, Vermont: Bear& Company, 2004.

Campbell, Joseph. *Occidental Mythology*. New York: Penguin Books, 1964.

Campion, Nicholas. *The Great Year: Astrology, Millenarianism and History in the Western Tradition*. London: Penguin, 1994.

Chomsky, Noam. *Year 501: The Conquest Continues*. Boston: South End Press, 1999.

Cribb, Julian. *The Coming Famine: The Global Food Crisis and What We Can Do to Avoid It*. Berkeley: University of California Press, 2010.

De Vore, Nicholas. *Encyclopedia of Astrology*. New York: Philosophical Library, 1947.

Diamond, Jared. *Guns, Germs, and Steel: The Fates of Human Societies*. New York: W.W. Norton & Company, 1999.

Douglas, David. *Mayan Prophecy 2012: The Mayan calendar and the end of time*. New York: Fall River Press, 2009.

Flandes, Robert Sieck *The Sun Stone or Aztec Calendar: Literature and Drawing Reconstruction of the Original*. Mexico: Lito Selder, 1936.

Gould, Stephen Jay. *Ever Since Darwin*. New York: W.W. Norton & Company, 1992.

―――― *The Mismeasure of Man*. New York: W.W.Norton & Company, 1981.

Greene, Liz. *The Astrology of Fate*. York Beach, Maine: Samuel Weiser, Inc., 1984.

―――― *The Outer Planets and Their Cycles: The Astrology of the Collective*. Reno: CRCS Publications, 1996.

Grosso, Michael. *The Millennium Myth*. Wheaton: Quest Books, 1995.

Hamblin, David. *Harmonic Charts: A New Dimension in Astrology*. Wellingborough, Northamptonshire: Aquarian Press, 1984.

Hand, Robert. *Horoscope Symbols*. Rockport, Massachusetts: Para Research, 1981.

―――― *Planets in Transit*. Atglen PA: Whitford Press, 1976.

Hayakawa, S.I. *Language in Thought and Action*. New York: Harcourt, Brace and Company, 1940.

Hollister, C. Warren. *Roots of the Western Tradition: A Short History of the Ancient World.* New York: John Wiley & Sons, 1982.

Holmes, George. *Renaissance*. New York: St. Martin's Press, 1996.

Jaynes, Julian. *The Origin of Consciousness in the Breakdown of the Bicameral Mind*. Boston: Houghton Mifflin Company, 1976.

Jenkins, John Major. *Maya Cosmogenesis 2012*. Rochester, Vermont: Bear and Company, 1998.

Jung, C.G. *Aion*. Princeton: Princeton University Press, 1959.

―――― *Modern Man in Search of a Soul*. New York: Harcourt Brace Jovanovich, 1933.

Korzybski, Alfred. *Science and Sanity*. Englewood, New Jersey: Institute for General Semantics, 1933.

Leon-Portilla, Miguel. *Time and Reality in the Thought of the Maya*. Norman: University of Oklahoma Press, 1990.

McKibben, Bill. *Deep Economy: The Wealth of Communities and the Durable Future*. New York: Henry Holt and Company, 2007.

Meadows, Donella H., Dennis L. Meadows, Jorgen Randers, and William W. Behrens III. *The Limits to Growth*. New York: Signet, 1974.

Meyer, Michael R. *A Handbook for the Humanistic Astrologer*. New York: Anchor Books, 1974.

Mumford, Lewis. *Technics and Civilization*. New York: Harcourt, Brace, and World, 1962.

―――― *The City in History*. New York: Harcourt, Inc., 1961.

―――― *The Myth of the Machine, Volume I: Technics and Human Development*. New York: Harvest, 1967.

―――― *The Myth of the Machine, Volume II: The Pentagon of Power*. New York: Harcourt Brace Jovanovich, 1970.

Neumann, Erich. *The Great Mother: An Analysis of the Archetype*. Princeton: Princeton University Press, 1963.

——— *The Origins and History of Consciousness*. Princeton: Princeton University Press, 1973.

Norberg-Hodge, Helena. *Thinking Outside of the Box* (audio recording*)*. Boulder: Alternative Radio, 2009.

Oken, Alan. *Complete Astrology*. New York: Bantam, 1988.

Percy, Marge. *He, She, and It*. New York: Fawcett, 1993.

Postman, Neil. *Amusing Ourselves to Death: Public Discourse in the Age of Show Business*. New York: Penguin Books, 1986.

Rudhyar, Dane. *An Astrological Mandala: The Cycle of Transformations and Its 360 Symbolic Phases*. New York: Vintage, 1974.

——— *Astrological Signs: The Pulse of Life*. Boulder: Shambhala, 1978.

——— *The Astrology of Personality*. New York: Doubleday, 1970.

——— *The Lunation Cycle*. Boulder: Shambhala, 1974.

Ruperti, Alexander. *Cycles of Becoming*. Reno: CRCS Publications, 1978.

Sapir, Edward. *Culture, Language, and Personality*. Berkeley: University of California Press, 1956.

——— *Language: An Introduction to the Study of Speech*. New York: Harcourt Brace and Company, 1921.

Scofield, Brian. *Day Signs: Native American Astrology from Ancient Mexico*. Amherst: One Reed Publications, 1991.

Shipley, Joseph T. *Dictionary of Word Origins*. New York: Philosophical Library, 1945.

Simon, Tami (Ed.). *The Mystery of 2012*. Boulder: Sounds True, 2007.

Smith, Adam. *An Inquiry into the Nature and Causes of the Wealth of Nations*. New York: Modern Library, 1994.

Thompson, J. Eric. *The Rise and Fall of Maya Civilization*. Norman: University of Oklahoma Press, 1954.

Thompson, *William Irwin: The Time Falling Bodies Take to Light*. New York: St. Martin's Press, 1981.

Tierney, Bil. *Dynamics of Aspects Analysis*. Reno: CRCS Publications, 1983.

Toynbee, Arnold. *Mankind and Mother Earth*. New York: Oxford University Press, 1976.

Trager, James. *The People's Chronology*. New York: Henry Holt and Company, 1994.

Trungpa, Chogyam. *Shambhala: The Sacred Path of the Warrior*. Boston: Shambhala, 1988.

Vallee, Jacques. *Dimensions: A Casebook of Alien Contact*. New York: Ballentine Books, 1988.

Von Franz, Marie Louise. *Projection and Re-Collection in Jungian Psychology*. London: Open Court, 1985.

——— *Psychotherapy*. Boston: Shambhala, 1993.

Waley, Arthur. *The Way and Its Power: A Study of the Tao Te Ching and Its Place in Chinese Thought*. New York: Grove Press, 1958.

Waters, Frank. *Mexico Mystique: The Coming Sixth World of Consciousness*. Chicago: Swallow Press, 1975.

——— *Mountain Dialogues*. Chicago: Swallow Press, 1999.

Williams, William Appleman. *The Tragedy of American Diplomacy*. New York: W.W. Norton, 1996.

Wolfe, Honora Lee. *The Breast Connection: A Laywoman's Guide to the Treatment of Breast Disease* by Chinese Medicine. Blue Poppy Press, Boulder, Colorado, 1989.

www.ingramcontent.com/pod-product-compliance
Lightning Source LLC
Chambersburg PA
CBHW080537170426
43195CB00016B/2593